Words of Love

Volume 1

Radio Sermons

A BOOK OF SERMONS BY:

J. WAYNE McKAMIE

First Edition
Published By
Robinson Digital Publications
P.O. Box 2634
Weatherford, TX 76086

First Edition Hardback
ISBN: 978-0-9972589-3-6

First Edition Paperback
ISBN: 978-0-9972589-4-3

First Edition eBook
ISBN: 978-0-9972589-5-0

All scripture quotations are taken from the Holy Bible, King James Version unless otherwise noted.

For additional copies contact:
Gary Robinson
P.O. Box 2634
Weatherford, TX 76086
parables@sbcglobal.net

Table of Contents

Introduction

In the fall of 2014, Brother George Hogland of the Lubbock, Texas, congregation and Brother J. Wayne McKamie of the McGregor, Texas, congregation discussed getting Wayne's radio sermons into print. Since I had recently republished Brother Wayne's sermons "The Parables of Jesus," they asked how we might accomplish that goal. We developed a plan and went to work producing this volume.

Fortunately, we have many more sermons than the sermons published in this book; so if the Lord is willing, we plan for this to be the first of multiple volumes of Brother Wayne's radio sermons.

As I began listening to the sermons and reading the transcripts for this first volume, I realized the practicality of Wayne's sermons as he challenges his hearers to think and to consider their actions along life's path. Wayne has a way of always challenging his audience. I believe all who read these sermons will find many nuggets of spiritual nourishment and will find them helpful as they face serious spiritual challenges in living for Jesus Christ. The messages are truly inspiring!

We hope and pray these sermons will encourage and challenge Christians to be the best we can be and will encourage all to submit to the Lord in humble obedience to His gospel. Certainly we pray that in all, God will be glorified by our sharing these sermons!

Gary Robinson
P.O. Box 2634
Weatherford, TX 76086
parables@sbcglobal.net

History of the Radio Program in Lubbock, Texas.

The Lubbock, Texas, congregation began a radio program on an area station in the early 70's with George Hogland as the speaker and a quartet from the Lubbock congregation doing the singing. When Wayne McKamie came here to conduct a gospel meeting in the summer of 1974, we made arrangements with him to send us sermons; and we began using recorded songs by our brotherhood.

The first sermon broadcast was "The Plan of Salvation," which was aired on KFYO/790AM in Lubbock August 11, 1974. The program has continued on KFYO for the past forty-two years.

In the early 80's, Wayne gave a series of sermons on the Lord's Supper, and they were answered on KFYO each Sunday by Grover Stevens of the Caprock Church of Christ on that congregation's program that aired just before ours. From that series a challenge to discuss the subject publicly was made: the debate was between George Hogland and Grover Stevens and was moderated by Wayne McKamie. Also, the preacher of a church in Levelland, Texas, requested a series of public studies. These studies involved a desire to know the truth and were conducted in a non-debate format for several weeks. We have received requests for sermons from as far away as Weatherford, Abilene, Amarillo, and Midland in Texas; also, requests came from Eunice, Clovis, and Portales in New Mexico.

We are blessed to be able to hear Wayne McKamie preach every Lord's Day. You can hear him also. The radio station has advised us: "KFYO streams the programs online. The stream is available on http:/kfyo.com. Just click on the 'Listen Live' button on the right side of the page. KFYO is on iPhone, iPad, and android devices. Go to the app store for your device and search for radioPUP. Select Lubbock, and then select KFYO to listen on the mobile device."

May these seeds of the Kingdom be planted in many good hearts for years to come and may God make them grow: that is our prayer in the name of Jesus Christ, the Son of the living God!

George Hogland

In Dedication to . . .

… my wife, Jean, without whose influence I might have never come to a knowledge of the truth.

… my four sons, who have heard these lessons since their earliest recall and in whom I hope to see them come alive as a beautiful blending of the human and the divine.

… my home congregation, in McGregor, Texas, whose members have listened patiently through the years.

… the cause of Him from whose lips these great truths first fell.

"To the only wise God our Saviour, be glory and majesty, dominion and power, both now and ever. Amen" (Jude 25).

J. Wayne McKamie

Acknowledgments

This book would have never been done had not some who heard the broadcasts decided to take on the long and tedious task of bringing it all together.

All of the brothers and sisters listed below have mastered their craft and contributed to the goal of retaining the style and manner of the speaker so that the lessons would live ever to those who did hear them in person. I am greatly indebted to all who have so willingly labored together to make this work possible.

Special mention is in order for George and Louva Hogland of Lubbock, Texas. More than forty years ago, George began to set this project in motion and has made many sacrifices to bring it to pass. My utmost gratitude to Louva, whose clerical skills and tremendous tenacity made this work possible.

Gary Robinson accepted the task of publishing this work. Gary is a brother with many talents and skills. He is one who has great patience and one who can set a goal and follow through to completion. He has wisely enlisted the help of skilled people for various parts of the project. David Robinson produced the artwork and the cover. Ashley Robinson reviewed the manuscript for readability.

My deepest appreciation goes to Joe Norton who contributed his superb work in so many areas. His formatting, editing, reading, and revision of the text manifest a technical scholarship second to none.

Many thanks to all of you who were willing to do what you could in such a time as this!

J. Wayne McKamie

J. Wayne McKamie

Biography

God's kingdoms have always included men who rose above the ordinary and became exemplary in performing the responsibilities God had for them to do. In each case, they had a deep and abiding love for God and developed a close relationship with Him. During the First Age, the patriarchs worked closely with God and led the people as God directed them. During the Mosaic Age, the same happened as God used men like the prophets, priests, and judges to lead His people. These men had the advantage of direct communication with God and, many times, the use of the miraculous in fulfilling their tasks.

During the opening years of the Christian Age, God set in place a system in which men would no longer have the use of the miraculous. Rather, God wanted men who would rise up and perform service for Him because of their love and dedication to Him and the cause of His Son—men who would perform their responsibilities without the use of the miraculous. The church has always been blessed with such men—and J. Wayne McKamie is such a man.

Background

Having been born into a staunch Baptist family, Wayne grew up in a rural environment, faithfully attending a Baptist church in Moody, Texas. He was born April 26, 1933, near Moody in McLennan County. His father was Dudley Clarence McKamie, and his mother was Mary Ellen McKamie. He was the youngest of four children.

From his earliest remembrance, his parents taught him to believe in and love God. As well, they maintained extremely high moral standards and taught him to do the same, warning him against drinking, gambling, dancing, and immorality. He heard some of the strongest sermons he has ever heard against such from his home and from the pulpit during his early years. He has related that he grew up with the conviction that a bottle of beer or a deck of cards would be as welcome in his home as a rattlesnake.

Wayne's first exposure to the New Testament pattern of worship was in 1949 when he attended a service of the Jones Hill Church of Christ about seven miles south of McGregor, Texas, at the invitation of a classmate, Jean Cherry (they later married). Billy Jack Ivey, a young preacher from Oklahoma, spoke that day. Wayne remembers being quite taken by the uniqueness of the building as well as simplicity of the worship:

> The building was a small typical one-room country school house. Gray weathered walls supported a steep wood-shingled roof. The well that served the school for so many years was still near the old front porch. Two doors opened in from the porch. Once inside a choice of short benches or ancient desks afforded one a seat. A raised section completely across the opposite end of the building, which once served as the teacher's vantage point, had been converted into the preacher's platform.

From that time, Wayne continued to visit the Jones Hill congregation as well as other congregations in the area. One such place was the Whitehall Church of Christ just outside of Moody, only about eight miles from the community where he grew up. He also visited the services of various other congregations in the vicinity of Waco, Temple, and Belton, all in Texas, hearing gospel sermons preached by such men as Homer A. Gay, James R. Stewart, Irvin Waters, E.H. Miller, Lynwood Smith, Homer L. King, C.S. Holt, Gillis Prince, Isom Hayes, Billy Jack Ivey, Fred Kirbo, and Barney Welch. He remembers well some of the gospel meetings at the Jones Hill congregation when the brethren set up lights outside and had an open-air service because of the hot Texas summers. Crowds were always good during those times because "people came to church back then."

During one of the first gospel meetings he attended, he heard Lynwood Smith preach at the 29th Street congregation in Temple. One of the first debates he heard was between Irvin Waters and John Staley about whether the church could use fermented wine in the Lord's Supper. Another debate he remembers was by E.H. Miller and John O'Dowd discussing whether it was scriptural to use individual communion cups in the Lord's Supper and whether they could divide the assembly into Bible classes.

In February 1950, after much searching and Bible study, Wayne decided to leave the Baptist Church and obey the plan of salvation as taught in the New Testament. He was almost seventeen years old at the time. Barney Welch, who was conducting a gospel meeting at the

Vaughn Blvd. congregation in Fort Worth, Texas, baptized him into Christ.

Wayne was married to Jean Cherry June 29, 1951. To them, four sons were born: Charles Wayne, Carlis James, David Neal, and Brian Dudley.

Evangelistic Work

Receiving much encouragement from brethren who had been in the church for a long time, Wayne began to speak publicly. He preached his first sermon at the old 4th Street congregation in Waco in early 1951. Because of his obvious understanding of the scripture, his exceptional talent as a public speaker, and his booming resonant voice, brethren continued to encourage him to become a full-time preacher of the gospel. Making the decision to follow their advice, Wayne's first opportunity to do evangelistic work came August 8, 1951, when he began working with the congregation in Harrodsburg, Indiana; thus, he has served the Lord as an evangelist for sixty-three years. Wayne and his wife, Jean, loaded up all of their possessions and their wedding gifts and headed for Indiana in a car that was a gift from Jean's father.

Wayne remembers the tremendous spiritual rewards of those years but also the difficulties that accompanied those rewards. He was extremely busy, and he realized the sacrifices his new wife was having to make. He says, in fact, that few really realize the great sacrifices preachers' wives must make so that their husbands can preach the gospel. Their situation was an extreme case. They were eighteen years old and they had been married only two months when they moved into this work that had taken them more than one thousand miles from their home.

While living in Harrodsburg, Wayne was ordained as an evangelist by Homer L. King in 1952. During the two years he and Jean spent there, he undertook a tremendous workload for a young Christian and a new evangelist. In fact, for the first six months, they did not stay at home for even one evening because they were busy with visitation and other responsibilities for the church. In addition to edifying and building up the church there, he also began a radio work, conducted home studies, began mission work at nearby points, and performed numerous other duties connected with a located evangelistic effort. Preaching three times a week and preparing a radio sermon for every Sunday morning plunged Wayne into an intensive study of the Bible that kept him busy almost day and night. Out of that study, however, came a knowledge of the Bible that has served him well throughout his years of preaching.

Jean reminisces, too, about their move to Indiana when they settled into the little house behind the historic big red-brick church building: "The church in Harrodsburg was the largest Church of Christ we had ever seen or had been a part of. There were about one hundred members. I will never forget our first Sunday there. A huge bell was rung at 10 o'clock and again at 10:30, calling the worshipers to come in. The singing was beautiful." She commented on how extremely friendly all of the people at Harrodsburg were and how much she appreciated that. "Even so, I got so homesick I thought I would die."

"We actually grew up in Harrodsburg," she said. "It was hard times, money was scarce, but we were happy." She becomes philosophic when she reflects on her years as a preacher's wife: "The Lord had something special planned for me. He had Wayne McKamie waiting and a life of preaching. Since I was a little girl, I wanted to be a preacher's wife." She says they never gave much thought for the future when they first began their spiritual journey together: "We wanted to be together, and together we were for the next eleven years more than most couples would be." She made this statement in reference to those years of traveling and preaching across the United States before they settled back in Texas to rear their family. They celebrated sixty-three years together in 2014.

While in Indiana, Wayne endeared himself to the Christians there and established a reputation that has stayed with him. He is still loved and highly respected wherever he works or conducts meetings. The fact that he is called back over and over to some of the same congregations for meetings testifies to the regard his fellow Christians have for him.

The first wedding he performed was in Harrodsburg in 1951, and the first funeral was also there in 1952.

Returning to the site of his first sermon, Wayne conducted his first gospel meeting at the 4th Street congregation in Waco in 1951.

While living in Indiana, Wayne took voice lessons and studied music under Dr. Ross at Indiana University. He also attended the Stamps Quartet School of Music in Dallas in 1959 where he studied under Videt Polk and Bobby Burnett. He has sung with and made records with the Sunny South Quartet, The Lamplighters, Celebration, and various other gospel singing groups.

After completing his work in Indiana, Wayne spent the next eleven years doing located work in a number of other states and conducting gospel meetings in many parts of the United States. Even after that time when he settled back in McGregor, Texas, to rear his family, he continued to conduct gospel meetings all across the U.S. as time allowed. The places where he did located work include Wayne, West Virginia; Memphis, Tennessee; Greenville, South Carolina; and in Andrews, Midland, Odessa, Waco, McGregor, and the congregation on Green Oaks in Arlington, in Texas.

Wayne has preached and/or conducted gospel meetings in every state where we have faithful congregations except the state of Alaska. He remembers the "hey day" of gospel meetings in the 1950's and 1960's when brethren would arrange to use "brush arbors" or set up tents for mission meetings either in their own city or in cities where there was no faithful congregation, and they would attract large numbers of people from a community to hear the gospel. These meetings were usually highly successful as evidenced by the large number of responses. Wayne recalls that brethren would find a vacant lot, clean it up, string lights or hang lanterns, get some funeral home fans, and advertise the meeting. During one such meeting in 1956 in Greenville, SC, Wayne and Bro. E.H. Miller preached what he called a "double header": both of them preached every night of the meeting. His wife Jean recalls, "they preached and preached while we sat for hours on metal folding chairs." Gospel meetings were longer back then, some lasting two full weeks and over three Sundays. Some went even longer if people continued to show an interest in the gospel. Buildings were filled to capacity many times with people standing outside and listening through open windows.

During those years, he and his fellow evangelists preached in any venue to which a crowd could be gathered: in country schoolhouses, court houses, prisons, municipal auditoriums, old store fronts, and others. And many people responded to the gospel. He remembers that during some of those meetings his "baptizing clothes never got dry."

For Wayne, the largest number ever responding during any gospel meeting was forty-one, and the largest number baptized in a new work was thirty-five. Gospel meetings were really a big occasion during those times. Preachers could go into any community and begin preaching, assuming that people already believed in God and in the Bible as the Word of God. Many times young men who wanted to become preachers of the gospel showed up to help with the singing, to assist in other ways during the services, and just to learn as much as they could.

"Preaching was our life, our work, our world," Wayne said. He remembers one tour in California when he preached thirty-five nights without a break, going from one meeting to another—that tour was in 1956. There were others when he preached from one end of that state to the other to enthusiastic audiences eager to hear the gospel.

Besides assisting countless souls in obeying the Lord and in remaining faithful, Wayne has conducted numerous weddings and funerals for fellow Christians across the nation. He has also participated in many brotherhood preachers' studies in this country.

Educational and Professional Career

All of Wayne's public school education was completed in the Moody Public School System. After several years as a well-known and respected evangelist, he moved back to his home in McGregor and continued his education at Temple Junior College, receiving his Associate in Arts degree in 1962. While at Temple, he was selected to be a member of Phi Theta Kappa, a national junior college honor society. Transferring to Baylor University, he completed the requirements for a Bachelor of Arts degree with a major in education in 1964. He was an honor student at both Temple and Baylor.

Having completed his bachelor's degree, Wayne decided in the fall of 1964 to teach school during the winter months and preach during the three summer months plus over weekends and during holiday periods. His goal was to provide a stable environment for his four boys while they were in school. He actually continued that rigorous schedule for the next twenty-four years. His first position was as a sixth grade teacher in the Waco Public Schools as well as helping in special education as needed.

In 1966, he became a master teacher with the Hallsburg schools, assisting other teachers and helping with some of the responsibilities of the principal, who was looking toward retirement. After the principal retired, Wayne did some teaching but also took on the responsibilities of the principal. In preparation for this position, he had begun working on a Master of Science degree in education at Baylor University, a degree he completed in 1970. Soon his position was upgraded to a combination of superintendent and principal, a position he held until his retirement in 1988. At that time, he returned to full-time preaching, the work he loved the most.

Radio Work

Having begun his radio work in Indiana, Wayne has also had programs in several other states. He has had extended broadcasts across the state of Texas, including Midland, Hillsboro, and San Antonio. At this time he has a program broadcasting from Waco, Texas, and from Lubbock, Texas, which has been on the air continually for the past thirty-five years. Radio was as effective in earlier days as television and the Internet are today.

In 2002, Wayne spent a little more than a year going to a professional studio in Dallas to make a recording of the entire New Testament. The congregation located on Grauwyler Road in Irving, Texas, sponsored this work.

Mission Work

For the past forty-seven years, Wayne has been involved in missionary work in Mexico, having made his first trip in 1967, accompanied by this writer. He has made many trips to visit congregations and mission points in Mexico, has accompanied native preachers into areas to explore the possibilities of new mission points, and has observed native preachers in their performance of evangelistic responsibilities. He has also conducted countless numbers of studies for preachers in the villages and has conducted many major studies for preachers in Saltillo, in Monterrey, and in Mexico City with all of the Mexican evangelists in attendance.

Studying the Spanish language at both Temple Junior College and Baylor University facilitated his work among the Spanish-speaking brethren in Mexico. He also became involved in the Texas Bilingual Institute in Waco.

Wayne continues to communicate with Juan Rodriguez, Jr., about the work there and occasionally with other native preachers. He also communicates with brethren in this country about the work in Mexico.

As well, Wayne has been involved in mission work in South America in the countries of Peru and Ecuador. He has made two mission trips to the continent of Africa: one was to Ghana with this writer where he assisted in conducting intensive Bible studies for the local preachers and the other was to Zambia where he worked with Roger Boone and Duane Permenter. In the 1980s, he and this writer made a good-will trip to England and Scotland to visit brethren and to establish ties with faithful churches there.

Conclusion

An asset that has stood well with Wayne in preaching is his phenomenal memory. Having been an avid reader not only of the scripture but also of the classic literature of the church, Wayne has found that his memory has allowed him to have at his disposal vast amounts of information that he can insert on the spot, enhancing his preaching and making the scriptures really come alive for his audiences. Because of his memory, he has always been able to preach his sermons from abbreviated notes rather than manuscripts.

Few who have heard the masterful persuasiveness of Wayne's sermons have gone away untouched in some way—saint or sinner. No sincere Christian has ever sat in the audience and listened to the gospel preached with Wayne's deep resounding voice without feeling a need to live a little more closely to the Lord.

Aside from the fact that his preaching is informative and inspirational, Wayne has always set before the people a model of a Christian witness in every aspect of his life. He is always diligent in doing the work of an evangelist and has proved to be a most congenial work fellow to many. He loves the souls of men and puts forth every effort toward their salvation. It has been while listening to Wayne preach that many, young and old, have made decisions that put them back on a stable course in their Christian lives. It is perhaps the message of penetrating practicality that causes people to be moved to action more than any other one characteristic of Wayne's preaching.

Wayne's basic philosophy really sums up the foundation upon which he has built his years of service to the Lord: "I believe in the inspired, inerrant, once-for-all-time handed down Word of God."

Joe L. Norton
Mansfield, Texas

Preface

"Words of Love" is an effort to give wider circulation to the word of God. These sermons of our Lord and His apostles were first heard in the cities, highways, and by-ways of Judea, and eventually in the regions beyond.

The idea of presenting these lessons in this form first came from George Hogland and his wife Louva. George asked if I would be willing to preach on radio for an extended period of time—extended it truly became! For forty-two years of continued broadcast, the Word has gone forth from KFYO in Lubbock, Texas.

These sermons, for the most part, were not written but recorded on the media available at the time. I would send the sermons to George and Louva, who would reduce the sermons to a transcript (a tremendous, tedious chore) to return to me for corrections.

I drew from the experience I gained from 1951 to 1953 when the brethren in Harrodsburg, Indiana, arranged for weekly broadcasts on WTTS in nearby Bloomington. Since then, I have conducted broadcasts in a number of states, more extensively across Texas.

I must draw your attention to the sermons themselves. These lessons are not examples of literary excellence on my part. I claim little originality. My story is that of John 4: "other men labored, I have entered into their labors." Enter into any of these lessons, and it will be evident that this work was neither written by a scholar nor for scholars. It was designed for those who love the Lord and his Word—and who want to know His ways more perfectly. "And this is life eternal, that they should know thee the only true God, and him whom thou didst send, even Jesus Christ" (John 17:3).

No person, says the great teacher, lights a lamp and then covers it under a basket, but rather that it may give light to all in the house. If we have lifted a candle to the candlestick, if we have shed light into the dark corners of unbelief, if a lost sheep has returned to the fold, we rejoice with joy unspeakable and full of glory. To God be the glory—great things He has done!

J. Wayne McKamie

Sermons

The Plan of Salvation

"Go thy way: for he is a chosen vessel unto me, to bear my name before the Gentiles, and kings, and the children of Israel." Our Lord spoke these words concerning Paul in Acts 9:15. This verse portrays clearly that our Lord planned for the salvation of those who would heed His word. We can see that this planning was begun even before the beginning in Genesis 1. Paul says in Ephesians 1:4, "According as he hath chosen us in him before the foundation of the world, that we should be holy and without blame before him in love." That the manner in every detail was known of God at this time is verified by Peter in 1 Peter 1:2: "Elect according to the foreknowledge of God the Father, through sanctification of the Spirit, unto obedience and sprinkling of the blood of Jesus Christ: Grace unto you, and peace, be multiplied."

The Bible teaches that when man was first made, he had perfect fellowship and communion with God. After the sin in the Garden, however, man was separated from God and in need of redemption. But before pronouncing punishment upon man, God made a promise concerning the plan He would implement to reconcile man unto Himself. In Genesis 3:15, He says:

> And I will put enmity between thee and the woman, and between thy seed and her seed; it shall bruise thy head, and thou shalt bruise his heel. (These words God spoke to the serpent, or in effect, to Satan) (Revelation 12:9).

The full revelation of God to man shows that the seed of woman is Christ (Galatians 4:4) and that He was to win the victory over Satan (Hebrews 2:14; Romans 8:3). Carefully consider these two verses that show it was in God's plan for Christ to redeem man and for His blood to be the redemptive power.

In 1 Peter 1:18-19, Peter says that men are redeemed by the "precious blood of Christ." Then he says in verse 20, "Who (Christ) verily was foreordained before the foundation of the world, but was manifest in these last times for you." On the day of Pentecost, this same apostle says about Christ, "Him, being delivered by the determinate counsel and foreknowledge of God, ye have taken, and by wicked hands have crucified and slain" (Acts 2:23). We can understand by God's word that He was working out this great plan throughout the history of the Old Testament. The Spirit of Christ, which was in the prophets, testified before him concerning the sufferings of Christ and the glory that should follow. But these prophets were not able to comprehend the full scope of this mystery. Peter says in relation to this salvation that the "prophets inquired and searched diligently" as to what it would really be or "what manner of time" it would come (1 Peter 1:10-11).

I am simply emphasizing today that God does have a plan. He completed this plan and revealed it unto us. It is the only plan and the only way. This knowledge is encompassed in such statements as the one given by Jesus in John 14:6, when He says, "I am the way, the truth, and the life: no man cometh unto the Father, but by me." His statement in Luke 13:3 also shows there is only one way: "Except ye repent, ye shall all likewise perish." "He that believeth and is baptized shall be saved" (Mark 16:16) emphasizes the same point.

Salvation is of the Lord, according to Jonah 2:9. And the Lord says, "Not everyone that saith unto me, Lord, Lord, shall enter the kingdom of heaven; but he that doeth the will of my Father which is in heaven" (Matthew 7:21).

Consider in God's great plan that His grace is sovereign and that we are saved by the grace of God. Possibly the best answer to the question of the grace of God is found in Acts 15:11, "But we believe that through the grace of the Lord Jesus Christ we shall be saved, even as they." No follower of the Lord could refuse to believe in salvation through grace. Grace means unmerited favor.

God does not save us because He has so much invested in us that He cannot afford to lose us. He does not save us because we are worth saving. He does not save us because we are too good to be lost. Many times we hear people say, especially at funerals, that God would not condemn a man who is honest, upright, good to the orphans and widows, and has other qualities that commend him to God.

But may I assure you today that God is not obligated to save anybody, not one of us, because of any number of good qualities or traits in us.

No one is capable of living such a good life as to put God under obligation to save him. The reason God saves us upon any condition is to be found only in God Himself. God's own mercy—spontaneous, undeserved, and condescending—is that which moved Him. God is His own motive. His love is not drawn out by our loveableness but rather wells up like an artesian spring from the depths of His own nature.

Salvation by grace is in contrast (1) with our own goodness and wisdom—that is, our own righteousness; or (2) with salvation by the works of the law of Moses, which we are told could not bring salvation; or (3) with perfect obedience on our part. If perfect obedience is a condition of salvation, then none of us will be saved. We are saved by the grace of God in spite of our imperfections.

The passage in Ephesians 2:8 has often been used to prove that man is saved by grace alone and not conditioned upon obedience to God. Grace does not forbid obedience—please remember that. Grace does not forbid obedience but rather makes it conditional. Since God has declared that the disobedient are lost because they obey not the truth, we must conclude that obedience is a condition of salvation by grace (1 Peter 4:17; 2 Thessalonians 1:9-10). Ephesians 2:8-9 reads, "For by grace are ye saved through faith; and that not of yourselves: it is the gift of God: Not of works, lest any man should boast." In these statements, Paul attributes our salvation to the mercy, the love, the kindness, and the grace of God.

At no time does Paul intimate that our salvation is on account of our goodness. In fact, he pictures the contrary. He points out how the world was lost and ruined by sin— that is, walking according to the course of the world, living in the lust of our flesh and of our mind—so that he might emphasize the wonderful love and the kindness, the mercy and the grace of God. Thus, we conclude that salvation is provided to man as a favor unmerited. But, man must be obedient to God's commands to receive such grace. In fact, the Apostle Peter says we must work righteousness to be acceptable to God (Acts 10:35). Paul says we are justified by a faith that works through love (Galatians 5:6).

I would like for you to consider next, after thinking of the grace of God, about the sinfulness of man. Certainly, the great plan of salvation encompasses such things as the grace of God and certainly the sinfulness of man. Of course, many things remind us of our sinfulness. Since our parents, Adam and Eve, sinned in the very beginning, man has continually suffered the effects of sin. The weeds and the thorns that grow, the sorrow and sickness and suffering that we endure, the tragedies that come all remind us that we are sinners and need to be saved. Paul tells us in Romans 3:23 that "all"—"all have sinned, and come short of the glory of God."

Some of the best men who have ever lived have openly confessed their weaknesses and their sins.

> In 2 Samuel 12:13, we read David's humble confession to God in the presence of Nathan, the prophet, "I have sinned."
>
> Paul says he had been the chief of sinners.
>
> John says that if we say we have no sin, we are liars and the truth is not in us and furthermore, we make God a liar. Thus, we know that none of us can say we have not sinned.

We sin because we are imperfect and because of the temptations of the flesh. The Bible teaches us that we do not inherit sin, but we sin because of our own weakness in the flesh. Ezekiel 18:20 declares, "The son shall not bear the iniquity of the father, neither shall the father bear the iniquity of the son." Paul tells us that God will hold each of us responsible for our own sins, so then every one of us shall give account of himself to God. Those who teach that children are born sinners fail to recognize the teaching of God's word on this subject. Please listen—the awfulness of sin is shown by the price that had to be paid that our sins might be forgiven.

Before Jesus died, men were commanded to offer animal sacrifices for a sin offering. These sacrifices could not bring complete atonement for sin but served to push the guilt of the sacrificer forward for a time. Hebrews 10:4 reminds us that "it is not possible that the blood of bulls and of goats should take away sins." Though man could pay the interest on sins by offering animal sacrifices, it was not until God gave His only Son that the principal could be taken away. Jesus had to die so that sin might be forgiven (Hebrews 2:9). Thus, sin is so terrible that the only one who could take away the guilt of it had to come from God. And the only sacrifice that would be powerful enough for its remission was the sacrifice of Jesus' blood.

We all need to come to Christ today to have our sins forgiven. The scripture teaches that "though our sins be as scarlet, they shall be as white as snow; and though they be red like crimson, they shall be as wool" (Isaiah 1:18). Such terms as "remission of sins" (Acts 2:38), "washing away sins" (Acts 22:16), "forgiveness of sins" (Ephesians 1:7), and "atonement" (Romans 5:11), all remind us that God through Jesus Christ now completely erases all of our sins when we submit to His divine will. And how thankful we should be that we live under the Christian dispensation where we can have the forgiveness of our sins rather than just a temporary atonement.

With the grace of God and the sinfulness of man in mind, surely one question that we should be ready to ask is, "What must I do to be saved?" This is undoubtedly the most important question that ever fell from mortal lips. It is asked essentially three times in the book of Acts, the book of conversions in the New Testament. These words are found in Acts 16:30 when the heathen jailer asks Paul and Silas, "Sirs, what must I do to be saved?" The question implies that something must be done by each accountable being in order to be saved.

Man, then, becomes immediately active, not passive, in the plan of redemption. This question makes salvation a personal, individual matter. There has never been a rational being who could spend a lifetime on earth without sometime, somewhere, surely, being vitally concerned about his own salvation. There have been some who waited too long to obtain the salvation that is in Christ with eternal glory (2 Timothy 2:10). And through no fault of the Saviour, these condemned men spurned the invitation of the Lord (Matthew 11:28; Revelation 3:20).

Jesus makes it plain in His last instructions to the apostles concerning the requirements of salvation. These are the requirements that would begin to be preached in Jerusalem (Acts 1:8) and would last until the end of the world (Matthew 28:20). He teaches every accountable being from Pentecost until Judgment that faith, repentance, and baptism for the remission of past sins would be necessary (Mark 16:16; Luke 24:47; Acts 2:38; Acts 22:16). These requirements are necessary to obtain the removal of the guilt in our past lives. And that is what the plan of salvation is all about.

To those who manifested faith in asking the apostles how to remove the guilt of their former manner of conduct, Peter answers, "Repent, and be baptized every one of you in the name of Jesus Christ for the remission of sins, and ye shall receive the gift of the Holy Ghost" (Acts 2:38).

To Saul of Tarsus, who had faith in Christ by asking what he should do to be acceptable unto the Lord (Acts 9:1-6) and who repented in fasting and prayer for three days, these words yet needed to be spoken: "And now why tarriest thou? arise, and be baptized, and wash away thy sins, calling on the name of the Lord" (Acts 22:16).

To a heathen in a pagan land where the gospel had never been preached, Paul says, "Believe on the Lord Jesus Christ, and thou shalt be saved, and thy house. And they spake unto him the word of the Lord," so that he might believe (Acts 16:31-32; Romans 10:13-17). The Bible teaches that he repented of his sins, indicated by the washing of the stripes on the backs of Paul and Silas, and was baptized the same hour of the night (Acts 16:33).

Thereafter, to remain in a saved condition, we must live righteously, worship consistently and scripturally, and work ardently in the Master's service, according to Philippians 2:15, Acts 2:42, and John 4:24.

The question today that is so relevant is: Are you a child of God? Have you done these things that you might be saved?

In a discussion of this nature, concerning the plan of salvation, I think we should want to know why people are lost. Now, when the Lord talks to us about the plan of salvation, He immediately implies that we are lost and need to be saved. So I am concerned this morning about why men are lost.

In answering this question, we are "not going all the way back to the nature of man," which renders him unable to do righteousness without God's help, but rather we want to mention some of the things that are easily evident by association with man.

The men who are lost are those who refuse to accept the help God has so graciously offered. Many are lost because of a lack of knowledge. This was the plight of the Israelites about whom Paul speaks in Romans l0. He points out that they had a zeal for God, but it was not according to knowledge. Being ignorant of God's righteousness, they sought to establish their own righteousness. In doing so, they failed to submit themselves unto the righteousness of God.

In many cases, men today are failing to submit themselves unto the righteousness of God because of their lack of knowledge. But the men of whom we are speaking now are those who have had every opportunity to know how to submit unto His righteousness but have failed to take advantage of such privileges.

Men are being lost, and many of them supposedly members of the Lord's body, because they are not learning what God has spoken to them. Men are being lost today because of prejudiced minds. Many people have preconceived ideas as to what members of Jesus' church think about their own status. The world thinks we believe we are especially endowed above others, and this idea leads them to be prejudiced against us and prevents them from listening to the truth. They fail to hear us explain that any righteousness we might have had imparted to us by God was because His word has led us to the truth. And this benefit is available to every human—not just some, but to everyone.

Men are lost today because they fail to recognize the sovereignty of God. They fail to see that God is God. As Paul says to the Israelites in Romans 9:16, "So then it is not of him that willeth, nor of him that runneth, but of God that sheweth mercy." "Shall the thing formed say to him that formed it, Why hast thou made me thus?" (Romans 9:20).

Men are lost today because they fail to heed the words of our Lord in Matthew 4:4 when He says, "Man shall not live by bread alone, but by every word that proceedeth out of the mouth of God." In James 2:24, the writer states clearly and emphatically that we must work to be justified, that pardon will not come by faith alone. Despite the clarity of this verse, millions in the world adhere to a faith-only doctrine. Jesus is the author of eternal salvation unto all them that obey him, according to Hebrews 5:9.

Christians are being lost today because of their failure to understand the inner workings of their own religion. It is so much in natural man to depend upon his own strength, and it is hard even for Christians to understand that the mature Christian life is not just the result of struggling self-effort nor of earned justification. They are both gifts of God by faith. They fail to realize that God "is able to do exceedingly abundantly above all that we ask or think, according to the power that worketh in us" (Ephesians 3:20). They fail to see that it is Christ in them that makes possible the hope of glory, according to Paul in Colossians 1:27.

These are reasons, along with others, that show men are being lost because of their own choosing—however ironical that may sound. God has done His part and will do His part. It remains for man simply to choose to do his part by obeying God's divine will.

Paul at Athens

Good morning, everyone. Once again we have the privilege of studying the Lord's word with you. Jesus states in Matthew 28:18, "All authority hath been given unto me in heaven and on earth. Go ye therefore, and make disciples of all the nations" (ASV). Since our Lord thus commissions us to preach the gospel to all nations and to all people in all nations, certainly we should be grateful for times and opportunities like these. There has never been given to anyone a commission that had a higher authority than that possessed by the Great Commission because Jesus says, "I have ALL authority .... Go ye therefore." It is interesting that in the early church, in the early days of evangelism, they went EVERYWHERE preaching the word.

Mark records it, "Go ye into all the world, and preach the gospel to EVERY creature." Luke says, "That repentance and remission of sins should be preached in his name unto all the nations, beginning from Jerusalem" (Luke 24:47) (ASV). In response to such teaching, the apostles and early Christians went everywhere preaching the gospel.

For our lesson today, we invite your attention to one of the cities to which the Apostle Paul turns to carry out the Great Commission. Open your New Testament to Acts 17, and let's study this morning about Paul and his preaching in the ancient Greek city of Athens. Luke says Paul and his company pass through Amphipolis and Apollonia and come to Thessalonica where Paul reasons with the Jews in their synagogues for three sabbath days. As he preaches Christ to them, some believe and others are moved with envy and stir up opposition to Paul. Then Paul and Silas go to Berea, about sixty miles southwest. Notice the compliment Paul gives these Bereans. "These were more noble than those in Thessalonica, in that they received the word with all readiness of mind, and searched the scriptures daily, whether those things were so" (verse 11). Now these are great qualities for us to emulate. We should open our minds to receive God's word readily, and we should search the scriptures daily.

We are not surprised at the success of the preaching in this particular place and verse 12 so aptly states, "Therefore many of them believed; also of honourable women which were Greeks, and of men, not a few." But men from Thessalonica come and stir up the people against Paul, and then he goes to Athens.

Ancient Athens was a great city. In fact, it was the capital of the province of Attica. It was noted for its learning and for its great beauty. Its free investigation and discussion gave assent to the spirit of democracy and gave to the world some of the basic principles for freedom and government. Many beautiful temples and buildings of outstanding architectural design were erected. Men from all over the world for many centuries had studied in this place; they came to study its art and its music and all the many things the Greeks knew.

To speak of Athens has come to mean to speak of learning—whether it be of philosophy, art, architecture, or democracy or just of the general desire to gain knowledge through study. But the Bible teaches that Athens was a city of idolatry. On every hand were their heathen temples and idols. The Bible says of Paul in Acts 17:16-17, "His spirit was stirred in him, when he saw the city wholly given to idolatry. Therefore disputed he in the synagogue with the Jews, and with the devout persons, and in the market daily with them that met with him." It was enough to stir the spirit of this great defender of the faith. He simply had to say something to the people.

Bro. J. W. McGarvey so aptly wrote, "In Athens where flourished the most profound philosophy, the most glowing eloquence, the most fervent poetry and the most refined art which the world has ever seen there was the most complete and studied abandonment to every vice which passion could prompt or imagination could invent."

It was Petronius who wrote, "It is easier to find a god than a man in Athens." But with all of their gods and with all of their idols came much sin. It's important to know this—that learning does not necessarily mean the knowledge of the true God. I think this generation of ours needs to hear that, and we need to emphasize it over and over—learning does not necessarily mean the knowledge of the true God.

Often people say they can't understand how brilliant and educated men could know so little about the Bible, or about God, or about the true church of the New Testament. Well, here is an example. These Athenians were interested in many philosophies, in many kinds of learning, but not interested in Jehovah. Man's wisdom has always led away from the true God. In speaking of man's early history, this same Apostle Paul writes in Romans 1:21-24:

> When they knew God, they glorified him not as God, neither were thankful; but became vain in their imaginations, and their foolish heart was darkened. Professing themselves to be wise, they became fools. And changed the glory of the uncorruptible God into an image made like to corruptible man, and to birds, and four footed beasts, and creeping things. Wherefore God also gave them up to uncleanness through the lusts of their own hearts.

And this, my people, has ever been the history of man. It is true today. Some of the greatest centers of worldly learning are centers of the rankest infidelity and the most brazen opposition to the Bible and to the true religion of our Heavenly Father. When secular learning becomes the standard of religion, you may easily observe that the simplicity of Christ's standards for Christianity will be erased. That simply has been a fact that has repeated itself too many times to be ignored. American universities and American denominations are no exception. People of our time would do well to observe the condition of Athens and be warned thereby. Some men point with seeming pride to the many religions of America, but many religions lead away from God. God's religion is ONE, and all who would please Jehovah must worship Him as He has directed in His word.

Let's notice some of the philosophy of the people in ancient Athens. Certain philosophers of the Epicureans and of the Stoicks encountered Paul. Now the Epicureans were not believers in life after death. Their idea was to get the most pleasure out of the present, to enjoy life as it passed—the gratifications of the lusts and the passions of the flesh obsessed them. Their philosophy is expressed by the rich fool in Luke 12:19 "Soul, thou hast much goods laid up for many years; take thine ease, eat, drink, and be merry." It is evident that we have their counterpart in the day in which we live because if there is anything that seems current today it is to eat and to drink and to be merry and to get all you can get because you are going to go this way only once.

The Stoicks that Paul encountered in Athens taught that one should be totally indifferent to both the sorrows and the pleasures of life. They believed in subjecting the appetites and the passions to reason and that all things were governed by irresistible fate—they believed virtue was its own sufficient reward and vice its own sufficient punishment, and that all of that occurred within this life. It is no wonder that some said of Paul, “What will this babbler say?”

Have you ever thought about this? Here is one of the greatest, if not THE greatest, preacher of all times—besides the Lord Jesus—the greatest preacher who ever walked the earth; and these, the wisest men in worldly philosophy, simply said of him, “What will this babbler say?” Others said, “He seemeth to be a setter forth of strange gods: because he preached unto them Jesus, and the resurrection” (verse 18). Please notice, these things were strange to their ears. They “spent their time in nothing else, but either to tell, or to hear some new thing,” but they had never learned of the one true God.

So the Apostle Paul begins to preach to them about God, even though they were educated men. He knows their ways, he knows their poets, he knows all these things, but these are not the things that Paul discusses. Paul does not simply try to fit in with the group: he tries to preach to them about those things that must inevitably be and those things that must happen, that must come to pass.

Remember they brought Paul to Mars Hill, to the Areopagus, which is the meeting place of the supreme court of Athens. It was a hill dedicated to Mars, the Greek god of war. Nearby stood the lovely Parthenon, a tremendous structure dedicated to the heathen goddess Minerva. Here in such surroundings, and before an assembly of people devoted to these idols, Paul preaches the one true God.

Notice how he begins the sermon—one of the greatest sermons you will ever read anywhere. He begins, “Ye men of Athens, I perceive that in all things ye are too superstitious” ... or as one translation puts it ... “ye are very religious. For as I passed along, and observed the objects of your worship, I found also an altar with this inscription, TO AN UNKNOWN GOD. What therefore ye worship in ignorance, this I set forth unto you” (verses 22-23) (ASV). We may observe these points: (1) they are religious people, (2) they have an altar to the unknown God, (3) Paul says they worshiped Him ignorantly, and (4) from this point Paul preaches to them about the one true God.

I want you to take a look at Paul’s sermon. A masterpiece! First, Paul introduces God as the one true God that made the world and all things therein. Paul sets God forth as the Creator of all and He is Lord of heaven and earth. No idol could compare to Him because He is Lord of all. Secondly, God does not dwell in temples made with hands. God could not be limited to the four walls of some temple built by men, however grand and great and ornate it may be. He is far too great for that. Stephen says of God:

> Howbeit the most High dwelleth not in temples made with hands; as saith the prophet, Heaven is my throne, and earth is my footstool: what house will ye build me (Acts 7:48-49)?

What kind of house could you build the Lord, One whose throne is heaven and whose footstool is earth? No house that man can build can house the God of heaven. The Greeks thought their gods dwelt in their temples, and they had to go there to communicate with them. Even today some feel they can't pray to God without walking to some great cathedral or to some meeting house. We are inclined to limit God with the limitation of idols. God is everywhere. His ear is ever open to our cries (that is, if we are His children), in every hour of need no matter where we may be: at home, at work, at play, in joy or in distress or sorrow. Let us not limit the greatness of our God.

Notice the third point that Paul makes. "Neither is worshipped with men's hands, as though he needed anything, seeing he giveth to all life, and breath, and all things" (verse 25). Their idols were supposed to have devoured their meat and drink offerings and to be enriched by their gifts; but God is not in need of help, like man, that He may exist. He is the One who gives. He gives to man and from Him comes the blessings of our very lives. We cannot enrich God with the gifts of our hands. It is from His unwasting fullness that all our blessings come. As James says, "Every good gift and every perfect gift is from above, and cometh down from the Father of lights" (James 1:17).

Paul set forth God as the God of all. "He hath made of one blood all nations of men for to dwell on the face of the earth" (verse 26). Listen to the American Standard Version, "And he made of one every nation of men to dwell on all the face of the earth, having determined their appointed seasons, and the bounds of their habitation." The races of men all have a common origin. They all came from the creative hand of God, no matter where they may now dwell on the face of the earth. God gave their seasons, their spring, their summer, their fall, their winter, their seed time, and their harvest. God also has appointed the bounds of man's habitation. The different nations are a part of the work of the one true God, and He is to be recognized in every nation. His providence is to rule over all human kind.

Notice fifthly, Paul sets forth the great principle that all men are to worship and to serve God. No person is exempt. Paul says:

> That they should seek the Lord, if haply they might feel after him, and find him, though he be not far from every one of us: For in him we live, and move, and have our being; as certain also of your own poets have said, For we are also his offspring. Forasmuch then as we are the offspring of God, we ought not to think that the Godhead is like unto gold, or silver, or stone, graven by art and man's device (Acts 17:27-29).

Paul is simply saying that God is near to all of us, and all men may know Him and serve Him. It is in Him that we live and move and have our very being. We should recognize that the God who has given us life and who sustains us is the Creator of the world. We are also His offspring; Paul, then, makes the grand argument that as the offspring of God, we should not degrade our origin by thinking that our Creator is like gold or silver or stone graven by art and man's devices. In other words, man did not come into being by some idol but was made by the true and living and powerful God. And so Paul is saying let us then worship and serve Him and Him alone.

Paul has so beautifully and adequately set forth the true God. He shows the utter uselessness of their idols and their heathen temples and points out the folly of their worship and then declares to them the greatness and the grandiose nature and the power of the one God of all the universe—the One whom all men of all ages should serve. He is our God today; and every man today, just as in ancient Athens, should worship Him.

I would like to make this point before we close: God will not overlook our ignorance. Paul continues his sermon by saying, "The times of this ignorance God winked at"...that is—He OVERLOOKED ... "but now commandeth all men EVERYWHERE" ... that is a pretty comprehensive statement ... "all men everywhere to repent" (verse 30).

Paul says God will not overlook their ignorance; and He will not overlook ours. Men have ample opportunities to know God and to know His plan of salvation. We live in a land of Bibles where Jesus is preached. Everyone has the responsibility to study the Bible and to obey God. As Paul writes in 2 Thessalonians 1:7-9 in regard to the second coming of Jesus, "The Lord Jesus shall be revealed from heaven with his mighty angels, In flaming fire taking vengence on them that KNOW NOT GOD, and"—please notice the other part of this verse—"that OBEY NOT THE GOSPEL of our Lord Jesus Christ." And what shall happen to those who do not know God or those who do not obey the gospel? "Who shall be punished with everlasting destruction from the presence of the Lord, and from the glory of his power." So the question today is, "My friend, do you know God?"

I don't know where you are today as you listen to this broadcast. I don't even know what you think about the broadcast, but I want to ask you the question today—as a soul that is eternity bound to another one who is eternity bound—let me ask you the question, "DO YOU KNOW GOD?" Have you repented of your sins? Have YOU obeyed the gospel?

When Jesus sends out His apostles, He says, "Go ye into all the world, and preach the gospel to every creature. He that believeth and is baptized shall be saved; but he that believeth not shall be damned" (Mark 16:15-16). Have YOU believed the gospel of Christ? Have YOU been baptized? Are YOU striving to observe all things that Christ has commanded you? (Matthew 28:20).

Remember, God is not going to overlook your ignorance. You have an opportunity to know Him and to know His word and to obey Him. You have a Bible (if you don't, we'll see that you get one); but you do, I'm sure, have a Bible, so you have an opportunity; and your opportunity is so much greater than that of the idolatrous Athenians. And if God will hold them responsible and God will not overlook their ignorance, may I assure you that He will not overlook our ignorance today.

Then Paul closes his sermon on the note of judgment when he says:

> He hath appointed a day, in the which he will judge the world in righteousness by that man whom he hath ordained; whereof he hath given assurance unto all men, in that he hath raised him from the dead (Acts 17:31).

The Lord, of course, speaks of that Day. The apostles speak of that Day, and Paul tells these people who were not Christians—who were idolaters—that they must repent and obey the gospel because they will face these things in the Day of Judgment. Then, as now, when they came to the close of the sermon, the scripture says "some mocked" and did not receive Paul's teaching; others, however, believed "among the which was Dionysius the Areopagite, and a woman named Damaris and others with them" (verse 34). Please remember, "God is not mocked: for whatsoever a man soweth, that shall he also reap" (Galatians 6:7). As you sow in this life, you must reap in judgment and for all eternity. We thank you for listening.

Authority in Religion

Good morning, everyone. Today our study concerns "Authority in Religion." We are pleased to be able to come to you today to study with you the word of God. Our subject today is one we believe to be most vital, probably one of the most vital questions a person could consider in his thinking about religion, and that is, "What is your authority in religion?"

This question should present the greatest of challenges to us. Other questions are important, but this one hits at the very heart of the things we practice in religion; and the answer will, of course, ultimately determine whether we will be lost or saved.

A related question is "Why do you believe the way you do about religion?" Is it because you were taught that way by your parents, is it because of the practices of your friends and neighbors, or do you have a concrete standard by which you examine all that you hear about religion? There is so much confusion and there are so many conflicting teachings that we must have some means of arriving at a safe and right conclusion as to what is right and what is wrong. What should we accept, or what should we reject? What should govern the decisions that will determine the salvation of our soul?

I think many people, today, have doubts and fears as to whether they are pleasing in the sight of Jehovah God. They face life's problems with uncertainty. In the time of hardship and difficulty, they have no strong arm of faith to sustain them. The discussions of matters of religion are offensive to them because they are not really sure of the basis of their own faith and practices. In such unsettled faith, there can be little comfort or little peace. Is this not true of many listening today—do you really have the comfort or the peace of mind that you ought to have regarding your practices in religion?

I think, today, how different was the unwavering faith of the Apostle Paul? He endured hardships and severe persecutions. He faced death with the conviction that he could say, "I know whom I have believed, and am persuaded that he is able to keep that which I have committed unto him against that day" (2 Timothy 1:12).

Jesus Christ was the one in whom Paul believed. Paul's faith had no place for doubt. Rather, Jesus became the ever-present source of strength to Paul, and that was the reason he could say, "I can do all things through Christ which strengtheneth me" (Philippians 4:13). And I ask you this morning—Do you not want to be sure and have the comfort and the confidence that Paul had in his religious convictions? Do you want the same thing in your life today? I tell you this morning that this same confidence can be true for you. There is but one answer, and Jesus Christ is the answer.

In Jesus, we have the full assurance of faith and the strength to meet every trying circumstance in life. In the teachings of Jesus Christ, we can find the solution to the problems that we must encounter day by day. In Him, we find the right standard for right and for wrong—the way to know what to do and what not to do—what to believe and what to classify as false teaching. His word should be the law to govern us and to tell us what to believe, what to do, how to live, how to worship God, how to treat our fellow man, and how to prepare for the time of death so that even in death we might have the confidence that we will make it into eternity and live in the presence of Christ in heaven. Jesus Christ is the only answer to all of these things.

Jesus Christ, while here on earth, spoke with authority. I am pleased that He spoke with authority so that it can remove us from this realm of doubt and wondering, thinking that perhaps we are not living as we ought to live. Listen as Matthew tells us, "The people were astonished at his doctrine: for he taught them as one having authority, and not as the scribes" (Matthew 7:28-29). This same reaction was true in the Master's teaching in the Sermon on the Mount. It was true in all that He taught. His teachings were from God. Jesus says:

> For I have not spoken of myself; but the Father which sent me, he gave me a commandment, what I should say, and what I should speak. And I know that his commandment is life everlasting: whatsoever I speak therefore, even as the Father said unto me, so I speak (John 12: 49-50).

Later He tells His disciples, "All power (or authority) is given unto me in heaven and in earth" (Matthew 28:18). God bore witness to His teaching through the miracles that Jesus did among the people. In John 20, we are told:

> And many other signs truly did Jesus in the presence of his disciples, which are not written in this book: But these are written, that ye might believe that Jesus is the Christ, the Son of God; and that believing ye might have life through his name (John 20:30-31).

Many of the people from Christ's time on earth recognized His miracles as proving His authority from God. Nicodemus says, "Rabbi, we know that thou art a teacher come from God: for no man can do these miracles that thou doest, except God be with him" (John 3:2).

In scripture God declares the authority of Jesus—in fact, repeatedly:

> In particular, on the mount of transfiguration as recorded in Matthew chapter 17, we read that God says concerning Jesus, "This is my beloved Son, in whom I am well pleased; hear ye him" (verse 5).
>
> In Hebrews 1:1-2, we read, "God, who at sundry times and in divers manners spake in time past unto the fathers by the prophets, Hath in these last days spoken unto us by his Son, whom he hath appointed heir of all things."
>
> The Apostle Peter applies the prophecy of Moses to Christ when he says, "A prophet shall the Lord your God raise up unto you of your brethren, like unto me; him shall ye hear in all things whatsoever he shall say unto you. And it shall come to pass, that every soul, which will not hear that prophet, shall be destroyed from among the people" (Acts 3:22-23).
>
> The law of Moses and the prophecies of the Old Testament point to the coming of Jesus. In speaking of the law of Moses, Paul says, "The law was our schoolmaster to bring us unto Christ, that we might be justified by faith. But after that faith is come, we are no longer under a schoolmaster" (Galatians 3:24-25).
>
> In Colossians 2:14, Paul teaches that Christ blotted "out the handwriting of ordinances that was against us, which was contrary to us, and took it out of the way, nailing it to his cross." We are no longer to keep the ordinances or sacrifices or Sabbaths of the old Mosaic law. We are to hear Christ, not

> Moses and not Elijah nor the other prophets. Their testimony points us only to Jesus Christ.
>
> The Old Testament scripture should be read and studied in view of Romans 15:4: "For whatsoever things were written aforetime were written for our learning, that we through patience and comfort of the scriptures might have hope."

These scriptures point out God and His plan and His promise. They point out Jesus as the promised Messiah, but the law of Christ is for us today and is found in the New Testament. Jesus is our lawgiver. The Bible declares, "For the law of the Spirit of life in Christ Jesus hath made me free from the law of sin and death" (Romans 8:2). Jesus' word is to be our law, both as He Himself spoke and as He directed the writers of the New Testament to record it for us. May I stress, this morning, that we must obey the law of Jesus Christ? He obeyed God—listen—He obeyed God and set an example of beautiful obedience. And Hebrews 5:8-9 states, "Though he were a Son, yet learned he obedience by the things which he suffered; And being made perfect, he became the author of eternal salvation unto all them that obey him." Please notice that the promise is to those who "obey HIM."

Jesus says, "He that rejecteth me, and receiveth not my words, hath one that judgeth him: the word that I have spoken, the same shall judge him in the last day" (John 12:48). We cannot trifle with the teachings of Jesus and expect to be saved. His word is sufficient, and we must be obedient to it or be like the foolish man who built his house upon the sand. In the day of trial, his house could not stand; his house was destroyed. And so shall we be destroyed if we obey not Jesus Christ, the Son of God.

I would like to emphasize the fact that Christ's gospel is perfect—it is complete. The Apostle Paul says there were some who perverted the gospel of Christ, and then he gives this warning:

> But though we, or an angel from heaven, preach any other gospel unto you than that which we have preached unto you, let him be accursed. As we said before, so say I now again, If any man preach any other gospel unto you than that ye have received, let him be accursed (Galatians 1:8-9).

Paul had preached the gospel of Christ as he had received it from Christ. He says, "But I certify you, brethren, that the gospel which was preached of me is not after man. For I neither received it of man, neither was I taught it, but by the revelation of Jesus Christ" (verses 11-12). The gospel that Paul preached "is the power of God unto salvation to every one that believeth" (Romans 1:16). Those who obey not the gospel of Jesus Christ shall be punished when He returns, according to 2 Thessalonians 1:9.

In the light of all these things mentioned thus far, the question should be this: How shall we regard the New Testament? In what light should we view it? Or what should it mean to us today? I would like to emphasize that the New Testament contains God's complete revelation of the gospel. In fact, in 2 Peter 1:3 he declares that we have "all things that pertain unto life and godliness." John says in the book of Revelation, so it is true of the whole New Testament, that we are not to add to it and we are not to take anything away from it (Revelation 22:18-19).

We should determine in our minds today that we are going to speak where the New Testament speaks and we will insist upon being silent where it is silent. Let us do what the Lord Jesus has commanded in the way that He commanded it and call Bible things by Bible names. His law is for us to obey, not to change or to pervert to suit our own likes or dislikes. We should change our lives to conform to the New Testament pattern of living and of serving God.

We have far too much—listen—we have far too much of changing the word of God to suit us instead of changing us to suit the word of God. Jesus should be the supreme authority in our lives, in our homes, and in the church of the Lord Jesus. For God has given Him "to be the head over all things to the church, Which is his body, the fullness of him that filleth all in all" (Ephesians 1:22-23).

Recognition of Jesus' authority would end controversy today if we were to submit to Him and obey His word. And I think one of the greatest things that should cross the mind of any person today would be to realize that if we were to recognize the authority of the Bible and the authority of Jesus Christ over us today, controversies and divisions would soon be on the way out. First of all, if we recognized the authority of Jesus Christ relative to becoming a Christian, we would all find ourselves reading something like this and believing it:

He that believeth and is baptized shall be saved (Jesus says in Mark 16:16).
Except ye repent, ye shall all likewise perish (Jesus says in Luke 13:3).

The steps of obedience are plain.

The faith enjoined is based on God's word (Romans 10:17).
It is one faith (Ephesians 4:5).
It is a faith that causes men to obey (James 2:24).
The repentance is a change of mind that leads to a change of life (Acts 3:19).
The confession is of one's faith in Jesus (Matthew 10:32-33).
The baptism is in water (Acts 10:47).
And it is a burial in water (Galatians 3:27; Colossians 2:12).
Baptism is essential for the remission of sins (Acts 2:38).

Thus, one is "baptized into Jesus Christ," according to Paul in Romans 6:3. And the Lord adds him to the church, according to Acts 2:47. As a follower of Jesus Christ, he is to be called a Christian (Acts 11:26; 1 Peter 4:16).

The unity of the church would be established if we recognized the authority of Jesus just as it is. And by that I mean this: the Bible teaches in Ephesians 4 that the church is one body. There are many members "yet but one body" (1 Corinthians 12:20). These Christians, as members of the Lord's church or body, are to love one another (John 17:21-26). Furthermore, they are commanded to keep the unity of the Spirit in the bond of peace, according to Ephesians 4:3.

Think with me just a moment. If this unity were accomplished in our world, do you realize it would remove the confusion of conflicting sects, parties, and denominational bodies? All professing Christians would be united in one body, the church of our Lord. Denominational names and creeds would be destroyed if men would recognize Jesus' authority. And certainly they should be. No man, no council, no synod, no church, no priest, no pope, nor anyone else has the right to legislate to the eternal souls of men, save the Lord Jesus and God.

Denominational divisions exist in our world today and in our city here because we have ignored the teachings of Jesus and we have established the teachings of men as authority to govern them. Every distinguishing doctrine of every denomination is something not found in your New Testament. I would like to repeat that statement—please listen—every distinguishing doctrine of every denomination is something that is not found in your New Testament.

Jesus' teachings would unite men. Men's teachings divide men. Jesus Himself proclaimed, "I am the way, the truth, and the life" (John 14:6). We may ridicule the teachings of Jesus, but I will assure you that His teachings are the only way we can be saved—by obedience to them. Religious unity can be found and obtained and kept only by a complete submission to His authority in all matters in which He has spoken.

If, today, the authority of Jesus Christ were recognized, I propose to you that the simplicity of the worship would be restored. There are several items taught in the New Testament as far as worship is concerned. The early church sang their praises to God (Ephesians 5:19). They prayed and were steadfast in the apostles' teachings (Acts 2:42). Each first day of the week, they contributed of their means, laying by in store as they had been prospered (1 Corinthians 16:2). On the Lord's Day, each first day of the week, they ate the Lord's Supper together (Acts 20:7; 1 Corinthians 11:23-28). These are things the Lord taught them to do, and we are taught to worship Him in spirit and in truth (John 4:24). If today we would recognize the authority of Jesus, we would be worshiping God in this fashion.

Last, if the authority of the Bible, if the authority of Jesus Christ, would be recognized in our fair city today, and in our world, His way would give us one hope. Ephesians 4:4-6 teaches there is one Lord, there is one faith, there is one baptism, there is one God, there is one Father, and thus there would have to be one hope of life eternal. John writes, "Blessed are they that do his commandments, that they may have right to the tree of life, and may enter in through the gates into the city" (Revelation 22:14).

In conclusion this morning, may we ask you again, very seriously, this question? What IS your authority in religion?

Please don't just turn me off. Please don't think, "Well, I really should study these teachings—maybe some day when I have a little more time or when I am a little more inclined or when I am not so busy, I will study these teachings." These matters are most important now. I would like to plead with you today to ask yourself the question—What is your authority?

> Have you recognized the authority of Jesus Christ?
> Have you obeyed the gospel of the Lord?
> Are you fashioning your life after the life of Jesus?
> Are you loving and serving others as Jesus taught you to do?
> Do you worship God as the Saviour has taught you to worship Him?
> Are you a Christian today? Just a plain New Testament Christian?
> Do you seek first the kingdom of God and His righteousness (Matthew 6:33)?

These are questions that you must answer individually. We can't just lose ourselves in the crowd somewhere. We, today, must face the questions individually. Each of us can do something about these questions because we can obey the Lord Jesus Christ in all things if we will just get our faith firmly fixed in Him. Our prayer, today, is this: that we may encourage you to follow the teachings of our Master in all things. And then when the Day of Judgment comes, you will not be found wanting and it is to this end that we beseech you to study and to obey God's word just as you read it in the book we know as the Bible.

Honor thy Parents

Good morning everyone. Once again we invite your attention to a study of the Lord's word, specifically to Ephesians 6 where the scripture teaches:

> Children, obey your parents in the Lord: for this is right. Honour thy father and mother; (which is the first commandment with promise;) That it may be well with thee, and thou mayest live long on the earth (Ephesians 6:1-3).

These commands from the Lord apply to all of us today. The first one is of particular importance to little children as they grow up in the home. "Children, obey your parents in the Lord: for this is right." But the force of the obligation increases as children grow older and develop an ability to understand the deeper meaning of the teaching and as they can see the wisdom of the Lord's plan. The second verse says, "Honor thy father and mother," and all of us come within the scope of this command! Little children, teenagers, grown young men or women, those who are married and may be miles away from home—all of us are included in this responsibility before God. Even if our parents have crossed over the valley of the shadow of death, upon us still rests the duty enjoined by God: "Honor thy father and mother." This relationship is older than Christianity.

The Old Testament relates that more than nineteen hundred years before Christ was born, God chose Abraham to be the father of a people to serve Jehovah, the lineage through which the Savior would come. In Genesis 18:19, God says of Abraham, "For I know him, that he will command his children and his household after him, and they shall keep the way of the Lord, to do justice and judgment." No greater thing might be said of any Christian today than "God knows him!" I wonder, can the Lord say of you, "I know him that he will command his children and his household after him, and they shall keep the way of the Lord, to do justice and judgment?" Abraham's descendants had become a mighty nation and God had delivered them from Egyptian bondage at Mt. Sinai. God then gave Moses the law to govern them as a nation and the fifth of the Ten Commandments was, "Honor thy father and thy mother." Disobedience to this command carried the penalty of death! "And he that curseth his father, or his mother, shall be surely be put to death" (Exodus 21:17).

Our Lord gave us this example: At the age of twelve when he had been to the Temple with Joseph and Mary, the scripture says of Jesus, "And he went down with them, and came to Nazareth, and was subject unto them" (Luke 2:51). Even though Jesus was the son of God and had said, "I must be about my Father's business," he still recognized this relationship to Mary, his mother, and Joseph, his father. He was subject to them. Verse 52 says, "And Jesus increased in wisdom and stature, and in favour with God and man."

When Jesus was about to die on the cross, He was mindful of His mother. Mary, together with that disciple whom Jesus loved (John the apostle), stood beholding the Lord's suffering on the cross. Jesus says, "Woman, behold thy son! Then saith he to the disciple, Behold thy mother! And from that hour that disciple took her unto his own home" (John 19:26-27). Jesus was obedient as a child, and he was thoughtful of His mother to the very end of His life! His example is for us to follow even today. And this command is for life! We cannot discharge it in a day or in a few years. It lasts as long as life lasts, even when our parents are old and after they are gone. It is for every day that we live, to remember to honor our father and mother.

Special days have been designated to honor our parents, and we title one of these days as "Mother's Day." Many mothers who have been neglected will be remembered on that day, and many good mothers will have their hearts warmed with expressions of love and gratitude from their children, who "rise up, and call her blessed" (Proverbs 31:28). Then, when Father's Day comes, the same will be true of fathers. But I would emphasize this point: Every day of our lives should be so lived that they give honor to our parents! The love that we express, the devotion that fills our lives toward them, and the appreciation for their work and patience and training and guidance should be in our thoughts and actions and manner of life every day!

Now this fact is true, too: parents should be deserving of honor. They should discharge their duties and bear their responsibilities so as to merit the respect and honor of their children. There is more to being a parent than having a child; yet in many instances, when we refer to parents, we are simply referring to the biological process of bringing a child into the world. Fathers and mothers should shoulder the responsibilities of parenting and give to their children the thought, time, and attention they need so that they can become responsible adults and faithful Christians. God has given such direction to parents. The home is the whole world of the child in the early days of life. The love, tenderness, and affection of the parents are all the child knows, and these expressions provide the nurture the child needs. Every parent should make his or her life an example for the child to follow, and thus they are following the direction in the Bible to bring their children up in "the nurture and admonition of the Lord." Very simply, they should be devoted Christians. Their examples should be Christian examples; their homes should be Christian homes, built around the service of God and the teachings of our Lord and Saviour. In those childhood days, parents are to mold and fashion that little mind into the likeness of the Lord. The love of Christ, the real purpose and joy of Christian living, and the true ambition to serve the Master should be planted in the child's mind during those formative years. The scripture declares, "Train up a child in the way he should go: and when he is old, he will not depart from it" (Proverbs 22:6).

Now, for some questions: Are you a father? As you listen to this broadcast, are you a father? If so, your home depends upon you. If you discharge your responsibility as a husband and as a father as God intended, first of all, **you will be a Christian**! You will set a Christian example and you will obey the Lord! You will go to church, love the church of the Lord, and put the church first in your life—a **first** above business, pleasure, and every other consideration—and you will make it your aim to implant the same attitude into the child who will walk in the steps of your parental example.

Another question: Are you a mother? If so, please be deserving of this honor. You have the most influential position of all—holding your heart near to his or her little heart! Your winsome ways, your happy smile, your tenderness and affection mean more than anything else to the child. You too, should (or may I say must) be a Christian! As a mother, you should teach and train that child at your knee, in your lap, in your home, and in all of your busy activities to know the meaning of Christian motherhood. Teach your child to know the Lord!

The greatest heritage that any parent can leave to his or her child is the heritage of the knowledge of Christ enforced and engraved on his heart by the devout example of a Christian father or mother. There is no greater legacy—there is no greater heritage on earth than that!

Such a heritage is far greater than silver or gold or land or honor or any earthly consideration. To know the Lord is the primary business and blessing of life, for both time and eternity! Further, it is your solumn duty as a parent to turn that little child's footsteps to walk in the paths of righteousness that will lead to heaven. The training and example you give that child will determine the destiny of his or her soul in the Day of Judgment! Whether the child gives you the honor that should be yours, whether his life is useful to Christ and to the church, and where that precious soul will spend eternity—to a large degree—rests upon how you, as a parent, discharge your duty toward your child! God has made you responsible, as a parent, for the upbringing, the training, and the fashioning of your child into a real Christian; and may God help you to do your work well. All of us as parents need to pray continually for wisdom from the Lord to direct us in placing Christ in the hearts and lives of our children!

May I say to you today that this is the responsibility of both father and mother. The Lord never intended that a child should have to make a choice between the two dearest people on earth to him. He or she should simply look at both of you as one flesh, moving in the same direction, and leaving an example to follow. But some disagree, so we shall stop at this point to discuss those other points of view.

One school of thought is that religious choices should be left to the child entirely. Frequently, a parent is heard to say that the teaching of religion should be reserved until the child matures and then let him decide for himself. Such philosophy is unsound. Parents impart their sentiments in religion, or in their lack of religion, whether or not they intend to. It is done by the force of example. A child learns through the heart as well as through the head the things they do and the things they neglect. Whether you read your Bible or go to church and whether you are faithful, all make a deep impression a child. Your every action and remark make an impression that cannot be erased.

No child lives in a spiritual vacuum. We must be aware of this reality! His soul will be filled with Christ or with infidelity. His mind will decide for God or for the sinful world. His life will be dedicated to Christ or to some pursuit of materialism or vice of his choosing; and as a parent, you may hold the influence over that decision! You may be that one who weighs heavily on the side of right. So, the question is, which shall it be? Where will (not simply you spend eternity), but where will that little child, little boy or girl, spend eternity? Teach your child to honor you as a parent. Many parents hunger for the affection and honor they would like to receive, but they die without it!

I go from place to place over this country and often listen to the hungry cry of a parent who longs more than anything, for the respect and the honor that is due them as a parent, but many of them do not have it. So it raises the question: Why not? One reason is that they did not demand honor when the children were small and now that they have grown up, these boys and girls do not want to change.

I often think of one of whom I read some time ago: a widowed mother had one son who grew up pampered, humored, and spoiled, and with the curse of having his own way. Now that mother is old, lonesome, and neglected; and her son is far, far away. Only now and then does he find time to write a few lines to his aged mother whose whole life hangs anxiously in the balance of his selfish neglect. Day after day, and often many times a day, that mother walks to the post office, longing to see if she has received some mail from that boy! When I think of how happy just a little note—a few words—could make her, I am made to remember that I, too, may have been negligent. I think of the little things that mean so much to our parents—little things such as thoughtfulness and consideration. We might do well to ponder today: How can we honor our parents? The scripture says, "Honor your father and your mother." So, we need to stop and ponder, "How?"

First, we can give them the respect due parents. Don't be ashamed of this responsibility. Some parents have not lived up to their role as parents and may not have been the example they should have been, but they should be respected as parents, regardless of what your view of them is; one thing for sure today: THEY ARE OUR PARENTS!

Secondly, as children we may speak kindly to them. There is no excuse to justify the back talk and the disrespectful language that children often use to their parents. They are our parents—we should speak kindly and with respect both to them and about them.

Thirdly, we can obey our parents. The scripture says, "Children obey your parents in the Lord." This is the Lord's will. Of course, no parent should require his child to do anything unreasonable or unscriptural; but Christians should do all in our power to obey our parents.

Fourthly, we can live upright and useful lives that will reflect honor upon our parents. Others judge our parents by the way we live. If we live disrespectful lives, we will bring reproach upon the name of our parents. If our lives are good and honorable, then those with whom we come in contact will honor our parents through us.

Fifthly, we can be thoughtful and appreciative of their sacrifices for us, and we can show our thoughtfulness in a thousand ways. As we grow older and even have children of our own, the more we should learn about how much the thoughtfulness and devotion of children can mean to the parents who have loved us.

Last, we can supply their needs. Many parents are overlooked and neglected in their old age, and children fail to see they have the personal attention, companionship, and care they deserve. Even when a place to live is provided, a parent is often neglected on a personal level. Some of the most severe rebukes the Lord gave were directed against those who neglected the needs of their parents (Matthew 15:5-9). 1 Timothy 5:8 says, "But if any provide not for his own," … "he hath denied the faith, and is worse than an infidel."

As a son or a daughter listening today, regardless of your age—very young to very old—you can honor your parents by serving the Lord! Nothing will mean more to them than for them to know you are living a Christian life! The Lord wants you to live for Him, and you can do that. He requires you to recognize God as your Heavenly Father and to be born again, born into God's spiritual family, the church. The meaning of the new birth is made plain in Galatians 3:26-27. It is the result of faith in Christ and is completed in a burial in baptism from which we are to arise to walk a new life (Romans 6:1-7). Thus, we become the children of God by faith in Jesus Christ; and if today you are not a Christian, and you look back upon those who endeavored to teach you in the paths of right, and you would want to honor them, please remember godly lives will reflect honor upon our parents long after they are gone as well as while they live. Let us resolve to honor our parents by serving the Lord as faithful Christians in God's family.

We close our study today with the words we read in the beginning, "Children, obey your parents in the Lord: for this is right. Honor thy father and mother; (which is the first commandment with promise;) That it may be well with thee, and thou mayest live long on the earth."

Abuse of the Bible

This morning we invite your attention to the abuse the Bible has received. When Sir Walter Scott, the famous novelist and poet, was on his death bed, he said to his son-in-law, "Bring me the Book!" "What book?" asked his son-in-law. Scott replied, "There is but one Book." Someone has said concerning the blessed Bible—and I am sure you have read this many times—but listen to it again:

> This Book contains the mind of God, the state of man, the way of salvation, the doom of sinners and the happiness of the righteous. Its doctrines are holy, its precepts are binding, its records are true and all of its decisions are immutable. Read it to be wise, believe it to be safe, practice it to be holy. It contains light to direct you, food to support you and comfort to cheer you. It is the traveler's map, the pilgrim's staff, the pilot's compass, the soldier's sword, the Christian's charter. Here paradise is restored. Heaven opened, and the ways of Hell disclosed. Christ is its grand object, our good its design and the redemption of man its end. It should fill the memory, rule the heart and guide the feet. It is a mine of wealth, a paradise of glory, a river of pleasure. It is given you in life, will be quoted at the Judgment and remembered forever. It involves the highest responsibility, will reward the obedient and condemn all who trifle with its precepts.

These are some wonderful, beautiful tributes someone has paid to the Bible. The author of this article is unknown, as far as we know; but if it were possible to acquire all the compliments that have been paid to the Book, the Sacred Volume would be covered with a vast pyramid.

Yet there is another side to the story of the Wonderful Book, I am sorry to say. There is a side to this story that is indicated in the closing chapter of the Revelation. It says there would be those who would trifle with its holy precepts. John records, "For I testify unto every man that heareth the words of the prophecy of this book, If any man shall add unto these things, God shall add unto him the plagues that are written in this book: And if any man shall take away from the words of the book of this prophecy, God shall take away his part out of the book of life, and out of the holy city, and from the things which are written in this book" (Revelation 22:18-19). The application of this passage is first to the book that contains it and secondly, we believe, to all scripture that has been given by the inspiration of God. There are some who do not love the scriptures. And then, there are those who may feel that they do and yet they actually wrest the Holy Scripture. In many instances the Bible has been greatly abused. Like a two-edged sword, it cuts both ways; and if it is not skillfully handled, it will injure all who toy with its sacred contents. This is not the fault of the word of God: it is just simply a fact that any instrument that is capable of doing great good is also capable of doing great harm; and we must not charge the abuse of the Bible to the Book itself.

In 2 Peter 3:16, the apostle says concerning the epistles of Paul, "In which are some things hard to be understood, which they that are unlearned and unstable wrest, as they do also the other scriptures, unto their own destruction." Notice that the inspired writer uses a metaphor that pictures the abusive way men have handled the word of God. He says men "wrest" the scriptures to their own destruction. This word "wrest" literally means to stretch on the rack and was associated with human torture. The accused were stretched on the torture rack until their limbs were pulled from their bodies. This is the picture the apostle is giving us. It is expressive of the awe and the terror that will result from the misuse of Holy Scripture.

An outstanding Bible scholar once said, "One of the most melancholy factors in the development of Christendom has been this tormenting, torturing stretching on the rack of the words and sense of Holy Scripture." Christians have often used the letter to murder the spirit and by quoting texts have defended hideous crimes against the freedom and the rights of mankind. Recall, for instance, the days in the defense of slavery and man-stealing and the atrocities of the Inquisition. They have often, as the author truly said, turned it from a blessing into a curse. There are many ways to abuse the word of God. If, indeed, we may wrest the scriptures, this action involves many things. It can be involved in many facets of our lives.

I would suppose one of the most common ways of abusing the word of God is by lifting a verse out of its setting, out of its context, and giving it the meaning that we want it to have. Many have used Ephesians 2:8-9 in that manner. The Lord says in this particular passage, "For by grace are ye saved through faith; and that not of yourselves: it is the gift of God: Not of works, lest any man should boast." This passage, along with others, is used to prove that we are saved by grace through faith **only**, and this faith only is merely a mental assent. But the Lord did not say that we are saved by faith **only.** We are saved by grace through faith. But the faith that avails is the faith that works (Galatians 5:6). If we could be saved by faith **only**, we could be saved by faith without its own expression, which is obedience to God. This is James' conclusion in James 2:26 when he declared, "For as the body without the spirit is dead, so faith without works is dead also."

Some have gone so far as to say that Paul and James are at variance one with the other and by isolating a verse of scripture from all other verses on the same subject we can prove that we are saved by mercy alone (Titus 3:5), or we can prove that we are saved by hope alone (Romans 8:24), or even baptism alone (1 Peter 3:21). For these are passages of the Bible that say these things save us and there is nothing else mentioned in that particular passage. This fact is the reason some men have been led to say, "You can prove anything by the Bible." Yes, you **can** prove anything by the Bible just as men can prove anything by you or me **if they abuse and misuse our testimony.** I think it's a dangerous thing to say you can prove anything by the Bible. This simply is not the case. It takes an abusing, a wresting, a twisting, a torturing of the word to accomplish such.

To learn the truth on this subject, or any subject, we must not construe one passage to contradict another. By isolating scripture, men have placed the Apostle Paul in a dilemma. Let's consider this one: The apostle says, "Christ sent me not to baptize, but to preach the gospel" (1 Corinthians 1:17). This passage has been lifted out of its setting and used to prove that baptism is not essential because Paul said he was not sent to baptize. If this conclusion is true, Paul did something he had no right to do, for he **did** baptize Crispus and Gaius (1 Corinthians 1:14). But what did Paul mean when he said he was not sent to baptize but to preach the gospel? When we study the context or the setting of this statement, we see that Paul was glad he had not baptized many of the Corinthians because, he says, "Lest any should say that I had baptized in mine own name" (1 Corinthians 1:15). The people of Corinth wanted to honor the men who baptized them, and so they said they were of Paul or they were of Apollos or others said they were of Cephas. The Apostle Paul rebuked them and stressed that the men who did the baptizing were not to be so honored.

Another way in which the scriptures have been wrested and changed is on the subject of being born in sin. A statement of David is sometimes isolated from other scriptures and used to prove that we're sinners at birth. You recall that the Psalmist David says, "Behold, I was shapen in iniquity; and in sin did my mother conceive me" (Psalm 51:5). David does not say a word about his being a sinner when he was born, but he mentions the act of conception before he even existed and he says, "In sin did my mother conceive me." Those who misuse this scripture overlook the fact that the Lord said to Israel, "The soul that sinneth, it shall die. ... The son shall not bear the iniquity of the father, neither shall the father bear the iniquity of the son" (Ezekiel 18:4, 20).

By isolating Holy Scripture, men endeavor to prove the primacy of the Apostle Peter. Jesus says to this apostle on one occasion, "I will give unto thee the keys of the kingdom of heaven: and whatsoever thou shalt bind on earth shall be bound in heaven: and whatsoever thou shalt loose on earth shall be loosed in heaven" (Matthew 16:19). Those who use this passage to prove that Peter **only** had the authority to bind and to loose, ignore the fact that in Matthew 18:18, Jesus gives this power to all the apostles. A distinguished scholar, Mr. Farrar, says of Peter, "He was imminent among the apostles; supreme he never was."

Some have abused the word of God by changing it to suit the times in which they live. In the Bible, we read that baptism is a burial. Paul states in Romans 6:4, "Therefore we are buried with him by baptism into death: that like as Christ was raised up from the dead by the glory of the Father, even so we also should walk in newness of life." Also, Colossians 2:12 says we are "Buried with him in baptism." But in 1643, the Westminster Assembly voted on the question of substituting sprinkling for immersion. When the vote was taken, the assembly was tied. The vote was 24 in favor of sprinkling—24 in favor of immersion. The Chairman of the assembly was Bishop Lightfoot, and he was allowed to vote **only** in case of a tie. He cast his vote for sprinkling. Thus, **one vote** of an assembly of frail human beings changed the scriptural practice of immersion to sprinkling—simply to suit the times in which they were living.

Some have used the Bible to condemn individual liberty in reading and understanding the scripture. They have quoted the Bible to justify the punishment of those who disagree with them. One church authority says, "The church can inflict temporal and corporal punishments." This quote is from *The Elements of Ecclesiastical Law* by S.B. Smith, page 89. Cardinal Vaughn says, "The church has never spared the knife when necessary to cut off rebels against our faith or authority." This quotation is from *The History of the Inquisition* (Lee, chapter 1, page 228). What text is used to support this extreme position? One can hardly imagine that one could find a passage in the word of God that could be so turned and so twisted to say the Bible sustained such a position. But, Deuteronomy 13:10 was quoted in defense of this position, "And thou shalt stone him with stones, that he die; because he hath sought to thrust thee away from the Lord thy God." It is a misuse of the Bible to quote this passage to justify the punishment of heretics. The command was given under the Mosaic dispensation, and we are not living under that law today. It was given to prevent Israel from becoming idolaters by embracing the corrupt heathen religions of Palestine.

The New Testament scriptures also are quoted by men who would punish those who disagree with them. Christ's command to "go out into the highways and hedges and **compel** them to come in" is often used as proof that it is right to force men to accept the decisions of the church. But Christ was speaking of securing "guests" for a wedding feast, and the recent versions of the New Testament use the word "constrain" instead of the word "compel." The Lord said the master of the feast told the servants to go out and constrain, or urge, the people to attend the feast.

Another of Jesus' statements that is taken completely from its setting is when Jesus says, "The tares are gathered and burned in the fire" (Matthew 13:40), meaning, to some, that heretics are to be put to death. The passage has **absolutely** no such meaning. The Son of God says the reapers are angels and the day of reaping is the judgment. The time when the tares will be burned is the Judgment Day (Matthew 13:39).

It is interesting to read the quotations of the British author, Disraeli, who says if a person should come to his bishop to ask for leave to read the Bible, with the best intention, the bishop should answer him from Matthew 20:22, "Ye know not what ye ask." This is from the quotations of a man by the name of Solomon Goldman in *The Book of Books*, page 268. Such statements are flagrant abuses of the Holy Scripture and of this scripture text. It has always been an amazing thing that people who say, "We do not have to have scripture for what we do," are always the ones who cry, "scripture" when one can be supplied by either reason or trickery.

The Bible is also abused by some to justify their evil practices—not only to suit the times, or to suit their whims or fancies, but simply to justify an absolute evil practice. Paul's advice to Timothy to "use a little wine for thy stomach's sake" (1 Timothy 5:23) is sometimes quoted in defense of drinking—drinking of all sorts. But this is a misuse of the scripture. This scripture implies that Timothy **did not** drink any wine, and furthermore he was so strictly temperate that he would not take even a little wine for sickness until he received a prescription from an inspired apostle. What Paul writes to Timothy is a prescription for an individual and a part of that prescription is that Timothy is to refrain from drinking water **only** while he is ill.

We can see then from these many instances that the Bible has been abused when it is misquoted and misapplied. Satan misquoted and misapplied a prophecy of the psalmist when he tried to persuade Jesus to jump from the pinnacle of the temple (Matthew 4; Psalm 91:11-12). You recall he tried to make the scripture teach that the angels would take care of Jesus regardless of what He did. But the prophecy was that the angels would take care of Him as long as He was in the way of righteousness. In the play *The Merchant of Venice*, Antonio expresses a great truth when he says, "The devil can site scripture for his purpose" (*The Merchant of Venice*, from the works of William Shakespeare).

The Apostle Paul gives this advice and instruction to Timothy, "Study to shew thyself approved unto God, a workman that needeth not to be ashamed, rightly dividing the word of truth" (2 Timothy 2:15). One translation puts it, "Do your best to present yourself to God as one approved, a workman who has no need to be ashamed, rightly handling the word of truth" (RSV).

We plead with you today to take the word of God as the word from the eternal God and to use it in the way God intended.

Holy Spirit Baptism and Water Baptism

Good morning, everyone. Once again we turn your thoughts to the word of God and to a question this morning that is of concern to one of our listeners, and I believe it is also a concern to many of our listeners today. That question is this: "How do you know which baptism is of the Holy Ghost and which baptism is of water?" Every so often we hear someone quoting a passage of scripture and stating that it refers to Holy Ghost baptism; and then we have someone else quoting a passage and saying it refers to water baptism. Some people raise this question because they are rightly confused and have not studied the matter: "How do we know the difference?" It is vital that we turn to the word of God and try to learn the difference between the two.

In the Apostle Paul's letter to the Ephesians, we read these words: "There is one body, and one Spirit, even as ye are called in one hope of your calling; One Lord, one faith, one baptism, One God and Father of all, who is above all, and through all, and in you all" (Ephesians 4:4-6). At the time the apostle wrote these words, there was only one baptism. There is only one today, too. But someone says, "The Bible speaks of other baptisms." This statement is true; but at the time Paul wrote the Ephesian letter, about 60 A.D., there was only one. The others had passed from the scene. What were those other baptisms? Well, there was the baptism of John, the baptism of suffering, the baptism of the Holy Spirit, water baptism, and the baptism in fire. Let's look at them one at a time.

The baptism of John: John the immerser was the great forerunner of Christ, who was prophesied aforetime.

> The voice of one crying in the wilderness, Prepare ye the way of the Lord, make his paths straight. John did baptize in the wilderness, and preach the baptism of repentance for the remission of sins. And there went out unto him all the land of Judaea, and they of Jerusalem, and were all baptized of him in the river of Jordan, confessing their sins (Mark 1:3-5).

John's baptism soon became null and void. It was in force, until the baptism of the gospel began to be performed, that is, baptism in the name of the Christ. We recall that on one occasion John, speaking of Jesus, says, "He must increase, but I must decrease." To show conclusively that the baptism of John was not continued into the gospel age, we turn to Acts 19, and we read:

> And it came to pass, that, while Apollos was at Corinth, Paul having passed through the upper coasts came to Ephesus: and finding certain disciples, He said unto them. Have ye received the Holy Ghost since ye believed? And they said unto him, We have not so much as heard whether there be any Holy Ghost. And he said unto them, Unto what then were ye baptized? And they said, Unto John's baptism. Then said Paul, John verily baptized with the baptism of repentance, saying unto the people, that they should believe on him which should come after him, that is, on Christ Jesus. When they heard this, they were baptized in the name of the Lord Jesus (Acts 19:1-5).

This portion of scripture shows as clearly as is possible that John's baptism was no longer in effect. The baptism of the New Testament had taken its place. John's baptism did not carry with it the promise of the Holy Spirit, but the baptism of the Great Commission did. And thus these followers of John the baptist became Christians, followers of the Lord Jesus, to whom John had pointed them.

The baptism of suffering: Matthew's gospel records this significant conversation about the baptism of suffering:

> Then came to him the mother of Zebedee's children with her sons, worshiping him, and desiring a certain thing of him. And he said unto her, What wilt thou? She saith unto him, Grant that these my two sons may sit, the one on thy right hand, and the other on the left, in thy kingdom. But Jesus answered and said, Ye know not what you ask. Are ye able to drink of the cup that I shall drink of, and to be baptized with the baptism that I am baptized with? They say unto him, We are able. And he saith unto them, Ye shall drink indeed of my cup, and be baptized with the baptism that I am baptized with: but to sit on my right hand, and on my left, is not mine to give, but it shall be given to them for whom it is prepared of my Father (Matthew 20:20-23).

In ancient times, assassinations and executions were often performed by putting poison into a cup from which one must drink. Hence the expression "drink the cup." The "cup" in the baptism of suffering mentioned here denotes the "sufferings" Jesus must endure in becoming the Saviour of men. He died in order to purchase the church with His own blood (Acts 20:28.) These two sons of Zebedee shared His sufferings: James was beheaded by Herod; and John, through dying a natural death, lived a life of suffering for the Master's name.

The baptism of the Holy Spirit: This baptism was special—listen—this baptism was special and not general. The baptism of the Holy Spirit was not received by all believers for it served a very special purpose. Jesus promised His apostles that after He went away He would send the Holy Spirit and that He would guide them into all truth and bring to their remembrance all things whatsoever He had commanded them while on earth. This was a miraculous measure of the Spirit. It was to come when the kingdom came, and they were told to wait in Jerusalem for it to come. They were not to begin their teaching of the gospel until they were thus endowed with the Spirit.

When we read the second chapter of the book of Acts, we see the fulfillment of this promise—at which time the apostles preached the gospel in the name of Jesus for the first time. They spoke in foreign tongues so that men of sixteen different nationalities heard them in their own native tongue. The only other record of the baptismal measure is found in Acts 10:44 where the gospel is being introduced to the Gentiles for the first time. Cornelius and his household also received the baptismal measure of the Spirit and spoke in other tongues. There is not a man upon the earth today—listen—there is not a man upon the earth today that can duplicate these feats and speak in languages he has never studied; and, therefore, we do not hesitate a moment to declare and to affirm that no person today has received what they received—the baptism of the Holy Ghost. It was limited to a select few and for a particular time. It was special and not general. It was administered by the Lord and not by men. It was a promise and never—never a command. It is not being dispensed in the age in which we live.

Water baptism: As far as water baptism is concerned, it is administered by man in obedience to the Great Commission. Jesus says, "Go ye therefore, and teach all nations, baptizing them in the name of the Father, and of the Son, and of the Holy Ghost" (Matthew

28:19). This command, of course, is for the church age and is to continue until the end of time, for Jesus says, "Lo, I am with you alway, even unto the end of the world." Now this was predicated upon their fulfilling the commandments just received. On the day of Pentecost, ten days after Jesus had returned to the Father in heaven, the apostles received the Holy Spirit in the baptismal measure. For the first time, they began to preach the terms of the Great Commission. It was on this occasion that Peter commanded water baptism in the name of Christ for the remission of sins (Acts 2:38).

All true gospel preachers have preached it the same way since that day. It is during this period of Bible history that the Apostle Paul in the Ephesian letter writes that there is one baptism and it is, of course, water baptism. The only other baptism mentioned in the New Testament is the baptism of fire, and it was yet in the future.

The baptism of fire: Listen to the words of John the baptist:

> I indeed baptize you with water unto repentance: but he that cometh after me is mightier than I, whose shoes I am not worthy to bear: he shall baptize you with the Holy Ghost, and with fire: Whose fan is in his hand, and he will thoroughly purge his floor, and gather his wheat into the garner; but he will burn up the chaff with unquenchable fire (Matthew 3:11-12).

It is plain here that John is speaking in general terms to his audience. Some in his audience would receive the baptism of the Spirit, or at least they would receive the benefits of those who did, while others standing before him were to receive the baptism of fire. Now some have made a serious error in thinking this baptism is fulfilled in the experience of Christians. Some people even claim to have received the baptism of fire, but it is clear that John was talking about the future punishment of the wicked. Notice he likened it to wheat being gathered into the garner and the chaff being burned with unquenchable fire. This figure can have reference to nothing but the lake of fire prepared for the devil and his angels that is spoken of by our Lord. There were many of this type in John's audience. He called them a generation of vipers.

I think we have time for one more question: "Can one be saved if he fails to read the Old Testament?" I would say this is a question that is difficult to answer with just a yes or a no reply. We know according to Paul's language in Hebrews 10:9-10 that the Old Covenant had to be removed in order to make room for the New Covenant or Testament, and he adds that it is by this New Testament that we are sanctified through the offering of the body of Jesus Christ once for all. It is not by the law of Moses that we are justified but by the law of the Spirit of life in Christ Jesus (Romans 8:2).

The New Testament, however, cannot be fully understood or appreciated except by the light thrown on it by the Old Testament. I am persuaded this is what Paul means in Romans 15:4 when He says the "things that were written aforetime were written for our learning."

Someone has observed that the New Testament is the Old Testament revealed, and the Old Testament is the New Testament concealed. The inspired penman states that the law was a school master to bring them (the Jews) unto Christ (Galatians 3:24). The plan of salvation for us today is in the New Testament, but the underlying principles of obedience with examples of faith to strengthen them are found throughout the Old Testament. Without it, we would be poor indeed regarding many lessons we need to know. Every word of the Old Testament was put there at the direction of God. Holy men of God spoke as they were moved by the Holy Spirit, says the Apostle Peter; and it is truly a rich treasure for the spiritually minded Christian.

There is one other angle to this subject that I would like to mention. Sometimes people want to know just how much of their duty they can leave undone and still get to heaven. Others want to know just how much sin they can commit and get by with it. The danger here is not so much what is done or undone, but it's one's attitude toward it.

Some folks just don't like the Old Testament, and they don't want to study it. I am persuaded this attitude shows a lack of spiritual depth and an undeveloped appetite for the good things of the soul. In short, we will put the things in a few words. Love and cleave to the Lord, avoid and forsake all manner of evil. Obey the gospel of Christ as it is found in the New Testament, for that is the law unto us today, and then study all that God ever has said—whether it is in the Old or whether it is in the New. We should want to know the things that please the Lord and the things that do not please Him—whether it be then or now. The thing with which we should be most concerned today is to love our Lord and to obey Him so that we can be saved.

We want to thank you sincerely for listening today to these questions that have been proposed. We trust that we have given you an answer from the word of the Lord. We invite your questions and your comments. We will do our best to answer them from the word of God. Until this time next Lord's Day, we bid you one and all a pleasant good day.

Questions and Answers on Baptism

Good morning, everyone. Once again we turn our attention to the Lord's word and we trust that as we study from time to time you will find these things are simple and plain and forthright. If you, at any time, experience difficulty with the lesson or have any questions, please feel free to call or write for whatever assistance we can render.

We undertake this grave task, recognizing the tremendous responsibility that lies upon us as teachers of the word, fully aware of the words of James when he says, "Be not many masters (or teachers), knowing that we shall receive the greater condemnation." Therefore, it shall be our policy to proceed with caution, to speak as the oracles of God, and to leave all speculations to those who "rush in where angels fear to tread."

This morning we would like to proceed with two or three questions and answers from the word of God. The first questions is: **"If a person accepts Christ and feels in his heart that he is at peace with God and cannot be baptized because he is unable to leave his bed because of his physical condition, do you believe that God in His infinite mercy will save him?"** This question shows plainly that the one who asks recognizes that God, in His word, has placed baptism into Christ between the sinner and salvation. Otherwise, the problem would have never materialized in his thinking. Second, we wish to note that this question is a common one indeed. It is brought forth by different people on various occasions and for a variety of purposes. Sometimes the question is posed as a device to gain sympathy for the idea that baptism is a non-essential. Sometimes it is asked by those who are suffering anguish and heartache because of the deplorable condition of a loved one. At any rate, it is a good question and one that deserves proper consideration.

Let us take the question apart and analyze it carefully. Whether we believe this way or that is of little importance. What is important is what the Bible teaches. The Bible does teach that it is possible for one to believe a lie. We might want to believe something with all our heart; yet if the Bible does not teach it, our desire is in vain. Believing something will not make it so, unless it is so. Jesus says, "Ye shall know the truth, and the truth shall make you free" (John 8:32). Now since the word of God is truth and the supreme standard of all righteousness, we must go to it for the answer to all our spiritual problems. Again, our Lord says, "Sanctify them through thy truth: thy word is truth" (John 17:17). All the tears ever shed can never erase the written word supplied by the Holy Spirit. "Heaven and earth shall pass away: but my words shall not pass away" (Mark 13:31)—so says our Saviour.

The question describes a person who, they say, accepts Christ and feels in his heart that he is at peace with God. Recall that Jesus instructs His disciples not to let their peace be upon those who would not hear their words (Matthew 10:12-15). To have the peace that passes understanding, one must have God's assurance that he is saved; and this assurance comes only from the word of the Lord. In that word, we read that "Christ has become the author of eternal salvation to all them that obey him" (Hebrews 5:9). Now think about this statement and let me ask you a question: Can one really feel at peace knowing he has failed to obey the gospel of Christ? On what basis would this peace come? We know a person can be taught a false doctrine and feel at peace, for the scripture plainly says, "There is a way that seemeth right unto a man, but the end thereof are the ways of death" (Proverbs 14:12). Thus, we are made to see that the ways of death can be a comfort to a man who has been taught a lie and who has believed it. Paul says, "God shall send them strong delusion, that they should believe a lie: That they all might be damned who believed not the truth, but had pleasure in unrighteousness" (2 Thessalonians 2:11-12). The word of truth teaches that in order to be saved, one must hear the word, believe it, repent of his sins, confess the name of Christ, and then be buried with his Lord in the likeness of His death, unto the remission of sins. Until a person has done this, there is no assurance; and I would be less than your friend to extend to you the idea that there is any assurance or any liberty or any salvation outside of this complete obedience to our Lord. The Bible provides none—I must provide none. Now, if there are extenuating circumstances over which the individual has no control and he has finally realized the truth and has a deep, sincere desire to obey Christ and live for Him, we can do nothing but commend him to God's mercy. As to what disposition God, the righteous Judge, will make of his case, we dare not say. Clemency belongs to the Judge. It is ours to preach the rigid but righteous law of Christ that holds ajar the "strait gate," opening to a narrow way that leads to life. The Lord Himself states, "Few" there be that "find it" (Matthew 7:13-14). Only God knows what the man would do under different circumstances.

Sometimes, the fear of death can make people "very religious" for a time; but all too often when their physical health and strength returns, the power of sin in their lives also returns in full measure. Of course, many individuals have obeyed the truth at the eleventh hour of their lives. When the truly penitent soul learns that Christ has commanded baptism, he will **desire** to be baptized at once. Like the Ethiopian eunuch said, "Here is water; what doth hinder me to be baptized?" He wanted to do the will of the Lord. Now, if such a condition existed and the person involved did not desire to receive baptism, it would clearly indicate one of two things—either he had not been properly taught the significance of baptism, or he did not believe it when he heard it. In either case, he would not be a fit candidate for baptism. On the other hand, if he did understand the teaching of the Bible on the subject and had an earnest desire to obey his Lord, there would be few (if any) cases where he could not be baptized, even if he were an invalid. Countless numbers of sincere people, upon learning the truth, have been carried out of hospitals and baptized at their request then returned to their hospital bed. Others have been too sick to leave the hospital and have been baptized in the large bathtubs that many hospitals have. In most cases, there is a way made available to those who have the faith to say, "Lord, what wilt thou have me to do?"

God's mercy is infinite, but "He that turneth away his ear from hearing the law, even his prayer shall be an abomination" (Proverbs 28:9)—we must not forget that! Let us always remember that **man's extremity is God's opportunity.** I remember hearing that statement many years ago, and I think there is a great deal of truth in it. When we feel that man has reached the place where he can do nothing else, this is sometimes God's great opportunity. By that I simply mean this: There are many situations imagined by people where we suppose one can't obey the gospel; but I am persuaded if there is life present and one wishes to obey the gospel, there **will be a way** that will be made. Unless, and until, man has sued for mercy on the terms of the gospel, he can find no assurance that comes from the fountain of truth. The gospel is God's power to save, and Jesus sums it up by saying, "He that believeth and is baptized shall be saved."

The second question we would like to consider concerns baptism, and it reads as follows: **"If you have once been baptized but now feel**

that you might have obeyed simply because a cousin did, should you be re-baptized?" There is only "one baptism" (Ephesians 4:4). If one has been scripturally baptized once, he can never be baptized again. In the case mentioned, however, it is clearly apparent that this person has never been baptized but merely placed under the water since he did not render obedience to Jesus Christ. He was motivated by the action of another without any true purpose or conviction of his own. Hence, he has not as yet experienced the one baptism of which the Bible speaks.

No doubt there are many people in this same condition who have given it little thought. I would not knowingly—listen—**I would not knowingly** baptize any person who was doing it to please a relative or a friend, for I am persuaded that such would be mockery. Some have been baptized for other reasons just as wrong, evidently. Only they and God know if they were or were not. No baptism at all is as good as the wrong kind! Some are baptized after confessing that they are already saved. Now, this is not true baptism for the simple reason that it is not based on a proper understanding of the word of God. How can a person be in a saved condition before he is **IN** Christ? This is what they are affirming, in effect, when they confess before baptism that they are saved already. Those who read and believe the Bible know that baptism is **INTO** Christ (Galatians 3:27). They also know that it is for the remission of sins (Acts 2:38). It does no good to ignore or deny these scriptures, for they will be there in the judgment to face an unbelieving world! Because preachers who call themselves "Doctors" or "Masters," or whatever, deny the necessity of baptism does not make it any less binding. If you have been taught that you are saved without obedience to the gospel, you have been misled! I would be less than your friend not to say that to you today. May we urge you "not to think of men above that which is written" (1 Corinthians 4:6) but rather to inquire diligently at the fountain of truth. Jesus says, "Search the scriptures; for in them ye think ye have eternal life: and they are they which testify of me" (John 5:39). The way to destruction is a broad way, "and many there be which go in thereat" (Matthew 7:13). Our Lord says, "Every plant, which my heavenly Father hath not planted, shall be rooted up" (Matthew 15:13). Again, our Lord states, "If the blind lead the blind, both shall fall into the ditch" (Matthew 15:14).

I often get the idea that there are those who feel they do not need to study the word of God and that if someone, indeed, is leading them astray—well, that won't be their fault, but it will be the fault of the person leading them! But Jesus says, "If the blind lead the blind, **both** will fall into the ditch." Death is too real and eternity too long to gamble with one's soul. Surely, we should realize that procrastination often precedes destruction. To put off doing what one knows to be right is sinful and it is only prolonging and agitating a dangerous condition. "To him that knoweth to do good, and doeth it not, to him it is sin" (James 4:17).

A third and last question we would like to answer from the word of God is this: **"What is baptism for, and what does John 3:5 mean?"** In answer, I would like to say that the leading purpose of baptism is to bury the man who has decided to be dead to the world (through faith and repentance) and to raise him in Jesus Christ. It is for the purpose of immersing a penitent believer and bringing him out of darkness into light. Jesus says, "Go ye therefore, and teach all nations, baptizing them in the name of the Father, and the Son and the Holy Ghost" (Matthew 28:19). Baptizing them in the name of the Father and the Son and the Holy Ghost puts them into the enjoyment of all the blessings to be received in Christ—the blood of Christ, the remission of sins, and the fellowship of God, Jesus Christ, and all those who are in fellowship with God. Man dies to the world and to himself. If the body of sin is put off—buried in baptism—he is "raised to walk in newness of life in Christ Jesus" (Romans 6:3-6; Colossians 3:10-15).

What does John 3:5 mean? I am persuaded that it just simply means to believe and to be baptized. Our Lord says, "Except a man be born of water and of the Spirit, he cannot enter into the kingdom of God." Now, often times it is taught that John 3:5 refers to natural birth—that is, when Jesus says a man must be born of water, that means a natural birth and then later we are born of the Spirit and that is all there is to the spiritual birth. But I would like to point out that a child in his **natural** birth **is not** born of water! Whatever water is present at the birth is born of the mother—just as the child is. Water comes forth from the womb of the mother just as the child does. The water is born **with** the child from the mother. We might as well say when twins are born that one is born of the other because they both came forth from the womb of the mother as to say that a child is born of water because water came forth from the womb just as the other child did. The idea is a violation of the common use of words. It is a strange and ridiculous interpretation to avoid the force of a truth that is taught in other places, even if it were not taught here. We can read and study and learn that all scholars agree (at least for fourteen centuries after Christ) this simply refers to baptism, and Jesus says, "Except a man be born of water"—(that is, be baptized)—"and of the Spirit"—(that is, begotten of the Spirit, believing the gospel, repenting of our sins)—"he cannot enter the kingdom of God." For fourteen centuries, as far as I know, no man **ever** thought of this passage as applying to anything other than baptism.

We want to thank you for listening to our questions and answers this morning, and again we would like to continue to solicit your questions or your concerns in regard to the Holy Scripture. Remember, the scripture declares, "To him that knoweth to do good and doeth it not, to him it is sin." Certainly, we should be most concerned about the teaching of the word, for as our Lord says, "Search the scriptures, for in them ye have eternal life."

Not My Will

Good morning, everyone. We are grateful that you are with us this morning. We express the gratitude in our hearts for your continued interest in this broadcast. Certainly any letter or any word from you is encouraging to those of us who are sustaining and delivering this broadcast. So may I encourage you to write us a card or letter? We hope you will continue to listen each Lord's Day as we search the scriptures, as the Bible says, to see whether these things are so.

For our lesson this morning, we invite you to turn to Luke 22:42 and read with us, "Father, if thou be willing, remove this cup from me: nevertheless not my will, but thine, be done." Our theme for today comes from this verse—"Not my will, but thy will be done." These words are from the prayer Jesus prayed to our Father in Gethsemane. The time was at hand for Him to be delivered into the hands of the enemy to be crucified. You will remember Jesus took with Him Peter, James, and John and went to the garden to pray. He withdrew Himself from them about a stones throw and prayed the words that we read. He then went back and found His disciples sleeping. To them He said, "Watch and pray that ye enter not into temptation: the spirit indeed is willing, but the flesh is weak" (Matthew 26:41). Matthew says He went away again the second time and prayed saying:

> O my Father, if this cup may not pass away from me, except I drink it, thy will be done. And he came and found them asleep again: for their eyes were heavy. And he left them, and went away again, and prayed the third time, saying the same words. Then cometh he to his disciples, and saith unto them, Sleep on now, and take your rest: behold, the hour is at hand, and the Son of man is betrayed into the hands of sinners (Matthew 26:42-45).

Thus, our Lord was willing to submit to the Father's will, even to the point of dying on the cross—"even the death of the cross" as Paul says in Philippians 2:8. It was easy for our Lord to say, "For I came down from heaven, not to do mine own will, but the will of him that sent me" (John 6:38). He always lived in this spirit, and this is the frame of mind we should always have—that is, "Not our will, Father, but thine be done." The child of God, like the Lord Jesus, will desire to do the Father's will and to accomplish His purpose on earth because it will be the most satisfying thing he can do.

Let us observe, with Christ as our example, how the Father's will must be done. First, God's will should always be done in the church. Paul says, "Unto him be glory in the church by Christ Jesus throughout all ages, world without end" (Ephesians 3:21). Could there ever be any misunderstanding between brethren that would result in church fusses and factions if every member prayed, "Father, not my will but thine be done," and then lived in that particular spirit? Is it not God's will "that there be no divisions among us; but that we be perfectly joined together in the same mind and in the same judgment"? (1 Corinthians 1:10). Jesus says to His disciples, "It is impossible but that offences will come: but woe unto him, through whom they come!" (Luke 17:1). Differences sometimes do arise between us; but, if we are willing to let God's will be done instead of our own, then all matters can be settled for the good of all and the glory of God. The main difficulty in settling such disturbances is that there are so many who are saying, "I will have my own will and my own way instead of the Father's will." If all would sincerely pray, "Father, not my will but thine be done," there would never be any unfaithful members of the Lord's church, for God wills that we be faithful "unto death" (Revelation 2:10; Matthew 10:22).

It is the Father's will that Christians assemble for worship and observe the Lord's Supper upon the first day of the week as the first Christians did (Acts 20:7). The Hebrew writer says, "Not forsaking the assembling of ourselves together, as the manner of some is; but exhorting one another: and so much the more, as ye see the day approaching" (Hebrews 10:25). Therefore, when a member of the church sleeps too late to come to worship on the Lord's Day or if he spends the day in pleasure, he does not have the desire of the Father in mind. It is the will of the Father that we "go into all the world, and preach the gospel to every creature" (Mark 16:15). Luke says of the Jerusalem church, "And daily in the temple, and in every house, they ceased not to teach and preach Jesus Christ" (Acts 5:42). Hence, a church that has no program of evangelism has no disposition that the Father's will be done through its members. If we would just sincerely pray, "Father, not my will but thine be done," there would never be introduced into the doctrine of Jesus Christ the doctrines and commandments of men. Neither would there be imposed upon the church any practice that is unlike the practice of the New Testament church. In 2 John 9, we read, "Whosoever transgresseth, and abideth not in the doctrine of Christ, hath not God. He that abideth in the doctrine of Christ, he hath both the Father and the Son." Why will men teach the doctrine of justification by faith only when the New Testament says, "Ye see then how that by works a man is justified, and not by faith only" (James 2:24). Why will men teach that it is impossible for a child of God to fall from grace when we read in the New Testament such divine declarations as this, "Wherefore let him that thinketh he standeth take heed lest he fall" (1 Corinthians 10:12).

Here is another question. Why will men practice sprinkling for baptism when the Bible authorizes immersion? In recording the baptism of the Ethiopian eunuch, Luke says:

> And he commanded the chariot to stand still: and they went down both into the water, both Philip and the eunuch; and he baptized him. And when they were come up out of the water, the Spirit of the Lord caught away Philip, that the eunuch saw him no more: and he went on his way rejoicing (Acts 8:38-39).

Paul says, "Buried with him in baptism, wherein also ye are risen with him through the faith of the operation of God, who hath raised him from the dead" (Colossians 2:12). The New Testament teaches beyond a doubt that first century baptism was by immersion. The New Testament, which contains the Father's will, does not teach sprinkling and pouring as well as immersion. Many will admit the Bible teaches immersion; but when asked, "Why do you practice sprinkling?" they reply, "What difference does it make? Who still believes the Bible contains the will of God?" Many honest souls have been sprinkled or had water poured upon them thinking this is what the New Testament teaches and believing their minister when he tells them this practice is New Testament, but it isn't. Why is it hard for many to accept what Jesus and His disciples taught on this subject? Is not the answer simply, "My will be done and not yours, Lord"?

If all would pray devotedly, "Father, not my will but thine be done," then there would not be given to the professed followers of Christ any name but the divine name of Christian (Acts 11:26), for in this name we glorify God. Peter says, "Yet if any man suffer as a Christian, let him not be ashamed; but let him glorify God on this behalf" (1 Peter 4:16). We have noticed briefly that God's will is to be done in the church. Let's observe another place where God's will is to be done.

God's will is to be done in the home. If the Father's will were done in every home, there would never be another divorce case brought into the courts. God's will in this relationship is well expressed in Matthew 19:8-9. No, there is no doubt about what the Father's will is in the home. He has spoken to every member of the family declaring just how each should feel and act toward each other.

> To husbands, He says, "Husbands, love your wives, even as Christ also loved the church, and gave himself for it" (Ephesians 5:25).
>
> In Colossians 3:19, the same writer says, "Husbands, love your wives, and be not bitter against them."
>
> To wives, He says, "Wives, submit yourselves unto your own husbands, as unto the Lord ... . Therefore as the church is subject unto Christ, so let the wives be to their own husbands in every thing" (Ephesians 5:22-24).
>
> To parents, He says, "Train up a child in the way he should go: and when he is old, he will not depart from it" (Proverbs 22:6).
>
> "And, ye fathers, provoke not your children to wrath: but bring them up in the nurture and admonition of the Lord" (Ephesians 6:4).
>
> "Fathers, provoke not your children to anger, lest they be discouraged" (Colossians 3:21).
>
> To children, He says, "My son, hear the instruction of thy father, and forsake not the law of thy mother" (Proverbs 1:8).
>
> "Children, obey your parents in the Lord: for this is right. Honour thy father and mother; (which is the first commandment with promise)" (Ephesians 6:1-2).
>
> "Children, obey your parents in all things: for this is well pleasing unto the Lord" (Colossians 3:20).

What a wonderful home your home and mine would be if every father, mother, husband, wife and youth would truly say, "Father, not my will but thine be done in our home." Think what a change would occur in this world and in our lives if all of us would say, "Father, simply let me become a doer of your will."

I would like, in the remaining time, to cite an example I have learned in the Old Testament about this matter of doing and not doing the will of the Father. It has to do with a study about the rebellion of Jeroboam. You recall the efforts Jeroboam made to establish his own religion for the people. He fled into Egypt for plotting against Solomon, when he was a young man, after Solomon had given him an office of honor according to 1 Kings 11. You recall that on the death of Solomon and upon the request of his friends, Jeroboam returned from Egypt. Ahijah had prophesied that ten of the twelve tribes would be given into his hands, and he made haste to fulfill this prophecy. So Jeroboam and all the congregation of Israel came to Rehoboam, the son of Solomon, and said:

> Thy father made our yoke grievous: now therefore make thou the grievous service of thy father, and his heavy yoke which he put upon us, lighter, and we will serve thee. And he said unto them, Depart yet for three days, then come again to me. And the people departed. And king Rehoboam consulted with the old men, that stood before Solomon his father while he yet lived, and said, 'How do ye advise that I may answer this people?' (And I want you to notice their answer.) If thou wilt be a servant unto this people this day, and wilt serve them, and answer them, and speak good words to them, then they will be thy servants for ever (1 Kings 12:4-7).

You recall that Rehoboam forsook the advice of the older men and consulted the young men who grew up with him and who stood before him. They answered him:

> Thus shalt thou speak unto this people that spake unto thee, saying, Thy father made our yoke heavy, but make thou it lighter unto us; thus shalt thou say unto them, My little finger shall be thicker than my father's loins. And now whereas my father did lade you with a heavy yoke, I will add to your yoke: my father hath chastised you with whips, but I will chastise you with scorpions (1 Kings 12:10-11).

When Jeroboam and the people heard this, they cried, "What portion have we in David? neither have we inheritance in the son of Jesse: to your tents, O Israel: now see to thine own house, David. So Israel departed unto their tents" (1 Kings 12:16). Thus, the once united kingdom of Israel is now divided, but the matter didn't stop here, you remember, because Jeroboam built Shechem in mount Ephraim and dwelt there.

> And Jeroboam said in his heart, Now shall the kingdom return to the house of David: If this people go up to do sacrifice in the house of the Lord at Jerusalem, then shall the heart of this people turn again unto their lord, even unto Rehoboam king of Judah, and they shall kill me, and go again to Rehoboam king of Judah. Whereupon the king took counsel, and made two calves of gold, and said unto them, It is too much for you to go up to Jerusalem: behold thy gods, O Israel, which brought thee up out of the land of Egypt. And he set the one in Bethel, and the other put he in Dan. And this thing became a sin: for the people went to worship before the one, even unto Dan. And he made an house of high places, and made priests of the lowest of the people, which were not of the sons of Levi (1 Kings 12:26-31).

In the 13th chapter of 1 Kings, we read that God sent a young prophet to cry out against the altar worship at Bethel. My point in reading this account is this—there is a lesson for us today. First of all, we notice that this matter was the product of Jeroboam's imagination. He conceived this thing in his heart (1 Kings 12:26). He had no concept whatsoever of saying, "Father, not my will but thine be done." It is evident that he was concerned only with his will and his desires. It seems that his chief concern was not abiding by the will of God—a willingness to do right and God's will thus come about—he simply wanted what he wanted and what he thought. God declared that His thoughts are not man's thoughts, you remember? And it is always true that religious effort that follows man's opinion in preference to the plain and explicit word of God is the product of man's imagination. Jesus says, "In vain do they worship me, teaching for doctrines the commandments of men" (Mark 7:7). In the religious world today, men make the same tragic mistake. How many times have you heard people contend that one does not have to be baptized to be saved? Or they say I surely don't believe baptism has anything to do with one's salvation. But who do we think we are to follow our own judgment?

Our own judgment—in rebellion to the will of the Almighty God!! We can never by any wild stretch of the imagination think we are saying, "Not our will, Father, but thine be done."

We notice again that Jeroboam's effort had a selfish view in mind. You remember that he set up golden calves in Bethel and Dan. He did so lest the people continue to go to Jerusalem and worship and the hearts of the people be turned from himself back to Rehoboam. So it is today that many religious efforts crowd God entirely out, and they become efforts that exist with the sole purpose of honor and aggrandizement of some individual. The Papal system with all its pomp and ceremony bestows undue honor upon a mere man. God only is to be the object of our devotion—not man. His will is to be our aim—not the satisfaction of our own selfish whims. The validity of religious things can largely be measured by a consideration of the respect shown to God. I would like to re-emphasize that point. The validity of religious things can largely be measured by a consideration of the respect shown to God. Jesus says, "My meat is to do the will of him that sent me" (John 4:34). Acceptable service is not concerned with the desires and the aims of man but those of God. The pride of life, that is, man's desire to selfishly do his will rather than God's is the basis of all sorts of schemes that are palmed off on men in the name of religion today.

Thirdly, I would like for you to notice this thing that Jeroboam did fostered convenience rather than conviction. God had decreed that Jerusalem was the place for men to worship, but Jeroboam said it was too much for the people to go to Jerusalem. He was catering to the people—he was a man pleaser. He was not the last one, however, to make that mistake. Many a man is willing to sell out today—I mean, all the way—they are willing to sell out to soothe the feelings of the people. The religion of the Lord demands that we serve through conviction rather than through convenience. It is concerned with obedience—not ease. It may lead us into some rough and difficult places. It may well demand that costly sacrifices be made, but God requires obedience. Jeroboam pleased men but displeased God, and that was a sin.

Last, we notice that Jeroboam did not respect the law of God because he built altars in Bethel and altars in Dan rather than allowing the people to go to Jerusalem to worship. Jerusalem was the place where God had decreed for men to worship Him.

It is tragic but true that men still follow their own desires rather than the plain declaration of the scripture. Let us learn these valuable lessons from this tragic story of one who rebelled against God. May we be inspired to follow without question our Father's will. We should remember that Jesus says, "Not everyone that saith unto me Lord, Lord, shall enter into the kingdom of heaven; but he that doeth the will of my Father which is in heaven" (Matthew 7:21). Our entrance into the celestial city is dependent upon our doing the Father's will.

The question today: What are you doing to accomplish the Father's will in the church and in your life and in your home? It does no good to pray, "Father, not my will but thine be done," unless we endeavor to live in harmony with this, the Father's will.

Thank you for listening.

Old Time Religion

Good morning, everyone. Once again we turn your attention to the word of God and we would like to discuss with you the subject, "Old Time Religion." It is so true that much ink has been used and many tears have been spilled in sentimental reminiscing concerning that which is sometimes called "Old Time Religion." Several years ago on a nation wide radio program, an internationally known evangelist discussing the present day need for old time religion defined such as "the doctrines taught by Jesus Christ and as embraced in all creeds today." Now this man was only partially correct. It is true that old time religion must come as a result of following the doctrine of the Lord Jesus, but by no stretch of the imagination can it be said of such that it is embraced by all creeds today.

The word "creed" comes from the Latin word "credo" meaning "I believe." In times past we have talked about the "good confession" which was made by people in the first century before they were baptized into Christ. They simply stated, "I believe that Jesus Christ is the Son of God" (Acts 8:37). In other words, Christ was their creed; and that creed was enough. Christ is still the creed of those who have renounced the doctrines and commandments of men with all their human creeds and disciplines. If we believe Christ, we believe His New Testament; we believe His Father's word that Christ gave to the apostles to teach and to bind. It is true, old time religion is Christ's religion. To label the religious systems of men today as old time religion is to mis-name them for they are not old enough to be the real commodity. The Apostle Paul writes, "All scripture is given by inspiration of God, and is profitable for doctrine, for reproof, for correction, for instruction in righteousness: That the man of God may be perfect, throughly furnished unto all good works" (2 Timothy 3:16-17). If the scriptures really provide these benefits, what business do men have in composing their own human creeds, church manuals, and church disciplines? By what authority do they impose these human doctrines upon others and say they don't recognize them and, therefore, they cannot partake of the Lord's Supper with them since they will not subscribe to their man-made creed? These people seem to be generous when they say that other religious folks are Christians.

But, in reality, when they make such an acknowledgement, they are being hypocritical because they refuse to allow others the right to eat with them. That is sectarianism gone to seed—as I see it.

A great number of people are quite sentimental in regard to old time religion; but when they ignore the authority of Jesus Christ contained in His word, they are pitifully mistaken. It is impossible to have old time religion and deny any part of the word of God, which is almost 2,000 years old. In order for any man to practice true old time religion, he must be willing to accept and embrace the supreme authority of Christ and His word as opposed to all the creeds, manuals, disciplines, confessions, and catechisms that men are capable of bringing into existence.

Let us seriously and prayerfully take notice of some necessary characteristics a church must possess before it is capable of practicing the old time religion of the New Testament. First of all, if, indeed, we are claiming to possess old time religion, then we must have the oldest Head of the church. The Head of the true church does not consist of any apostle or group of apostles nor of any supposed successor to the apostles. The New Testament instructs us that Jesus Christ was raised from the dead and ascended into glory where He was seated on the right hand of the Majesty on high and crowned both Lord and Christ and made "head over all things to the church, Which is his body, the fullness of him that filleth all in all" (Ephesians 1:19-23, Acts 2:36, Hebrews 1:3).

We are also made to understand that He is not only the author of our faith but the finisher of it as well (Hebrews 12:2). You recall that Jesus told Peter, "Upon this rock I **will build** my church" and that is precisely what He did. John the Baptist was already dead and buried when Jesus made the statement, "Upon this rock I will build my church," so certainly John did not build the church. The Lord built it and first began to add men to it in Jerusalem on the first Pentecost following His ascension into heaven, exactly 53 days after He shed His blood on Calvary (Acts 1 and 2). Consequently, we must conclude that any church that is not this old—almost two thousand years old, with Jesus as its founder and its Head—is not old enough to have had the old time religion committed unto it.

But again—please think with me—for a church to practice the true old time religion, it must engage in the oldest worship. In old times,

Moses prophesied about the coming Christ and the new law He would bring with Him. It was God who said:

> I will raise them up a Prophet from among their brethren, like unto thee, and will put my words in his mouth; and he shall speak unto them all that I shall command him. And it shall come to pass that whosoever will not hearken unto my words which he shall speak in my name, I will require it of him (Deuteronomy 18:18-19).

The Apostle Peter made reference to this prediction, and he applied it to Christ, the great lawgiver of the church. He is the only figure—listen—the **only** figure who fits the description of the prophets. He is the perfect ante-type of Moses who was the lawgiver of the old dispensation. Jesus was given all authority in heaven and in earth, according to His own affirmation. Now when Jesus was conversing with the Samaritan woman at Jacob's well, the subject of worship arose. Remember? The Lord said:

> The hour cometh, and now is, when the true worshippers shall worship the Father in spirit and in truth: for the Father seeketh such to worship him. God is a Spirit: and they that worship him must worship him in spirit and in truth (John 4:23-24).

In these words, we see a pattern or an outline that true worship was to follow. The worship of the early church was in spirit. Men and women were completely dedicated to the spiritual development of their souls. If need be, there were those of that number who would willingly lay down their very lives for the gospel's sake; and thousands did so in times of persecution.

They truly realized that God is a Spirit and that it did not require a lot of noise, a lot of physical exertion and excitement, to worship the Father. They realized that worship is for spiritual communion and not for the purpose of putting on a show or entertaining the crowd. New Testament worship was a worship that was in spirit but it was also a worship that was in truth, that is, it was conducted not according to what men might think fitting and proper or what might best fit the times or what might best fit on the television program or what the people of that particular time wanted ... not according to that which pleased the physical senses but in accordance with apostolic teaching. They worshiped in truth or as truth directed.

New Testament worship consisted of teaching and preaching, singing without the use of mechanical instruments of music, the regular weekly observance of the Lord's Supper, and the giving of one's means for evangelistic and benevolent purposes. In fact, "They continued steadfastly in the apostles' doctrine and fellowship, and in breaking of bread, and in prayers" (Acts 2:42). Old time religion, then, does not consist of worship that is not authorized by apostolic teaching and practice. Anything that has been added as an item of worship by uninspired men since the days of the apostles is simply not old enough to be classified as "Old Time Religion." It is not far enough to go back to Grandpa's time: we must go all the way back to the time of the apostles and the original church of Jesus Christ (Romans 16:16).

But let us notice further. If a church is to practice the old time religion, it must have the oldest church organization. Modern churches have everything under the sun, it would appear to me. They have their official boards, their pastors, their board of deacons, their general conferences, hierarchies, synods, along with their branch organizations, Sunday Schools, womens' auxilaries, societies, circles and what-not. Any resemblance between these and what we read about in the New Testament is only coincidental. It is impossible to find similarities. Such does not exist in the Bible. I know these statements sound like the voice of one crying in the wilderness of modern times. There are those, I am sure, who would classify us with the apostle as Festus did so long ago as he cried out, "Paul, thou art mad." But the fact is that such things did not exist in apostolic times. Such things did not exist among those who truly practiced the old time religion.

The New Testament church, with Christ as its Head, was composed of independent congregations fully autonomous with a group of elders or bishops in each congregation and assisted by a group of men known as deacons. There were no super organizations and there were no nation wide hook-ups. Churches cooperated with each other in the great work of saving the lost and providing for those in need but each congregation maintained its own independence, its own autonomy. It was accountable unto God alone. You recall that when Paul sent a letter to the church at Philippi he addressed it to "all the saints in Christ Jesus which are at Philippi, with the bishops and deacons" (Philippians 1:1). The words "elder," "bishop," and "pastor" are various terms that describe one single office or work in the church.

They are spiritual overseers of a congregation. These are not to be confused with the work of a preacher or an evangelist. The preacher is not the "pastor" of a church. That is not Bible terminology. The preacher has no authority in church affairs except to preach the word. He works in close cooperation with the elders, the leadership of the congregation, and under their spiritual supervision. I think that we should realize his specialty is and ought to be evangelism and not the oversight of congregational affairs. Evangelism is a broad term that includes many responsibilities. Certainly the preacher is not one who simply punches a clock at 5 p.m. He is never "off duty." As far as the deacons of a congregation are concerned, they have no authority either except for that which is delegated to them by the elders who are their spiritual overseers. It is their task to assist the elders and render whatever service is needed—that is, whatever they are capable of fulfilling. This statement does not mean a deacon cannot engage in spiritual service. A deacon may do anything that any other Christian may do.

I would like to point out also that there is no caste system in the New Testament. Never is there any such thing in the New Testament as a distinction between clergy and laity. We still hear people talking about "clergy" and about the "lay" members of the church. This modern concept has its roots deeply embedded in Roman Catholicism. The New Testament church consisted of saints—that is, its members, its elders, and its deacons. There is no official office of evangelist. Every son of God is expected to spread the glad tidings; however, there are some who devote their entire lives to the task and forego all secular employment in order to do a more efficient job of it. They are evangelists or in common language we would simply speak of them as preachers of the word. Now this is Old Time Religion because we can read it in the New Testament.

I would like to point out one other thing in closing. Another characteristic of the church that practices old time religion is this—it must preach the oldest law of pardon. Such additions as the mourner's bench and faith-only are much too modern. The preachers of the early church preached the gospel of Christ. They preached the Great Commission. Our Lord told them to "Go ye into all the world, and preach the gospel to every creature. He that believeth and is baptized shall be saved; but he that believeth not shall be damned" (Mark 16:16). And we find them going forth and carrying out this Great Commission. They went everywhere preaching the word, including to

Samaria where the scripture declares in Acts 8:12 that many of these people believed and were baptized. They went to Corinth, and the scripture says that many of the Corinthians, hearing, believed and were baptized. They preached the word of God in Caesera. The Apostle Peter commanded Cornelius to be baptized. So on the word of God went throughout the entire known world as they went preaching the good news of our Lord. They preached that men must believe and they must repent of their sins. They must confess the Holy Christ—His death, His burial, His resurrection—and they were immersed upon their confession of faith in Christ as the Son of God. They were baptized for the remission of their sins (Acts 2:38). I propose to you that anything short of this is not ancient enough to be that Old Time Religion of the New Testament. I would like to impress upon you today the necessity of insisting upon the Old Time Religion. In fact, in Jude 3, he teaches us that we are to earnestly contend for the faith that was once for all handed down to the saints. That is the Old Time Religion.

The question today: Have you obeyed that Old Time Religion? Are you contending for that Old Time Religion? Think about it!

Enemies of Christianity

Ladies and gentlemen, we invite your attention this morning to a study that we believe is something needful. We would like to say also in the beginning that we are grateful for the privilege of coming into your home and studying with you the Lord's word. Our lesson pertains to the greatest force in the world today, and that is Christianity.

Christianity, when defined in the light of Bible teaching, would be the religion of Christians. Or, to speak from a different point of view, Christianity is that body of followers of Christ who stand as a mighty army for the spreading of the gospel of our Lord and for the defense of His cause among men. It is indeed the cause of Christ, God's own Son. Christianity has always had enemies! It would seem that if there would be anything that would never have an enemy, it would be Christianity, when we think of what the term really means. But the fact is there have always been those who have been opposed to the teaching of Jesus Christ. May we ever trust in the ultimate triumph of the worthy forces of our Lord. When truth has seemed to be crushed and defeated, it has always come forth to victory! Opposition and persecution have only fanned the flames of Christian zeal into a whiter and more intense heat! The rulers of the Jews thought by putting Christ to death on Calvary, they would win; but they only aided in carrying out the plan of God. When persecution was heaped upon the church in Jerusalem and the disciples were scattered abroad, they that were scattered went everywhere preaching the word! (Acts 8:4). Paul spoke of the hardship he had endured at the hand of his enemies by saying, "But I would ye should understand, brethren, that the things which happened unto me have fallen out rather unto the furtherance of the gospel; So that my bonds in Christ are manifest in all the palace and in all other places; And many of the brethren in the Lord, waxing confident by my bonds, are much more bold to speak the word without fear" (Philippians 1:12-14).

There are two classes of enemies: Some are recognized by all, or are universally labeled as enemies. But often, the most deadly enemies are those whom some might call friends. They are forces that serve more as a "fifth column," fighting from within the gates, in a sense, for they bear such similarity to the true forces of our Lord that they deceive the multitudes of men. Christians must "put on the whole armour of God that they may be able to stand against the wiles"—that is the cunning craftiness—"of the devil" (Ephesians 6:11). I think we should face this fact, that Satan is the leader of the forces of the enemy! He has been the enemy of good from the very beginning of man's existence, and he has been the enemy of Christianity from the time of its establishment. He brought sin into the world in Eden, and he sought to overthrow Christ. Three times he tempted Him in the wilderness only to be put to flight! Throughout the ministry of the Master, he tried to gain advantage over Him; but Satan and all his hosts could not win! Christ spoke of those who opposed Him saying, "Ye are of your father the devil, and the lusts of your father ye will do" (John 8:44). Satan still, even in our own time, is the leader of those who fight against the church of our Lord, and the teaching of truth! Christ pictured him in the parable of the sower, as taking the word of God out of the hearts of men, lest they should believe and be saved (Luke 8:12). The devil sowed false teaching in the world, according to the parable of the tares, and the tares are the children of the wicked one; the enemy that sowed them is the devil (Matthew 13:38-39). And, the colleagues of Satan are still sowing tares among men today!

Let us consider together, some of these enemies of the cause of Christ (contemporary enemies) and the teaching of His word. I would like to point out that "modernists" are the enemies of Christianity. These are individuals who profess some faith in Christ; in fact, they may profess a great deal of faith in Christ! They hold to some of the teachings of the Bible, but they deny, for example, the virgin birth of Christ and label His miracles as matters of deception and some of His teachings as being impractical. They claim to believe only what they think can be applied to us today without realizing or recognizing that all of Christ's teachings are practical and that all of His teachings can be applied to us today in the same way in which He gave them nineteen centuries ago! The so-called modernists say the Bible is out of date and is not inspired of God in the first place, and that it is not the authority for men to recognize in religion in our modern generation! The modernists would destroy confidence in God, in Christ, in the Holy Spirit, and especially in the Bible as the word of God! They have nothing to offer in place of the faith they seek to destroy any more than they have proof for any of their accusations and denunciations. They often hide behind the guise of learning and not infrequently in some of the pulpits of the land! Their positions make them the more dangerous, and they prey upon the young people of our day, seeking to undermine their faith in Christianity. They are called modernists, but their work is actually the same as the false teachers of the time of Paul. So, they are not actually "modern" in this sense. In 2 Corinthians 11:14-15, we read, "... for Satan himself is transformed into an angel of light. Therefore it is no great thing if his ministers also be transformed as the ministers of righteousness; whose end shall be according to their works." We should not forget the exhortation found in 1 John 4:1, "Beloved, believe not every spirit, but try the spirits whether they be of God: because many false prophets are gone out into the world." God's children must prepare themselves to be able to stand against the forces of modernism, and they must be prepared to teach their young people the truth of God. They must be able to show why God's word is inspired and how we must obey God in order to be saved from sin—and eventually be saved in heaven! The world today needs the firm foundation of eternal truth that is found in the Bible to save us from chaos! The gospel of Christ is God's only power to save men, and it must be preached to all the world (Romans 1:16).

Not only is a modernist an enemy of Christianity but the moralist is an enemy of Christianity. He claims to live a good moral life, to be honest in his dealings, to be a good neighbor, and to be a good citizen. He points to the moral quality in Christ's teachings and says that is all that is required! He says the church is not necessary and that a man can be saved out of the church as well as in the church! But the moralist ignores the teachings of the Bible in the most fundamental points. He fails to recognize that man, even though he does his best to be moral, is still not perfect. He overlooks that "all have sinned, and come short of the glory of God" (Romans 3:23), and man cannot cleanse himself of his own sin. God's word says, "Without shedding of blood is no remission" (Hebrews 9:22). Christ shed His blood for the remission of sins (Matthews 26:28), and it is in Christ that we have redemption through His blood, the forgiveness of sins, according to the riches of His grace (Ephesians 1:7). Men must obey the gospel of Christ to be saved. Mark 16:16 says, "He that believeth and is baptized shall be saved." Acts 2:38 tells us, "Repent, and be baptized every one of you in the name of Jesus Christ for the remission of sins." And in this obedience, our sins may be washed away by the blood of Christ (Acts 22:16). The Lord will add us to the church (Acts

2:47); and by our faithful living for Christ, His blood will continue to cleanse us from sin (1 John 1:7). The church was purchased with the blood of Christ (Acts 20:28). Christ purchased the church for man's good and man's salvation! Yet, the moralist ignores all these fundamental truths of God's word! If indeed the moralist is true, then my Lord died in vain on the cross of Calvary because there were some good people living before Jesus ever died!

Denominationalism is also an enemy of truth in our day because denominationalism causes division and confusion in religion. Its forces are many and great and powerful, and that we do not deny! Its doctrine and creeds have long been the cause of strife and discord. Many good, honest people have been so confused by its very claims that they have chosen to remain in unbelief. I think often of the missionary who tried to teach the heathen idolater about the true God, but he was met many times with this answer: "Is your God a god of division?" or "Why don't you Christians get together before you come over to teach us about God?" Christ taught His followers to be one. He prayed that they might be one (John 17:20-21). But the claims of denominationalism defeat the purpose of Christ's teachings and serve to nullify the prayer that He made to the Father.

Churches of Christ are pleading for the unity of the followers of Christ—a unity based upon the plain and simple teachings of the Bible. Unity is not something that is impossible! It is the will of God for men. It can be done … it must be done if we will win the world to Christ, the only Saviour that God has given to a sin-sick and lost world!

Humbly, and in the name of the crucified Son of God, we make this plea today: The Bible is the basis for our faith, and the doing of God's will is our sole purpose and claim; the direction of the Holy Spirit through the Inspired word of God is our only guide; heaven is our great goal; and as children of God, we want to point out God's way that we might all enter that home some day. May we plead with you today to lay aside the barriers of denominationalism and let us all be Christians, nothing more and nothing less. Let us do away with the creeds and names that separate men, and let us bow humbly and obediently at the foot of the cross of Christ, seeking to do His will in all things. Let us consider these matters in view of the Day of Judgment and in light of where we will live in eternity!

We are living in perilous times, more perilous I think than many of us realize! There are powerful and insidious enemies who are seeking to destroy the liberty and freedom that we have enjoyed in this great country of ours. There has been a continuous and rapid growth of sin in the ranks of our citizens. Satan's forces are alert to every opportunity to tear away the foundation of Christianity. Christ and His church is the ONLY answer! Men of faith and courage must stand united in the Lord's great army, the church of our Lord, to defend the cause of Christ and to preach the gospel of peace and salvation! Can the Lord depend on you? Will you place Christ foremost in your life? Will you, through obedience to the gospel of Christ, unite with God's children in this great work?

Not only are these enemies and hindering forces, some church members are hindering forces also! They stand as a "fifth column" fighting against the cause of Christ. Some are lukewarm, lacking in zeal and love for the Christ. They are like those at Laodicea whom the Lord condemned in Revelation 3:15-16. Some have become members of the Lord's church but are friends to the sins of the world. James writes, "Ye adulterers and adulteresses, know ye not that the friendship of the world is enmity with God? whosoever therefore will be a friend of the world is the enemy of God" (James 4:4). Some are lovers of pleasure more than lovers of God (2 Timothy 3:4). Some would compromise the truth of God with the teaching of sin and the teaching of error. There are extremists and hobbyists who exalt their opinions above the teachings of Christ, and cause strife and trouble in the ranks of the children of God! From them, the Lord bids us to turn away and and to avoid them! (Romans 16:17; 2 Thessalonians 3:6). Paul says, "they are the enemies of the cross of Christ: Whose end is destruction ... " (Philippians 3:18-19).

I would like to point out, however, that in spite of all the enemies, be they organized or individual, be they weak or be they powerful, regardless of what they may be, or who they may be, our Lord will be victorious over His enemies! You will recall that while He was here, He was victorious over His enemies and over the grave. "But thanks be to God, which giveth us the victory through our Lord Jesus Christ" (1 Corinthians 15:57). We also read in 1 John 5:4, "And this is the victory..."—Now think about this!—"THIS is the victory that overcometh the world, even our faith." The enemies of Christ and the enemies of Christianity will not prevail; even the last enemy that shall be destroyed is death! (1 Corinthians 15:26). The Lord shall come to receive His own and He will be glorified in His saints (2 Thessalonians 1:10). But the question today is: Will you be in that number? Will the Lord call you home at last? Are you living for Him now? Jesus says, “He that is not with me is against me” (Matthew 12:30). He also says, “Ye are my friends, if ye do whatsoever I command you” (John 15:14). Christ laid down His life for us; let us ever be faithful to Him, in His service to the very end of life!

Thank you for listening.

Secret Sins

Ladies and gentlemen, it is a distinct privilege to come into your homes today to study with you the Lord's word. We are very grateful to be able to be here and study with you on a subject that we believe is of vital interest and concern to your soul. We invite you to open your Bibles to the nineteenth Psalm. Every person should be a student of the book of Psalms. The one hundred fifty Psalm should be read frequently and prayerfully, I believe. Their beauty and their devotion are unexcelled in all of the Old Testament. Actually, only the teachings of our Lord in the New Testament can be considered surpassing them in their devotional and spiritual value. One of the most familiar of the Psalms is the one to which I have made reference, the nineteenth. It combines praise to God and prayer to Him as the One who knows and understands the hearts of men. It strikes deep into our hearts in our meditation and our realization of our own sins. Notice that the twelfth verse says, "Who can understand his errors? cleanse thou me from secret faults." The next verse contains that prayer, "Keep back thy servant also from presumptuous sins; let them not have dominion over me: then shall I be upright, and I shall be innocent from the great transgression."

The setting of this particular text should be noticed. The recognition of personal sins stands in contrast to the devout thoughts of meditation expressed in the first verses of this Psalm. Out of these spring the realization of the sinful condition of the individual. Let us now read together. "The heavens declare the glory of God; and the firmament sheweth his handywork. Day unto day uttereth speech, and night unto night sheweth knowledge. There is no speech nor language, where their voice is not heard. Their line is gone out through all the earth, and their words to the end of the world. In them hath he set a tabernacle for the sun, which is as a bridegroom coming out of his chamber, and rejoiceth as a strong man to run a race. His going forth is from the end of the heaven, and his circuit unto the ends of it: and there is nothing hid from the heat thereof" (verses 1-6). And then there is the consideration of God's law. "The law of the Lord is perfect, converting the soul: the testimony of the Lord is sure, making wise the simple. The statutes of the Lord are right, rejoicing the heart: the commandment of the Lord is pure, enlightening the eyes. The fear of the Lord is clean, enduring for ever: the judgments of the Lord are true and righteous altogether. More to be desired are they than gold, yea, than much fine gold: sweeter also than honey and the honeycomb. Moreover by them is thy servant warned: and in keeping of them there is great reward" (verses 7-11). Then follows the text, "Who can understand his errors? cleanse thou me from secret faults" (verse 12).

It is not possible for a man to understand his own errors without bringing his life into close comparison with divine truth. The deviation from God's rule for righteousness can be seen only when the standard of God is applied. Each person is himself his own greatest mystery. But each one of us should search diligently his own life to the end of understanding how little we actually know of ourselves. Even our physical structure passes our knowledge. All of the marvelous discoveries of science and medicine, as extensive and as revealing as they have been, still leave us to exclaim, "I am fearfully and wonderfully made" (Psalm 139:14).

Why do we do certain things? Most of us are brought face to face with the question, "Why did I do that?" The inward and sometimes not fully realized working of our mind fascinates every observant person in the study of his own mental relations. In this text, the psalmist seems almost to despair of understanding self, of being able to ferret out the inner faults of the heart. Jeremiah, the prophet, says, "The heart is deceitful above all things, and desperately wicked: who can know it?" (Jeremiah 17:9). Therefore, the importance of the exhortation of Proverbs 4:23 "Keep thy heart with all diligence; for out of it are the issues of life." Each one has his own hidden faults. If we had eyes like those of God, we could better see our true condition as God sees it. As Mr. Spurgeon once wrote, "The transgressions that we see and confess are but like the farmer's small samples which he brings to market when he has left his full grainery at home." We have but a few sins that we can observe and detect compared with those that are hidden from ourselves and unseen by our fellow creatures. In Psalm 90:8, "Thou hast set our iniquities before thee, our secret sins in the light of thy countenance." So it is that God sees and that God knows the secret sins, that is, sins that are secret in contrast to open sins. And all these sins shall be brought into judgment as we are told in Ecclesiastes 12:14: "For God shall bring every work into judgment, with every secret thing, whether it be good, or whether it be evil."

The American Standard Version gives our text like this, "Clear thou me from hidden faults," and I think the thought is apparent. The hidden faults are those that exist without our knowledge or at least our being aware of them. Each of us has faults that we do not realize, evidently. The evidence that these hidden faults can exist is clear. Think about this: How easy it is to see another's faults, the faults that the other man does not see in himself, evidently, and he does not know they even exist. Secondly, there is the outcropping of faults when under trial, when times of stress or strain or trial come upon us; we do things without realizing the "why" of our actions. Thirdly, let's observe Abraham. The Bible points out his great faith in God, but in the time of trial, he spoke of Sarah as his sister, thus denying the fact that she was his wife. Why?

As I study this passage, I often come up with that one lone question "Why?" Was not God able to protect them? Did not his faith reach to this point? Consider Moses who was the meekest of men, but he sinned with his lips under provocation; and his sin was of sufficient gravity that God determined that Moses should not enter the promised land of Canaan. Why did Moses so sin? And Solomon, the wisest of men, bowed to idols and was made to sin by outlandish women whom he had taken to be his wives. Why?

I think it is evident from those passages alone that self-examination is something needed by all of us. Like the psalmist, we need to realize each one of us has hidden faults. There is an abundance of faults that lie in our hearts, faults that have hitherto been overlooked. Such self-examination may not be pleasant, but it is most practical. It is most essential and such self-examination can have some great results. First of all, it can humble us before God when we come to their realization.

Secondly, it can vest us of our pride of personal perfection, a pride that may go before a fall. Thirdly, it can make us more considerate of the faults we see in others and more disposed to use love in dealing with them so that we may help others overcome those errors and shortcomings and in so doing, we will open the way for them to help us with the same consideration.

In our examination, we may find those faults that we have forgotten. Or we may find those hidden faults that we had never observed before; but with a better knowledge of God's word and teachings, they become more noticeable. Or we may find those faults we do not want to admit, not even to ourselves—faults that tend to cover our real nature. They may be our failure to study God's word. It may be that failure of yours to pray as you ought to pray or to be faithful in worship to God. Every person has a tendency to justify himself, to excuse his own actions and to cover his own shortcomings. Each has a love for self, for ease, for pleasure, for pride or self-preservation.

Sometimes a person excuses, in his own thinking, the sins of greed and avarice by calling them thrift. His failure, or lack of faith, is in his mind attributed to caution or to good business. But I would like to point out today that sin is sin. As trite as that may sound and as redundant as that may be, sin is sin. Whether it is secret or hidden or open, it is still sin. It may be different in its extent and the influence of the hidden fault may be far less, but it remains a sin. It is condemning to the individual, and that condemnation can be removed only by obedience to God's plan for the remission of sins.

The danger is this: Hidden faults are like germs that lie dormant for years, and then under favorable conditions they grow into a large proportion. It is said that almost every person carries within his body the germs of tuberculosis and that when the condition of his body becomes physically weak, he is susceptible to their growth. These germs grow and make the person a victim of tuberculosis. So we need to beware. Our hidden faults under provocation may spring out and grow and make us the victims of their control in our lives.

So there is a need for the knowledge of God and His word. We need to study the Bible. As James expressed it, we need to look into the "perfect law of liberty" (James 1:25). The Bible is like a mirror into which we can look by our study, there we can see God's perfect order, and there we can discover our own faults.

Secondly, our need is to obey what God teaches in His word. James tells us to "continue therein"—remember?—"Continue therein" and be not a "forgetful hearer, but a doer of the work." It is this man who will be "blessed in his deed" (James 1:25).

When the New Testament teaches faith in Christ as God's Son, we should learn to have that faith. When we see that "except ye repent, ye shall all likewise perish" (Luke 13:3), we should obey in repentance. When we read in the Lord's word, "He that believeth and is baptized shall be saved" (Mark 16:16), we should be ready to obey His command and be buried with our Lord in baptism for the remission of our sins. When we learn how the disciples "continued steadfastly in the apostles' doctrine and fellowship, and in breaking of bread, and in prayers" (Act 2:42), we should respond in faithful observance of the apostles' doctrine and teaching, in laying by in store as we are prospered on the first day of every week (1 Corinthians 16:2), in the eating of the Lord's Supper as it was laid down and given to us, and in regular and faithful observance of the privilege of prayer.

Now to obey the Lord's teachings would demand of us faithful Christian living—that is, that we will follow the example of Jesus Christ. It would mean, as John says, "If we walk in the light, as he is in the light, we have fellowship one with another, and the blood of Jesus Christ his Son cleanseth us from all sin" (1 John 1:7).

Here is salvation from all sin, even our hidden faults, through the blood of Jesus Christ. Here the grace of God saves us through our Lord and Saviour. We need to develop a conscience. It should be a good conscience that knows God's standard of sin, the New Testament. It should be a conscience sharpened by the truth of God and one that is strong and absolutely unyielding. It should be able to discern both good and evil (Hebrews 5:14). Conscience, taught by God's word, should be able to direct us in becoming Christians and in living a faithful Christian life. This development will be seen in our reliance upon God to help us overcome all our faults whether they be secret or open. It will mean our salvation, now and for all eternity. It may be expressed in the prayer of the book of Psalms:

> Keep back thy servant also from presumptuous sins; let them not have dominion over me: then shall I be upright, and I shall be innocent from the great transgression. Let the words of my mouth, and the meditation of my heart, be acceptable in thy sight, O Lord, my strength, and my redeemer (Psalm 19:13-14).

This marvelous benediction can be ours, but the purpose must be to obey the Lord, to meditate upon His truth, and to be kept from the great transgression of apostasy from the gospel of Christ. Without the meditation upon His truth, the words of our mouth are like the empty shell without a kernel and they are worthless and useless in God's sight. In conclusion, this morning, may we exhort you to be aware of the hidden faults of your life?

May we point you to Christ and to His gospel as the means of our salvation? May we encourage you to become a Christian so that the precious blood of Christ might cleanse your every sin as you walk in the light of God's truth? We would pray today that God would help us to realize our need of forgiveness for even those things that lie hidden within our hearts. We would ask that you would meditate seriously upon these words of David from the Psalms because they are, indeed, written for our learning and our admonition.

What is Your Conception of Religion?

Ladies and gentlemen, we invite your attention this morning to a question that I believe we need to consider seriously: "What is your conception of religion?" So many people have only a vague conception of religion. So many look upon religion as something that is unreal or unnatural or something not fitted for their every day practice in the ordinary affairs of life. The word "religion" has been so misused and abused that often people shy away from the very mention of the word. True religion is practical and understandable. It is even beautiful in its simplicity. It applies to the child; it is suited to the most profound. It would fill the need of the man on the street, or in his business, or in his home, or on the farm, or in the simplest game in which he may engage in his recreation. True religion is found in God's requirement for everyday living. God's religion is made up of fundamental principles that can be applied to the situations that come before us every day that we live.

At different times and under various circumstances, the divine writers have stated very plainly what Jehovah would require of man. Possibly one of the most striking summaries of religion in the Old Testament prophecies is found in the writing of Micah in Micah 6:8. I want you to listen to this great statement. It was given to a people who needed to have set before them the real essence of true religion. It was nothing new. He spoke of God's way saying, "He hath showed thee, O man, what is good; and what doth the Lord require of thee, but to do justly, and to love mercy, and to walk humbly with thy God?" Micah here summed up religion in three parts. God's requirements of men are (1) to do justly, (2) to love mercy, and (3) to walk humbly with thy God. These three truths have been expressed again and again and again both in the law and in the prophets. God had declared them in times past but they had not listened. The people of Micah's day were much like the people of our own time—they were more interested in other things. Ceremonials and things of show had more appeal to them than the practical principles of God's truth. They were disposed to separate their religion from their way of living. They wanted to continue to live as they pleased and have some ceremonials that would suffice with God. I propose to you that that's a picture of the generation in which we are living this very moment.

Notice the proposal of the people. Their idea is expressed in these words: "Wherewith shall I come before the Lord, and bow myself before the high God? shall I come before him with burnt offerings, with calves of a year old? Will the Lord be pleased with thousands of rams, or with ten thousands of rivers of oil? shall I give my firstborn for my transgression, the fruit of my body for the sin of my soul?" (Micah 6:6-7). Why would they propose such things? Are not ceremonials easier than true holiness? Such matters tend to pacify and to appease the perverted conscience. They make great outward demonstration, but they are not the true way to please God. True religion lies deeper than those things. The Lord's way is the way of heart and of life. Jehovah is interested in man himself. He wants man's heart. He wants man's life. He wants man's love, and God wants man to do that which is right and kind and humble before Him. This has always been true, and it is true today. May we learn these essential lessons from those of Micah's day?

Religion is more than ceremony. They were interested in "thousands of rams and ten thousands of rivers of oil," but outward ceremony cannot replace the heart. He wanted them to understand that God was not some vain monarch who could be pleased with big gifts and empty phrases. Samuel says, "Behold, to obey is better than sacrifice, and to hearken than the fat of rams" (1 Samuel 15:22). Many a man has desired to do as he pleased and then offer some gift or sacrifice as a ceremony of atonement. Thus, Samuel rebuked king Saul, Micah rebuked the people of his day, and the Lord condemned the Pharisees of His day for the same thing. He says, "Woe unto you, scribes and Pharisees, hypocrites! for ye pay tithe of mint and anise and cummin, and have omitted the weightier matters of the law, judgment, mercy, and faith: these ought ye to have done, and not to leave the other undone" (Matthew 23:23).

Outward ceremonies lead to hypocrisy. Please remember that. They make mere whited sepulchers devoid of the real qualities of the soul. Men are inclined to substitute them for godliness. Forms, rituals, and ceremonies often become liabilities to the soul. They ease the conscience but condemn the man himself. Let's examine the time in which we live today. Let us see if this ancient prophecy and these ancient words can have any meaning to the time in which we live.

Have men of our day become more interested in outward ceremony—have they become more interested in outward ceremony than in the weightier matters of judgment, justice, mercy, kindness, and the true humble faith that would make men more like God? I think we must admit today that this is true—that we are still following the same collision course they followed so long ago.

There are acts of obedience that God has required of us. I want to assure you today that whereever you are and whoever you are, there are some acts of obedience that God requires of you; and He requires them NOW. These acts are the simple expressions of our faith in matters of obedience, in matters of true Christian living and service, and in humble worship before God. But all too often men have yielded to the eye appeal and to the show appeal of elaborate ceremonies; and when that occurs, the true spirit of religion is crowded out.

True religion is not ostentatious. I want you to think of the great show and glamour of the gifts of THOUSANDS of rams. Try to visualize that—the gift of THOUSANDS of rams and TEN THOUSANDS of rivers of oil. The human tendency is to love the big things, those things that attract considerable attention and that will draw the praise of men. Micah, the prophet, pointed men away from these things. His desire was to declare God's plan of justice, and of mercy, and of an humble walk before God.

True religion is not fanaticism. It is not the offering of the first born as a human sacrifice. Such things had been done as in the case of the king of Moab who offered his son as a burnt offering upon the wall when he saw the battle was against him (2 Kings 3:27), but God has never approved of such things. God's religion has not a place in the world for fanaticism. Those people of the east had long abused and tortured their bodies. Thorn beds and such things as these had long been the thing that they proposed would help in serving their God. Heathen gods had been the objects of human sacrifices, but our God is to be served in a better way than these. God rebuked those who wanted to make a show of religion, remember that? He pointed out how some men sounded the trumpet before them that others about them would know about their alms to help the poor. He says some love to pray standing in such places that they will be seen of men, but our Lord sums it all up when He says, "They HAVE"—please notice the tense—"they HAVE their reward" (Matthew 6:1-6). In spite of all of this, men continue to think of religion in terms of outward demonstration and show. They are more concerned with personal praise than with God's approval. They prefer large and costly cathedrals to spending money preaching the gospel. They are attracted to the display of the crowd instead of the power of the gospel of Jesus Christ. Men are measuring the Lord's truth by the worthless standards of a world that is more interested in entertainment than in where it will spend eternity.

We need to stop today and listen to the words of Micah, the prophet. Stop and think! Remember the Master, whom we are to follow, was the little babe of Bethlehem, born in a stable, cradled in a manger. He was reared in the despised city of Nazareth and He was called the carpenter's son. He says, "I am meek and lowly in heart" (Matthew 11:29). Mark says, "And the common people heard him gladly" (Mark 12:37). Peter says He "went about doing good" (Acts 10:38). The religion of Christ did not appeal to the rulers of His day. The lovers of ceremony and of ostentation hated His rebukes. They thought His teaching was too plain and too simple for them. They despised Him, persecuted Him, and crucified Him at Calvary. But the way to heaven is still the way of that humble Teacher whom they rejected. God's true religion is still the way of the cross, and men need to turn back to the simplicity of God's plan! The fundamental principles of God's requirements for men need to be reiterated again and again and again. We need to have them in our lives day after day after day. Micah says the Lord required of men "to do justly, and to love mercy, and to walk humbly with thy God" (Micah 6:8), and these truths were pointed out by our Lord as "weightier matters of the law, judgment and mercy and faith" (Matthew 23:23).

These principles were often set forth in the writings to the early Christians. May I assure you, they are not out of date for men today. God's requirements are indeed reasonable. We can understand them. I have no problem understanding the things that the Lord requires. They are to make up the moral character of every Christian. Let's remember them, not only as the words of Micah, but as truths that are declared by our Lord. These things are taught also in the gospel for Christian living.

We are to do justly. What does that mean? To do justly means to do that which is just or right. It means right living, right dealing in all that we do. It is fairmindedness put into practice. To be "just" means to be free from blame. It means that as boys and girls, we play the game fair, even when the going is hard and the decision is close. It means that we will not cheat and do that which is unfair. This principle winds itself into the game of adulthood. It matters not who we are nor where we go, the same principle should still be there.

Justice. Justice should be the standard in our homes and should govern us in our attitudes toward our families. It should guide us in our business transactions. It should decide the way in which we deal with our neighbors and cause us to have the proper regard for our fellow Christians. The judgments that we make in every day dealings should be weighed in the balance of justice. In fact, the matters of our relationship to others should be considered as honestly and religiously as the way we handle the Lord's Communion when we gather to worship on the Lord's Day. To deal justly would be to practice honesty, to pay our debts, to give every man his due, and to be fair in all of the problems that come before us. The world seems to be forgetting this rule for living. Various surveys have shown such an increase of dishonesty that it is absolutely ridiculous. They indicate there are more dishonest people than honest ones. The rate of crime in our country is showing an appalling increase day by day by day, but God's standard is still the same. It doesn't matter what may occur or how the winds may blow, God's standard is still the same. True religion would demand of us to be honest and just in all our dealings with our fellow men. It doesn't matter what others may do; He has never changed our standards to go along with an ungodly world. He is spoken of as "the Holy One and the Just," you remember, in Acts 3:14. As our Lord was just and is just today so are we to be as disciples.

Not only did he say the Lord would ask you to do justly but he says also that we should love mercy. Now, mercy is a wonderful thing. We are dependent upon the mercy of our God. Our sins are, indeed, many. We are grateful that we have a God who is ready to pardon, that He is gracious, and that He is merciful. We are thankful for His love in sending our Lord into the world that we might know His mercy in the forgiveness of our sins because of the death of Christ. In His gospel, He sets forth the fact that He shed His blood for us on Calvary. In this we see the great plan of God's mercy. In the gospel of Christ, that mercy is extended to us that we might believe in Him and that we might be baptized for the remission of our sins (Mark 16:15-16). Surely, surely we realize that without the mercy of God and of Christ, we would be without hope.

QUESTION: How much do we appreciate that mercy? The prophet says that men ought to LOVE mercy. The mercy of God toward us should make us merciful toward others. Mercy is a beautiful compound of love plus forgiveness. Indeed we cannot receive God's mercy unless we are merciful toward others. Jesus says, "Blessed are the merciful: for they shall obtain mercy" (Matthew 5:7).

He says that true religion means to "walk humbly with thy God." We are to humble ourselves "under the mighty hand of God" (1 Peter 5:6). Surely when we think of God's greatness and of our utter dependence upon Him, we can humble ourselves before Him. We must bring our will into subjection to His. To be just and to be merciful is not enough; God asks that we be humble. He wants that humility to be part of our fellowship with Him. He desires, as the prophet says, that we walk humbly—please notice—not simply BE humble or HAVE humbleness, but to WALK HUMBLY with thy God; so we see it put to use. Christ humbled Himself before God in His obedience to Him, even to the death of the cross. That same mind of humility is to be ours as we walk with God. As Paul states in Philippians 2:5, "Let this mind be in you, which was also in Christ Jesus." Christ humbled Himself, and He would have us to humble ourselves if indeed we intend to live in that beautiful city of heaven.

Remember these principles today. They are God's requirements. These are the essentials of true religion. Let them be ever before you as you learn "to do justly, and to love mercy, and to walk humbly with thy God."

Honesty

Ladies and gentlemen, we invite your attention this morning to the subject of Honesty. Honesty may be defined as integrity, truthfulness, freedom from fraud. It implies a refusal to lie, to steal, or to deceive in any way. Possibly the word is most used in connection with the refusal to steal or the misuse of the property of another. God taught His people one of His fundamental principles, "Thou shalt not steal" (Exodus 20:15). It was also said in the law, "Thou shalt not covet" (Exodus 20:17). God intended that men should respect the property and the personal rights of other people. This principle has been overlooked so many times. There are tremendous crimes committed every day; in fact, I suppose we could say almost every moment in the United States. They fall into many categories: burglary, larceny, auto theft—tremendous examples of violation of God's law "Thou shalt not steal," and in violation of the principle of honesty.

It is said that more than three hundred years before the coming of Christ, there was a man by the name of Diogenes of whom it was said that he walked through the streets of ancient Athens in the day light carrying a burning lantern in his hand saying that he was seeking for an honest man. Honesty was a desirable trait in his day, and I assure you that it is so today. Occasionally you may find in the newspaper an ad stating that they want a young man whose education and training are desirable who has various other qualities they desire but above all he must be honest. May I assure you today that honesty is not only a good thing and one that is desired in the world, but honesty is a Christian virtue? It is one the world needs and the world admires and one that all should strive to possess at all times. There are, as we have already stated, tremendous violations of this quality; and it would appear that day by day by day it is becoming more frequent. Honesty is being walked over, thrown out the window, and considered simply to be not needed in the twentieth century.

There are several reasons we should be honest. We should be honest, first of all, simply because it is right. We have all heard the statement, "Honesty is the best policy." But the man who is honest just for policy's sake may prove dishonest when it is more convenient to be so. We should rather be honest for honesty's sake, not just as a matter of policy. We will be honest because it is right. We will be honest because God teaches us to be so. We will be honest, as He also taught, in the little things; and the big things will follow in the right way. The man who would be dishonest with a nickle will do the same with a thousand dollars. The one who would gamble for a dime may venture for higher stakes. More than 57 percent of American adults engage in gambling in all manner of games, office pools, lotteries and in otherwise good things such as sports and games, etc. that could be regarded for good, not evil. Gambling is within itself a form of dishonesty. So we should be honest because it is right.

Today, be honest with yourself. You know your own heart. Let it be kept pure and free from deceit, true to your own good. Exercise care in your thinking. Watch what you do. Search your motives. It is a fact that you must live with yourself. Can you actually respect yourself in your own thinking? Learn to think correctly. Jesus says as a man thinks in his heart, so is he. Solomon also made the same statement in Proverbs 23:7. In giving the things for the Christian to think on, Paul says, "Whatsoever things are honest ... think on these things" (Philippians 4:8). Fill your heart with honest thoughts and you will speak and do the things that are honest. If you cannot be honest with yourself, you cannot be honest with others.

So we should not only be honest with ourselves, but we should also be honest with other people. We should deal justly and fairly with others. The Lord teaches us, "Provide things honest in the sight of all men" (Romans 12:17). Again we read, "Providing for honest things, not only in the sight of the Lord, but also in the sight of men" (2 Corinthians 8:21). As Christians we are told to "walk honestly toward them that are without" (1 Thessalonians 4:12). In all things we are taught to be willing to live honestly (Hebrews 13:18). The Apostle Paul instructs Timothy to pray for all men "For kings, and for all that are in authority; that we may lead a quiet and peaceable life in all godliness and" ... what? ... "honesty" (1 Timothy 2:2). Peter says, "Having your conversation" ... that is, your manner of life ... "honest among the Gentiles: that, whereas they speak against you as evildoers, they may by your good works, which they shall behold, glorify God in the day of visitation" (1 Peter 2:12). We are to speak that which is right and truthful. The telling of that which is untrue, gossiping, tale bearing, and false witnessing are forms of dishonesty. You may rob a man of his good name by the use of your tongue. You recall that

Shakespeare had his character, Ophelia, say, "Who steals my purse, steals trash; 'Tis something, nothing. 'Twas mine, 'tis his; and has been slave to thousands. But he that filches from me my good name robs me of that which not enriches him and makes me poor indeed." How true that is.

Next, not only should you be honest with yourself and honest with others but above all things you should be honest with God. God is the source of every blessing that you have today. He has made you His steward—your life, your body, and all you possess are from Him. You are not true to your trust unless you use them for God in His service. You are to "present your bodies a living sacrifice, holy, acceptable unto God, which is your reasonable service" (Romans 12:1). Be honest with your abilities. God intends that you use them for Him in doing good. What are some of your abilities and your talents? First of all, you possess a mind, and your mind should be filled with the knowledge of Him through the study of His word. Your heart should be dedicated in love, "Thou shalt love the Lord thy God with all thy heart, and with all thy soul, and with all thy mind" (Matthew 22:37). Your tongue should be used to praise Him, to pray to Him, to tell others about Him and His wondrous love and salvation and about the Christ who died to save us. Your feet should be found in paths of righteousness. Your hands should be used to minister in His name. Your time should be used, not be consumed selfishly but given to work, to worship, to meditation, to service for Him, seeking first the kingdom of God and His righteousness.

Not only do we have our mind, our heart, our tongue, our feet, and our time, we also have that thing that is called "money." Your money should be recognized as part of your stewardship. Out of the abundance He has given, you should lay by in store upon the first day of the week as you have been prospered; in fact, you should **purpose** to do so (1 Corinthians 16:2). And not only this, but be mindful of the poor and the needy and the orphans and widows. We must all give an account of our stewardship on the Day of Judgment; therefore, always bear this in mind: Remember the parable of the talents that you may hear Him say in that day, "Well done, thou good and faithful servant: thou hast been faithful over a few things, I will make thee ruler over many things: enter thou into the joy of thy lord" (Matthew 25:21).

One cannot be honest with God—think with me on this—you may disagree, but think with me—one cannot be honest with God unless he is a Christian. The Christian life is the life of a just steward who has dedicated his life to Christ. One must believe in the Lord with all his heart (Acts 8:37); he must repent of his sins (Luke 13:3); he must acknowledge his faith in Christ (Romans 10:10); and he must be baptized in obedience to the Lord who says, "He that believeth and is baptized shall be saved" (Mark 16:16). Then his life must be spent as a faithful member of the body of Christ, which is His church (Ephesians 1:22-23). He must wear the name of Christ and be the light of the world and the salt of the earth (Matthew 5:13-16). There is no other way to discharge the God-given stewardship acceptably, is there? I propose to you there is no other way. And may I ask: Are you being honest with God in these matters? Have you really accepted the challenge of His word? Have you really given thought to this and decided whether you are being honest or not in respect to your life?

It is possible to be honestly mistaken; of this we have no doubt. Many a person has made a mistake in thinking he was right but his thinking he was right did not make it so. He was honestly mistaken. Many have heard the story of the storekeeper who weighed his merchandise on scales that he thought were accurate but later found he had been giving short weight all those years. In order to continue being honest with himself, he had to correct his mistake by using accurate scales that gave proper weight. He had been honestly mistaken.

It is true that men are honestly mistaken sometimes in the matter of religion. Saul of Tarsus persecuted and put to death Christians, thinking he was doing God's service. He did it in all good conscience but he did it ignorantly in unbelief (Acts 23:1; 1 Timothy 1:13). Paul was wrong, but he thought he was right. When he learned better, he sought to correct his mistake by living for the Lord whom he had persecuted. He never forgot that mistake. Remember? Over and over he would say he was "less than the least of all saints." He would insist that he was the "chief of sinners." He never forgot it. When Ananias came to him to tell him what to do for the remission of sins, he obeyed him immediately by saying, "And now why tarriest thou? arise, and be baptized, and wash away thy sins, calling on the name of the Lord" (Acts 22:16). From that day on, Paul lived and sacrificed and died for the Lord, trusting in His grace and His great abundant mercy.

In 1 Kings 13, we have the story of a young prophet who fearlessly denounced the idolatry of king Jeroboam. He refused the offer of the king to remain, but was honestly deceived by the old prophet who lied to him saying that God had spoken to him also. You remember how the lion met him in the way and killed him. He, too, was honestly mistaken but died because of his mistake.

In a similar way, one may be mistaken when he hears false teaching in the matter of religion today. The Lord teaches us to be buried with Him in baptism (Romans 6:4), but many have been mistaken and used other forms of baptism such as sprinkling and pouring. The Lord has plainly taught, "He that believeth and is baptized shall be saved" (Mark 16:16), and that this baptism is a burial in water (Romans 6:4; Acts 8:38-39). He shows us how it is done: "they went down both into the water, both Philip and the eunuch; and he baptized him. And when they were come up out of the water" he says, describing their actions. The act itself is described by Paul in Colossians 2:12 where he says, "Buried with him in baptism, wherein also ye are risen with him through the faith of the operation of God, who hath raised him from the dead." Now, if you have been honestly mistaken in this matter, why not be extremely honest today and correct this mistake just as Saul of Tarsus corrected his mistake. Paul was honest. He says simply, "What will you have me to do?" and upon hearing the answer, he did it.

Many have been mistaken in regard to the church. The Bible teaches that the church is the body of Christ (Ephesians 1:22-23). It further teaches there is one body (1 Corinthians 12:20). "For by one Spirit are we all baptized into one body" (1 Corinthians 12:13). Obedience to the Lord in baptism for the remission of sins means the Lord will add us to the church (Acts 2:47). You cannot separate the two. When one is baptized, he is baptized into Christ (Romans 6:3) and God adds him to the one church Jesus established and for which He shed His blood (Acts 20:28). You cannot—listen—you cannot be saved apart from Christ. Obedience to Him in baptism makes you a member of Christ's church; He adds you to the church. One is honestly mistaken who believes he can be saved without being a member of the church of our Lord Jesus Christ.

The name of Christ must be, and should be, supreme. "Neither is there salvation in any other: for there is none other name under heaven given among men, whereby we must be saved" (Acts 4:12). Followers of Christ were called Christians (Acts 11:26). The church was called by His name (Romans 16:16). And so it should be today.

The worship of God must be in spirit and in truth (John 4:24). The Lord's Supper and the laying by in store as we are prospered should be part of our worship each Lord's Day (Acts 20:7; 1 Corinthians 16:2). We should worship Him in singing (Ephesians 5:19) and continue in prayer and study of His word (Acts 2:42). These are items of worship that the Lord has outlined in His word, and we must not add to or take from them but faithfully discharge our duty in each of these.

The same principle—listen—the same principle applies to all of our duties and relationships to God. In all things let us know and understand the will of God and be not honestly mistaken but ever doing the will of God. Jesus says, "Not every one that saith unto me, Lord, Lord, shall enter into the kingdom of heaven; but he that doeth the will of my Father which is in heaven" (Matthew 7:21). May we be determined that we shall be honest with ourselves and with others and with our God and with our soul. Let us be determined that we will be known as honest people—as Christians. When we find that we are wrong, let's be honest and have faith enough to correct that wrong. When we find that we are right, let's be honest enough to contend for it until our Lord shall come again.

God's Immutable Laws

Good morning, everyone. We invite your attention today to a study of God's Immutable Laws. God has given us every reason and every incentive possible to encourage us to live for Him. The Bible clearly holds all these reasons before us. The passage of our study today was written to give encouragement to those who were wavering in their faith and I should think it would be a source of strength for us in regard to our faith today. Let's turn to Hebrews 6 for our reading.

The divine writer first exhorts them to go on unto perfection, leaving the first principles of the doctrine of Christ. Then he reminds them of the danger of falling away from God's teaching. He points them to matters in which they are well acquainted, saying in verse 7, "The earth which drinketh in the rain that cometh oft upon it, and bringeth forth herbs meet for them by whom it is dressed, receiveth blessing from God." All of us surely recognize this fact.

He continues, saying, "But that which beareth thorns and briers is rejected, and is nigh unto cursing; whose end is to be burned" (verse 8). This statement also must be remembered as a warning to those of us who may be unfruitful in our lives. God's blessings are upon the land and upon the life that is fruitful, but the unfruitful shall be rejected and destroyed. I think it is evident from reading this passage that God notices the life of each of us. We are reminded of this fact quite vividly in verse ten, "God is not unrighteous to forget your work and labour of love, which ye have shewed toward his name, in that ye have ministered to the saints, and do minister."

Over and over again the Bible teaches us how God is ever aware of all of man's acts, and He shall notice even the smallest of them. Jesus gives emphasis to this thought in Matthew 10:42 as He says, "And whosoever shall give to drink unto one of these little ones a cup of cold water only in the name of a disciple, verily I say unto you, he shall in no wise lose his reward." It is with this assurance that the believer is encouraged to press on. God does not forget and God does not fail to notice the good of such individuals among us.

The writer says, "And we desire that every one of you do shew the same diligence to the full assurance of hope unto the end: That ye be not slothful, but followers of them who through faith and patience inherit the promises" (verses 11-12). Faith in God would have us to be diligent in keeping the commands of God so that we might receive His blessings even as those who have in the past been faithful and often in the face of trials have developed patience. James writes, "The trying of your faith worketh patience. But let patience have her perfect work, that ye may be perfect and entire, wanting nothing" (James 1:3-4). The Hebrew writer would exhort us to be characterized with both faith and patience so that we might also inherit the promises of God. God's promises are true. He promised Abraham that He would bless him saying, "Surely blessing I will bless thee, and multiplying I will multiply thee. And so, after he had patiently endured, he obtained the promise" (verses 14-15). God's promises to Abraham were true, and God blessed him because of his faith and perseverance. Our faith and our hope are based upon the promises of the same great God, even as with Abraham. God kept His promises then, and may I assure you that God will keep His promises now. God has not changed.

The Bible teaches that God's word is immutable. The terms immutable and immutability occur in verses 17 and 18 and are used in connection with the counsel or the will of God. They are used to show us how God's law and God's promises are in keeping with the very nature of God Himself. God is unchanging and unchangeable. His purpose is fixed—invariable, not mutable, immutable. Every promise and every law of God can be depended upon by those who trust in Him. The plans of God never change. All of our hope of heaven is based upon this truth concerning the laws and promises of God. Today we have hope because we know God will keep His promises. We know His word can be trusted in all things and at all times. God is ever the same. It is even as David says, "Lord, thou has been our dwelling place in all generations. Before the mountains were brought forth, or ever thou hadst formed the earth and the world, even from everlasting to everlasting, **thou art God**" (Psalm 90:1-2). The Bible is saying that God shall never fail. His word is true. He cannot lie. As Paul says, "He abideth faithful: he cannot deny himself" (2 Timothy 2:13.

God has given His promise and He confirmed it by an oath so that by the confirmation of His own divine nature we might have the strong consolation of hope. God has left us no room for any reasonable doubt. If God were changeable, if God willed one thing today and changed tomorrow, who could trust in Him or have any hope through His promises? If He were governed by caprice, changing with different whims and fancies, we could not depend upon Him; but God is, even as the Bible says concerning Christ, the same yesterday, today and forever (Hebrews 13:8). God's laws are even as Jesus says in His word: "Heaven and earth shall pass away, but my words shall not pass away" (Matthew 24:35). Jesus says of God's law, "Till heaven and earth pass, one jot or one tittle shall in no wise pass from the law, till all be fulfilled" (Matthew 5:18).

It was in this regard that Robert Milligan once wrote, "No opposing force in Heaven, Earth or Hell can ever nullify or set aside a decree or a promise of Jehovah." I think we should never forget the truth of that statement. Every law of God is totally dependable. It is true in regard to the universe and all the material creation of God. It is true in the entire spiritual realm. In every one of the teachings and prophecies given to us in the Bible, we can be sure that God's law will never fail.

We are people who are parts of both the material and the spiritual creation of God. Our bodies are subject to the material because they are made of the earth. Our spirits are from God; and, therefore, the spiritual laws of God govern them. Many times we can better understand these matters through the understanding of things about us that we see and know to be true. I would like for you to notice God's material law. The Bible teaches that God made the whole universe. The Bible declares in its very first verse, "In the beginning God created the heaven and the earth." There was not anything in all of the earth or the heavens above that God did not create—the sun, the moon, the stars, the planets in the firmament above or in the earth beneath. Only the sin and the evil in the world did not come from God. God's unfailing laws govern the entire universe.

In Genesis 1, nine times we are told that everything brought forth "after their kind." This was God's law then, and it is God's law now. Every species of all the creation of God has always remained in the same basic nature in which it was created. Everything was arranged to continue by the same laws that governed from the beginning. Man's progress has been measured by his discovery of, and his application of, these fundamental and dependable laws of God.

I would like to point out that the law of God in the universe does not change. None of the laws in regard to the universe have ever changed. The laws of gravitation have always been the same, and man can depend upon their remaining so. The rising of the sun, the changing of the seasons can be calculated for as many years ahead as we desire should the earth remain. The principles of seed time and harvest exist and will do so until the end of time (Genesis 8:22). It is the cause of the accuracy and the dependability of these immutable laws in nature that men can produce electricity or make their many inventions or fly into the air and the space above, or plow through the depths of the sea or descend into the earth itself. By these same laws, they can split the atom and handle the powerful forces being discovered in the laboratories throughout the world. The pharmacist compiles his prescription by them. The farmer sows and reaps by them. The factories operate their machinery by these laws. All of the activities of our lives, every day we live, are governed by those laws. We know we can depend upon these material laws that God has given to govern the universe.

Man must obey these laws, whether they be the ones that govern the nourishment and proper care of the body or the laws of the universe in general. We know it is dangerous and sometimes fatal to disregard these laws. Even a slight disobedience might be the cause of physical death. The child must learn his lesson early in life and be governed by this principle of obedience to the laws of nature or suffer the consequences in his body. He must learn that fire will burn but when used properly it can be beneficial. He must learn all the dangers of violation in connection with every good thing that he has to enjoy. He must come to know that he can only enjoy them by respecting the laws that govern their nature and their use.

There is no respect of persons in regard to material law. The innocent child who grasps the electrically charged wire will die even as the hardened criminal who sits in the electric chair to be electrocuted or the man who deliberately electrocutes himself. The little fellow who accidentally stepped in the path of the train died even as the man who did it on purpose. The rich, the poor, the old, the young, the educated or the unlettered can all be blessed in their respect for God's law or they can be destroyed by their disobedience.

These laws can be trusted. If it were not so, the world would be filled with chaos. If we could not trust the laws governing electricity, certainly we would not be able to use this radio station. We would not be able to use these 50,000 watts or whatever it may be here today. It involves enough power to destroy us all; but when properly handled, this same great power can carry these words into your cars and into your homes, even though you might be many, many miles away. Because we can trust God's material law, we persue the conducting of our business, our farms and our homes. We go about what we call "the normal way of life." We are not afraid. We know we can trust them as the men of generations of the past have trusted those same laws.

These same facts are true concerning God's spiritual laws. God created our spirits, and He gave us laws to govern them. These laws are revealed to us in the Bible. They are similar to the laws that govern the universe about us. May we be able to understand them by comparison? First of all, God's spiritual laws are universal. They apply to all of us. They were to be preached to every creature. They were to govern every life of every accountable person in the world. It is God's perfect law of liberty found in the New Testament. The commands and the promises are made to all men and should be regarded with respect and obedience in every nation in all the earth and throughout all generations. The same seed of the kingdom, the word of God (Luke 8:11), will make Christians out of those who accept it whenever and wherever it is preached and believed. Only the pure seed of the gospel of Christ will bring forth the Christian life and produce salvation.

The gospel produces faith and leads to repentance and to a confession of faith in Christ and to a burial with Christ in baptism for the remission of sins (Mark 16:15-16; Acts 2:38; Acts 8:35-39).

The gospel leads us to become a new creature (2 Corinthians 5:17). It leads us to walk in newness of life (Romans 6:4). It leads us to all the spiritual blessings in heavenly places that are found in Jesus Christ (Ephesians 1:3). By obedience to God's law, we are saved (Acts 2:38, 47).

The church is brought together as the spiritual body of Christ, the family of God. By God's spiritual law, the church of Christ is to be governed in all its work, its organization, its life, and its hope. The name of Christ is the name to be honored and in which we are to glorify God and to have salvation (Philippians 2:9-11).

In all of this, one thing is sure—God's law can be trusted. Because of this fact we have hope. We can depend upon God's promises. They are immutable. They are as sure as God Himself. They shall never, never fail.

The Right Church

Good morning, everyone. One more time we have been allowed the privilege of coming into your home and we trust into your heart to study with you the word. Today we are inviting your attention to a subject which we believe is most vital. We hope that for a few minutes that we can sit down together and study and think on something that is most precious, and that is concerning the church of our Lord Jesus Christ. I believe the church of the Lord Jesus is indeed precious. Anything that cost the blood of the Son of God, cost His death upon Calvary, is bound to be precious. The Bible declares in Acts 20:28 that the church of God, the church of the Lord Jesus, was purchased with His own blood.

There are many people today who are confused in their thinking about religion. They are honest and conscientious and they want to be right, but the divided condition of the religious world causes them to be bewildered. They are longing for the truth and they want to please God, but the conflicting theories and teachings of the various churches confuse their minds. As a result, you will find some who never become a member of the church. Others are still seeking for the right one and asking the question, "How can I find the right church?" To all you good people, we kindly direct this study today and we ask you to seriously consider this matter.

First of all, think of the importance of our search. To find the right church is to find the kingdom of God. Jesus says, "The kingdom of heaven is like unto treasure hid in a field; the which when a man hath found, he hideth, and for joy thereof goeth and selleth all that he hath, and buyeth that field" (Matthew 13:44). That is how important the church should be to each one of us today. It is worth all that we have that we may find the right church, the kingdom of God, and possess it for our very own. The church is worth our search in the joy and happiness and salvation it will mean for us. It's worth the hours of study of God's word and all the prayerful seeking to find the Lord's church to be sure we have found the right way. It is worth every sacrifice we will ever make to have the blessing of God's kingdom.

Jesus says, "Again, the kingdom of heaven is like unto a merchant man, seeking goodly pearls: Who, when he had found one pearl of great price, went and sold all that he had, and bought it" (Matthew 13:45-46). We must search, the Bible teaches, if we would find the right church. It is a pearl of great price worth more than all the world. Further, there is but **one** pearl of great price and for it we must search. When we have found it, we must buy it by giving all that we have. The seeking of it should be more important than any other consideration in our lives. Jesus says, "Seek ye first the kingdom of God, and his righteousness; and all these things shall be added unto you" (Matthew 6:33). The eternal welfare of our souls depends upon it. We cannot ... we cannot afford to let our prejudices or our ignorance or our personal preferences hinder us in this search for the right church.

Let's appraise the conditions about us for just a moment. As I speak to you at this time, there are more than 250 different kinds of churches in the United States. Each body, large or small, must be recognized as men and women who believe in their particular doctrines. However, each one of these churches does not agree with others in their teaching, organization, or practice. Often the conflict is very pronounced and the opposition is very strong. It is evident that they cannot all be right because there is too much difference and too much confusion, and the Bible declares that "God is not the author of confusion, but of peace" (1 Corinthians 14:33).

Upon further study, I am sure you will be convinced that the distinguishing names and doctrines of all the denominations are not found in the Bible. The things that cause the dividing conditions, that bewilder the minds of men, are not of God. If they were of God, they would be contained in the Holy Scripture. They are men's opinions and men's personal inclinations and preferences and prejudices. The Bible teaches that God is a God of unity. Jesus prayed for His disciples and them also who would believe on Him through their teaching, and the Lord expressed that prayer in these words, "That they all may be one; as thou, Father, art in me, and I in Thee, that they also may be one in us: that the world may believe that Thou has sent me" (John 17:21).

God wants men to be in agreement, not in confusion. Whether we consider the nature of the Lord's people in all the nations of earth or the conduct of the worship of the local congregation, God's rule is,

"Let all things be done decently and in order" (1 Corinthians 14:40). Please let us notice together that the Bible teaches there is but one church. The church is the body of Christ (Ephesians 1:22-23). God gave Christ "to be the head over all things to the church, which is his body." The church is made up of the saved. Acts 2:47 says, "The Lord added to the church daily such as should be saved." In Ephesians 5:23, Paul tells us, "Christ is the head of the church: and he is the saviour of the body." In each reference to the church in your Bible, you will always have the oneness of the church before you. Christians are the members. That is, those who are saved, and they are many. Paul says in 1 Corinthians 12:20, "But now are they many **members,** yet but **one body.**"

This exhortation is found in Ephesians 4:3-6. Listen to it:

> Endeavouring to keep the unity of the Spirit in the bond of peace. There is one body, and one Spirit, even as ye are called in one hope of your calling; One Lord, one faith, one baptism, One God and Father of all, who is above all, and through all, and in you all.

This is God's plan for the unity of the church. The church of the New Testament is one. There were many congregations made up of many Christians in many different cities and different nations, but they were all one body or one church. When men in Corinth were more concerned about following personalities than following Christ, Paul raised the question, **"Is Christ divided?"** (1 Corinthians 1:13). "Is Christ divided?" Paul rebuked their divisions and taught them, "Now I beseech you, brethren, by the name of our Lord Jesus Christ, that ye all speak the same thing, and that there be **no divisions** among you; but that ye be perfectly joined together in the same mind and in the same judgment" (1 Corinthians 1:10). It is this kind of unity that the Lord wants today. He doesn't want 250 or 300 different churches teaching different things and conflicting doctrines and conflicting ways, but He wants people with no divisions among them. He wants them perfectly joined together "in the **same mind** and in the **same judgment.**"

Jesus Christ established the church. In Matthew 16:18 we have His words, "Upon this rock I will build my church." In Acts 2, we read about how that church came into being. It was established on the first Pentecost after the resurrection of Jesus. Christ became the head of the church. God raised Christ up to sit on David's throne. He made Him both Lord and Christ. From that day forward, through all the teaching of the New Testament, the church is always spoken of as being in existence and Pentecost is referred to by Peter as the beginning (Acts 11:15). So Jesus Christ alone established the church. To find the right church, therefore, we must find the church that Christ established, the one for which He is the supreme and only head. God gave Christ "to be head over all things to the church, which is his body, the fullness of him that filleth all in all" (Ephesians 1:22-23). In Colossians 1:18, the divine writer points out the preeminence of Christ when he says, "And he is the head of **the** body, **the** church." We must bear in mind that as the church is the body of Christ and Christ has but **one** body, we are searching for but one right church, not many of them. Christ has but one body or one church. Christ does not have many bodies. It is according to the parable, **one** pearl of great price, **one** kingdom of heaven.

But perhaps the most important question at this moment is this: Does the Lord's church exist on the earth today? I think as people read the scripture, they realize there was only one Lord Jesus and that the Lord Jesus established His church and all the denominations that exist today were not existent in that day. They did not even exist at the time Jesus said, "Upon this rock I will build my church." So the Lord's church was all there was, and Christians were all there were at that time. The question now is Does it still exist today? I would like to hasten to answer the question. Yes, the Lord's church does exist among men today. How do we know it exists? Because the seed of the kingdom is still here to perpetuate that kingdom, the church. Jesus says in giving the interpretation of the parable of the sower, "The seed is the word of God" (Luke 8:11). Where ever that seed is planted in the hearts of men and grows in obedient lives, there the kingdom of God exists among men.

It is not necessary to prove an unbroken line of succession through the generations of the past from the book of Acts down to this moment. Wheat seed always produces wheat. Whether the following season or many seasons later, as long as the germ of life remains in that seed, wheat will always and under all circumstances, produce wheat. The gospel of Jesus Christ will always produce Christians and Christians only—whether in the first century or the 20th century, whether in Palestine or in the United States. Where you find Christians after the New Testament pattern, there you have the church of our Lord—

because they constitute a church through the word of God as Peter says, "Being born again, not of corruptible seed, but of incorruptible, by the word of God, which liveth and abideth forever" (1 Peter 1:23).

God's word has not lost its power through the centuries. Peter says, "The word of the Lord endureth for ever. And this is the word which by the gospel is preached unto you" (1 Peter 1:25). Therefore, since the church of our Lord is in existence today—it has never failed, it has never passed away, it has never been destroyed—the next question logically follows: How can we recognize it? If it is here today, and the Lord promised it for ever would be, then how do we recognize it? First of all, the New Testament should be our means of recognition. The Lord has given us the marks of identity. Other religious bodies may be pointed out by their adherence to their creeds or their articles of faith or their catechisms. But the Lord's church can be governed by no authority except the authority of Christ. The church of our Lord can have no other law, written or unwritten, but the perfect law of liberty as given by Christ in the New Testament. This will be the matter of first consideration.

Surely there is but one standard by which to evaluate the church. The Lord's description is sufficient to lead us to recognize the His church, to distinguish it from all the other organizations that exist about us. As a building can be identified from the blue print by which it was constructed, so the church of the Lord in any community can be pointed out by the blue print by which it has been set in order, the New Testament pattern for the church.

First of all, thc names and terms used in the New Testament in reference to the church should help us recognize the right church. It is **the** church (Colossians 1:18). Jesus says, "I will build **my** church" (Matthew 16:18). Romans 16:16 says, "The churches of Christ salute you." The church belongs to Christ because He purchased it with His own blood on Calvary (Acts 20:28). He is the saviour of the body (Ephesians 5:23). In 1 Corinthians 1:2, it is called the "church of God." In 1 Thessalonians 1:1, we read, "The church of the Thessalonians which is in God the Father and in the Lord Jesus Christ." Also it is called the "kingdom," "the family of God," "the house of God," "the kingdom of His dear Son." Many figures were given and many parables were used to show the nature and work of the church. The individuals were called "disciples," "brcthren," and "Christians" (Acts 11:26).

Men may call the things they create by their own names or by the names of other men or by the names of movements of outstanding things and thus distinguish them. The Bible nowhere—listen—the Bible nowhere gives us any right to take upon ourselves any other names than those found in the New Testament or speak of the church by other names or terms other than those that are given by God. It does make a difference what terms we use.

The church is congregational as we see it in the Bible and as we should look for it today. Each congregation of the New Testament church is complete and is an autonomous unit, carrying on its own work. There is no association, no conference, no presbytery, no organization to tie one congregation to another congregation. Churches of our Lord are to work together in love and to help one another as the need arises (Acts 11:30). They can cooperate as long as they cooperate on a congregational basis. Each congregation that has men qualified, as described in 1 Timothy 3, is to have its own elders and deacons, selecting its own leaders, employing its preacher to work in the area if such is needed, and directing its own work in obedience to Christ in His word.

In looking for the church of our Lord, one should recognize the worship of the church. The worship of the church consisted of five things:

1. Early Christians taught the word of God (Acts 2:42).
2. They continued steadfastly in prayer.
3. They worshiped God in song, "Singing and making melody in your heart to the Lord" (Ephesians 5:19). The Lord did not teach us to use instrumental accompaniment in praising Him in the church; therefore, the songs you will hear on this program and in the worship in the churches of Christ is vocal music accompanied by heart melody.
4. They observed the Lord's Supper each Lord's Day. One should read carefully Matthew 26, Mark 14, Luke 22, and 1 Corinthians 10 and 11 to be sure that when he looks at the Lord's table he can recognize it by using those passages of scripture.
5. They gave willingly on the first day of the week as God allowed them to be prospered (1 Corinthians 16:2; 2 Corinthians 9:7-8).

Entrance into the church in the time of Christ was by obedience to the gospel of Christ. In searching for the Lord's church today, we must look for one that preaches what the people preached in that day. Each person must:

1. Believe in Christ as God's Son
2. Repent of sins
3. Confess faith in Christ
4. Be buried with the Lord in baptism for the remission of sins (Mark 16:16; Acts 2:38)

These five steps are in obedience to God's will, and then the Lord adds the saved to the church as we read in Acts 2:47.

It does make a difference, today, what you believe. In searching for the Lord's church, please remember it makes a difference what name you wear, what the church is, what it practices, how it functions. Obedience to Christ includes wearing the name we are commanded to wear. This name is "Christian," a divinely given name. The Bible only will always make Christians only. Please remember this teaching. It takes Baptist doctrine to make Baptists. It takes Methodist doctrine to make Methodists. It takes Lutheran doctrine to make Lutherans. You have never heard of someone becoming a Lutheran by believing and obeying some **other** doctrine. In all kindness, regardless of how honest and sincere a person is, the wearing of such names is unscriptural—that is, it isn't found in the scriptures. So it does make a difference; if you get down to searching for the church today as it was then, you will be searching for those who are known as Christians and Christians only—not this kind of Christian or that kind of Christian but just simply **Christians.** Certainly the church of the Lord Jesus Christ is most important to us. It **does** make a difference.

We might raise this question before we close today. How can a person live up to the Bible and belong to a religious body wearing a name that cannot be found in the Bible? How can a person live up to the Bible and wear a name religiously, as an individual that the followers of Jesus Christ in the Bible never did wear? How can a person live up to the Bible and belong to a religious body that teaches the wrong plan of salvation and is unscriptural in worship and name? The church of Jesus Christ ... and may I say this with all kindness to cause you to study the word ... the church of Jesus Christ is the only one in existence that is living up to the Bible in all these things. So it does make a difference as to which church a person belongs. It is the difference between belonging to the church of the Lord or to one that has been built by men. It means the difference between worshiping as the Lord teaches and as men teach. It means wearing the right name or the wrong name. It is the difference between obeying Christ and disobeying Him.

Please remember, **"It makes a difference."** And we propose that this difference should cause us to get down and study the word, think upon the word, and ask the Lord in earnest prayer that we might obey Him all the way—that we may obey from the heart that form of doctrine, and Paul says, "Being then made free from sin, ye become the servants of righteousness" (Romans 6:18). Please think on these things. Please study your Bible to see whether these things be true.

Abraham – A Man of Faith

Today our discussion will rest with a study of Abraham, a man of faith. There is no better way to learn what it means to have faith in God than to study the Bible examples of faith. Of those great examples, one of the clearest is that of Abraham. Consider with me such passages as Romans 4:2, Galatians 3:6, and James 2:23 where we are told Abraham believed God.

The name of Abraham is found at least 284 times in the Bible. He is one of the most outstanding characters in all the Old and New Testaments. The Bible teaches us he was born about 2,000 BC, the son of Tara, and was the 20th generation from the beginning of man's existence upon this earth as we read in Genesis 11. His name at the first was Abram, and when he was 99 years old, God said, "Thou shalt be a father of many nations. Neither shall thy name any more be called Abram, but thy name shall be Abraham; for a father of many nations have I made thee" (Genesis 17:4-5). Abram lived in the land of Ur of the Chaldees. It was from that land God called him, as Stephen says in Acts 7:3, "Get thee out of thy country, and from thy kindred, and come into the land which I shall shew thee." Hebrews 11:8 states of him, "By faith Abraham, when he was called to go out into a place which he should after receive for an inheritance, obeyed; and he went out, not knowing whither he went."

Abraham was a man who had a tremendous faith in God. I suppose to make that simple statement is quite an **understatement.** I want you to notice the kind of faith he had. When God called him, he obeyed. He didn't know where God would lead him. He could not see the future of all his journeys. He simply obeyed God. And from the example of Abraham, as well as so many other examples that God has given, we may correctly conclude that the faith that saves is the faith that **obeys.** I think we should let that become a "watch word" with us—to always remember that the faith that saves is the faith that obeys.

This same obedient faith that caused Abraham to leave Ur of the Chaldees caused him to leave Haran and go to Sichem and to Bethel in the land of Canaan. "There he builded an altar unto the Lord and called upon the name of the Lord" (Genesis 12:8). After his visit to Egypt, he returned to this land where again it is says, "And there Abram called on the name of the Lord" (Genesis 13:4). He was a devout man in his worship of Jehovah God, and his journeys can be traced by the smoke of his altars. When Abram returned from the slaughter of the kings who had taken his nephew, Lot, captive, he met Melchizedek, who was king of Salem and priest of the most high God. The Bible states that Melchizedek blessed Abram saying, "Blessed be Abram of the most high God, possessor of heaven and earth: And blessed be the most high God, which hath delivered thine enemies into thy hand." The Bible states that Abram "gave him tithes of all" (Genesis 14:19-20).

After these things, in Genesis 15 we read that God says to Abram, "Fear not, Abram: I am thy shield, and thy exceeding great reward" (verse 1). In verse 6, after the Lord had renewed His promise to him, we are told, "And he believed in the Lord; and he counted it to him for righteousness." His faith in God made him rejoice in the renewals of God's promise that even though he was an old man of 99 and his wife past the normal age of bearing children, Isaac would be born as the son through whom God would establish His covenant which he made with Abraham. So when he was 100 years of age, Isaac was born.

The Bible teaches us that it was at this time that God "tried" Abraham's faith. When Isaac, who was Abraham's only son according to God's promise, was a grown young man, God spoke to Abraham saying, "Take now thy son, thine only son Isaac, whom thou lovest, and get thee into the land of Moriah; and offer him there for a burnt offering upon one of the mountains which I will tell thee of" (Genesis 22:2). Abraham's faith in the Lord led him to begin his journey "early in the morning," you recall. He went prepared to do as the Lord had told him. The Bible states that he prepared the altar and "bound Isaac his son, and laid him on the altar upon the wood. And Abraham stretched forth his hand, and took the knife to slay his son" (verses 9-10). I want you to think how great the faith of Abraham was—to take his own son and prepare to kill him in obedience to the command of the Lord. In Hebrews 11:17-19, we are told, "By faith Abraham, when he was tried, offered up Isaac: and he that had received the promises offered up his only begotten son, Of whom it was said, That in Isaac shall thy seed be called: Accounting that God was able to raise him up, even from the dead; from whence also he received him in a figure." Abraham obeyed God, and when he had fully made clear his faith, the angel of the Lord spoke to him saying, "Lay not thine hand upon the lad, neither do thou any thing unto him: for now I know"—listen to this statement—"**now I know** that thou fearest God, seeing thou hast not withheld thy son, thine only son from me" (Genesis 22:12). Then God renewed His promise to Abraham and in verse 18 we read how God says of him, "Thou **hast obeyed my voice.**" This expresses so well to us what faith really is—**"Thou hast obeyed my voice."**

Abraham looked beyond this life. He looked to a time beyond dwelling in tents in the land of Canaan. Hebrews 11:10 says "He looked for a city which hath foundations, whose builder and maker is God." Together with Isaac and Jacob, he recognized he was a stranger and a pilgrim on this earth. He desired a better country, a heavenly country; and he knew that God was preparing for them a city.

Abraham lived almost 4,000 years ago, but he knew the eternal promises of God. He believed in that life which shall follow this life upon earth. He spent his days in the obedience of faith and the hope of the fulfillment of those promises. The Bible teaches that Abraham lived by faith, by faith in the great God who made him and who abundantly blessed him and in whom he trusted for the blessings of the life to be engaged in the presence of God eternally.

The thing that is wonderful about a study of the faith of Abraham is to come to the conclusion that we too can have the same kind of faith. Christ came into the world according to the promise which God made to Abraham as we read in Galatians the third chapter. He was the promised seed of Abraham, the one through whom all nations may know the blessings of God's salvation. These promises and these blessings are extended to us today in the 20th century. It is true now, even as Galatians 3:29 says, "And if ye be Christ's, then are ye Abraham's seed, and heirs according to the promise." It is possible for us now to be like they were. Paul says, "For ye are all the children of God by faith in Christ Jesus. For as many of you as have been baptized into Christ have put on Christ" (Galatians 3:26-27). In becoming children of God by faith in Christ, we are to be the children of Abraham and "they which be of faith are blessed with faithful Abraham" (Galatians 3:9). These blessings of salvation are not to be obtained under the Old Mosaic law but according to God's promise to Abraham. The law was given to last only until Christ came as he states in Galatians 3:19, "It was added because of transgressions, till the seed should come to whom the promise was made." The Bible teaches that we are to "walk in the steps of that faith of our father Abraham" (Romans 4:12). And we can be justified by faith even as he was, "Abraham believed God, and it was counted unto him for righteousness" (Romans 4:3).

Another thing that I would like to point out today is this: Abraham was justified by works. There is no conflict in these passages of scripture. The life of Abraham as a whole, from the time of his call by God in Ur of the Chaldees until the day he died, was a life of faith. It was a life that showed his faith in all the acts of his obedience to God. It is not strange then that we read in James 2:21-24, "Was not Abraham our father justified by works, when he had offered Isaac his son upon the altar? Seest thou how faith wrought with his works, and by works was faith made perfect? And the scripture was fulfilled which saith, Abraham believed God, and it was imputed unto him for righteousness: and he was called the Friend of God. Ye see then how that by works a man is justified, and not by faith only."

Now where is the conflict? It is not a conflict of one passage of scripture with another passage. The teaching of Paul and the teaching of James is in perfect, complete harmony. The Apostle Paul taught that Abraham was justified by faith, a faith that obeyed God so he was righteous through the grace of God, a grace that forgives men of their unrighteousness. James taught that Abraham was justified by faith but not by faith alone. "For as the body without the spirit is dead, so faith without works is dead also" (James 2:26). Abraham's faith was made perfect in his expression of that faith in works of obedience to God.

People often misrepresent the Apostle Paul and some try to twist his words to teach the doctrine of salvation by faith alone. But Paul did not teach justification by faith alone or by grace alone or by works alone. The Bible teaches that no man is righteous of himself. The scripture says, "There is none righteous, no, not one" (Romans 3:10). We are all dependent upon God to make us righteous. We cannot become righteous apart from the grace of God's forgiveness. That forgiveness can make us just as we believe in God and in Christ as the Son of God. We can be justified by faith in Christ. That faith must be a faith like that of Abraham, a faith that obeys God and therefore that faith is made manifest and made perfect in obedience to God.

The question that we ought to raise is this: Why should one think otherwise? Is there some command that men would seek to avoid? Is there some teaching that man wants to hold instead of holding the plain example of the obedient faith of Abraham? The answer to these questions can be found in the erroneous teachings heard all around us. They are the teachings that are so popular and so deceptive very simply because men **want** to hear them. Let's notice two of these. **Salvation by faith only is a very popular doctrine.** Many people say, "Just believe and you will be saved. Only believe and you will be saved this very moment." Or like one I heard some time ago on the radio who said, "Just believe where ever you are right now and you will be saved this very moment." What is wrong with such teaching? First of all, it is not Bible teaching. The gospel of Christ was preached on the day of Pentecost, as we read in Acts 2, and men believed what Peter says and when they ask, "Men and brethren, what shall we do? Then Peter says unto them, Repent, and be baptized every one of you in the name of Jesus Christ for the remission of sins" (verses 37-38). Saul of Tarsus is another example. Acts the ninth chapter tells us how Jesus of Nazareth appeared to him on the Damascus road. When Saul realizes who it was that spake to him, he says, "Lord what wilt thou have me to do?" (verse 6). The Lord directed him to go to Damascus. There, after Saul had continued three days in fasting and praying, Ananias, a preacher of the Lord's gospel, came to tell him what to do. As Paul later told it, as recorded in Acts 22:16, he says Ananias came and says to him, "Why tarriest thou? arise, and be baptized, and wash away thy sins, calling on the name of the Lord."

Saul was not saved the very moment he believed. One cannot read Acts the ninth chapter and believe that. His sins were still unforgiven three days later when Ananias came to tell him what the Lord wanted him to do to be saved. Peter and Ananias were quite different from modern denominational preachers who ignore the fact that the Lord had not promised salvation upon the basis of faith alone. The Bible pattern of faith is a faith that obeys God in order that the obedient believer might be justified by faith through the grace of God.

Secondly, **men have rejected God's commands.** The majority of people seemingly do not want to obey the Lord's command to repent and be buried with Christ in baptism. So many have chosen to twist this scripture, to misrepresent the teaching of the Bible, and to claim that Paul and James contradict each other. Let us not be deceived. The Bible is right. And the Bible examples of faith are all examples of obedience to God because of and in the perfection of faith in God. In each case where faith and justification are mentioned together, the justification as the result of faith is always evident after that faith in God has been expressed in obedience to God's commands.

Perhaps the best question at this moment would be: How may you **know** that you are right? The only answer I have for that today is this: Please study God's word. Have the faith that can come only from God's word (Romans 10:17). Then do what God has commanded. Believe that God's promises are true, that God will reward according to His grace. Don't stumble at God's commands. Have faith like Abraham; and that means what? ... obey God, trust Him for His promises. Accept Jesus Christ as your Saviour through obedience to the precious gospel and follow Him all the way to heaven so that with Abraham you may enter the heavenly "city which hath foundations, whose builder and maker is God." You can always rely—please listen—you can rely upon the teachings of our Lord. And if you have a faith like Abraham, you will always have the full assurance that God's blessings are yours.

We would close with the prayer that you may be so blessed.

Live Peaceably

Ladies and gentlemen, we invite your attention to a study that we believe is important and that should be a definite part of your life. Regardless of how talented you may be or how academically capable you have become, without this trait you will not be successful. Regardless of what you may know about God's word, unless you have this particular trait in your life—or at least are working to that end—you can accomplish little in the name of the Master. I am referring to the ability to get along peaceably with others.

The ability to get along peaceably with other people is of tremendous value, especially to a Christian. The Holy Spirit says, "If it be possible, as much as lieth in you, live peaceably with all men" (Romans 12:18). Our dealings with those about us should be pleasant, amiable, and beneficial. Our task is to develop our dispositions in accordance with His will. If we find that we are not particularly amiable or peaceable, we should certainly set out, today, to make that true within our lives. For the Holy Spirit insists that we are to live "peaceably with all men" as much as is possible.

If such ability is of great value to the individual, it's bound to be valuable in the home, in the community, in the church, and as nations with other nations. Many fail here: nevertheless, this ability is vital to our happiness and well being. Men may have keen intellects and be well trained by formal education but not be able to get along with others. Some have accumulated wealth and others have obtained great power but have lived lives of "quiet desperation." They have lived lives apart and lonely, robbed of the joys and companionship of others all because they didn't learn the lesson the Lord gave. I have known people skilled in their professions, even above many their equal, but they were not successful in their chosen field because they failed to get along with those with whom they came in contact day by day. We should remember that a man's success and his usefulness to others often depends on this important matter—getting along with others.

There are many things that hinder peace; and I think, especially as Christians, we should give our attention to it. **Selfishness** is many times a terrible hinderance. One can be so absorbed in his own likes and dislikes, in his own desires and interests, that he forgets the feelings and rights of others. He will behave like a small child who claims all the toys and attention for himself without regard to his playmates. Often this immature relationship is carried into adulthood, and selfishness separates him from those who could mean much.

Envy is another attitude that stands in the way of many. Some simply cannot bear to see others have success or possessions in which they do not share. It takes a big heart to "rejoice with them that do rejoice" (Romans 12:15) — to make the attainments of other people a matter of personal satisfaction and joy. But the green-eyed monster of envy has stood between many a man and his neighbor. It has blinded the eyes and closed the doors of service to others so, so frequently.

The desire to rule, to dominate others, may destroy an amiable relationship. Some cannot get along with others because they demand their own way. They want to rule, to have others bow in deference to them. A domineering personality is not conducive to friendly relations. Others fear being called weak or soft, so they run rough shod over others, not considering their feelings or wellbeing. God teaches us to "Be kindly affectioned"—listen—"be kindly affectioned one to another with brotherly love; in honour preferring one another" (Romans 12:10). Kindness should never, never be mistaken for weakness. Strength of character would cause us never to yield to deal unkindly with another. God's word says, "Be ye kind one to another, tenderhearted, forgiving one another" (Ephesians 4:32).

The word of God gives some "do's" and "don't's," and we would do well to sit down with pencil in hand, go through the Bible, and look at some of these things. Here are some do's and don't's: **Don't jump to conclusions** about others. Snap judgments are often wrong. Be sure you know before you decide—don't just "think" or "hear" or be without evidence. Many have robbed themselves of another's acquaintance and friendship because of a hasty and harsh judgment.

Don't let selfish motives warp your decisions about others. Too often we see a person through our own desires or motives. We think another is wrong because he does not agree with us. Give others the benefit of any doubt. When you are not sure, be charitable in your thinking of others. Your doubt may be unfounded. The other person may be deserving and good if you only knew the circumstances.

Don't be suspicious of others. Some question those about them. They can't get along because they are suspicious of them without reason. Such hinders understanding and consideration. It makes sympathy impossible. It makes its possessor most miserable and disagreeable.

On the other hand, **do look for the good in others.** Every man is bound to have some good in his life. At least he was made in the image of God. Look for the good, and you will find it. Help cultivate the good in others. Luther Burbank once said that every weed is a possible flower. I am not sure that is true, but I think the point he is making is well taken. Every man is capable of some good. We help him to flourish in good works by our insight into whatever good qualities he may have. Believe that the one at fault is capable of better things. Don't let some careless word or unthinking deed cause you to fail to see all the better qualities in that man's life. Even if you witness a fit of anger, you may be able to help him control his temper and to change his disposition by your patience with him.

Let's learn to acknowledge and to correct our own mistakes. We all make mistakes, do we not? But some people never recognize, evidently, their own shortcomings. It is easy to see faults in someone else. The mote in our brother's eye is much more recognizable and so much more apparent than the beam in our own (Matthew 7:1-5). Jesus says we need to first remove the beam from our own eye that we may see clearly to help others remove the mote from theirs. It takes real character—real character to admit our wrongs and then correct them. But this is the Christian way to order our lives before God and others.

Let's learn to take criticism. We are all fallable creatures and criticism just may be good for us. Let's examine every criticism that comes our way. The critic may have had a bad motive. His criticism may be too harsh. His words may be untimely, but they can be for our good if we value them correctly. Many show themselves to be a friend by criticism. We are told that the Mayo Brothers established their clinic—which has meant health to many a sick person—working on the basis that they would learn from their critics. Our critics can become our best friends if we will only let them. But be sure not to develop a feeling of self pity because someone criticized you.

Don't cultivate a martyr complex. Persecution may be turned to good. In fact, the Bible says ... and we should remember this ... "Yea, and all that will live godly in Christ Jesus shall suffer persecution" (2

Timothy 3:12). Jesus says, “Woe unto you, when all men speak well of you!” (Luke 6:26). When you are persecuted because of your faithfulness to the Lord, it should be an occasion of rejoicing. Our Master says, “Blessed are they which are persecuted for righteousness’ sake: for theirs is the kingdom of heaven. Blessed are ye, when men shall revile you, and persecute you, and shall say all manner of evil against you falsely, for my sake. Rejoice, and be exceeding glad: for great is your reward in heaven: for so persecuted they the prophets which were before you” (Matthew 5:10-12).

Don’t hate your persecutors, but be thankful that you may serve the Lord in the face of persecution. Persecution may cause your faith to be stronger and to develop the strength of your Christian character. You may even win your persecutors to become servants of the Lord for their own salvation. After all, there have been those converted who, as Paul says, “now preach the faith which they once destroyed.” In any event, don’t let them rob you of your eternal reward. Dwell with them in peace in every way that is possible and right.

Let’s have a real genuine interest in others. Each soul is important to our Lord. He died for that soul. Every person you meet is as important as the blood of Jesus Christ because He shed His blood for that individual. I think we ought to remember John 3:16. “For God so loved the world that He gave His only begotten Son, that whosoever believeth in him should not perish, but have everlasting life.” But I want you to put your name in there. Take out the word “whosoever.” “For God so loved the world, that he gave his only begotten Son, that” ... put your name in there ... “should not perish.” When you put your name in that verse, it becomes extremely meaningful to you. And then you should, in turn, look at others and realize that “God so loved the world, that he gave his only begotten Son, that” ... and name that individual, whoever he is ... “should not perish, but have everlasting life.” Have a real personal interest in those about you. The Lord did; how much more personal interest can you have than to give your life for an individual. That is exactly what the Lord did.

Christians cannot afford to be selfish. We cannot allow ourselves to become a spiritual introvert, to become a hermit in our thinking. Our lives are so interwoven with others about us; we are never islands unto ourselves. We should be interested in their welfare and especially in their spiritual welfare. We should have a desire to help others. Our Lord was born for others. He lived for others. He died for others. He was resurrected for others and now He lives to save and to intercede for others at the throne of God's mercy. If we would be a Christian, we must cultivate an interest in others. If you don't have an interest, then begin today. If we learn to get along with our fellow men, we must learn to help them and they will help us. We must be willing to treat others as we want to be treated. The measure that you mete to others will be their measure to you (Matthew 7:1-2). Our Lord says, "Therefore all things" **... all things ...** "whatsoever ye would that men should do to you, do ye even so to them" (Matthew 7:12). This is the golden rule. And I will assure you it is a good rule, but it is not just some golden rule that someone thought up; it just happens to be the command of Jesus Christ Who will judge us in the last day. The Christian must always hold this rule before him. It is one of the most important points of emphasis if we are going to get along with others.

Not only are we to treat others as we want to be treated, but we are to love one another. Jesus says, "Thou shalt love thy neighbor as thyself" (Matthew 22:39). This is a great love, when men learn to love to this extent ... **"as thyself."** Love helps more than anything else. "Love worketh no ill to his neighbor: therefore love is the fulfilling of the law" (Romans 13:10). When love is present, men can get along with one another. It makes us forget our petty differences and helps us to work out all our difficulties. It causes brethren to remember "we be brethren" (Genesis 13:8). It welds the heart of husbands to their wives with a devotion that makes them willing to give themselves for their wives (Ephesians 5:25). It binds the wives to their own husbands in loving submission (Ephesians 5:22). Parents who love their children will bring them up in the nurture and admonition of the Lord (Ephesians 6:4). And children who love their parents will learn to obey and honour their parents (Ephesians 6:1-2). When we have love as our Lord teaches us, we can be tender and kind and thoughtful to all those about us in every relationship of life. Yes, we can get along with one another. There is no doubt about that. This is the Lord's plan and it is right and it will work. If you don't believe it, just try it and see how well it will solve the difficulties of life.

The Bible teaches us that we are not only to love one another; **we are to "seek peace."** Please notice the term, "seek peace." The Apostle Peter says, "Seek peace and ensue it" (1 Peter 3:11). We can't seek peace and engage in strife at the same time. We can have peace if we are willing to extend the effort, and our Lord wants us to be peacemakers that we might be the children of God (Matthew 5:9).

Not only should we seek peace, **we should be friendly to others.** Solomon says, "A man that hath friends must show himself friendly" (Proverbs 18:24). That's a rule we may not disregard. Be friendly to others if you want to get along with them. As we sometimes say, "Smile and the world will smile with you." Solomon says in Proverbs 17:22, "A merry heart doeth good like a medicine." If you are merry and friendly, it will come back to you. Be friendly to others even when others are unfriendly toward you. It will break down the barrier between you. Few people can resist a friendly Christian disposition. Please remember: In your dealings with people at the office, on the farm, in school, or in the congregation, there are few who can resist the perpetual friendliness of a Christian disposition.

Scripture also teaches **we are to cultivate forgiveness.** Ephesians 4:32 says, "Forgiving one another, even as God for Christ's sake hath forgiven you." "If ye forgive not men their trespasses, neither will your Father forgive your trespasses" (Matthew 6:15). Christ is our example. He prayed on the cross for those who crucified Him saying, "Father, forgive them; for they know not what they do" (Luke 23:34). If we would follow His example, we must forgive one another. The extent of our forgiveness is given in Colossians 3:13: "Even"—listen to this—"Even as Christ forgave you, **so also do ye."** I would hasten to add that we must not sacrifice principle. We must stand for what is right, but we must do it in all kindness toward others. Never forget that each soul is of more value in God's sight than all the world (Mark 8:36-37). Offences will come, our Lord says, "but woe to that man by whom the offence cometh" (Matthew 18:7). Jesus says, "Whoso shall offend one of these little ones which believe in me, it were better for him that a millstone were hanged about his neck, and he were drowned in the depth of the sea" (Matthew 18:6). When you remember the value of each soul, then you can put forth every effort to get along with that person and try to win him or her to Christ.

Give your life to Jesus Christ. He wants to be your friend. He says, "Greater love hath no man than this, that a man lay down his life for his friends" (John 15:13). I would remind you. He did lay down His life for you. He says, "You are my friends, if ye do whatsoever I command you" (John 15:14). Believe in the Lord as He has commanded you, repent of your sins (Luke 13:3), be buried by immersion with the Lord in baptism (Acts 2:38; Romans 6:3-4), and then determine that you will serve your Lord; and if it be possible, as much as lieth in you, live peaceably with all men.

Who is a Wise Man?

Our subject today is concerning the question found in James 3:13. James asks, "Who is a wise man and endued with knowledge among you?" Have you ever stopped to consider this question? Could you select a wise man among your acquaintances? How would you determine who is wise and who is foolish?

Almost everyone has a general conception of what he thinks it would take to make a wise man, but all too often there is little thought given to this important question. Each one of us should desire to be wise. Solomon says, "Happy is the man that findeth wisdom, and the man that getteth understanding" (Proverbs 3:13). And he says wisdom "is more precious than rubies: and all the things thou canst desire are not to be compared unto her" (verse 15). In Proverbs 4:7, we learn, "Wisdom is the principal thing; therefore get wisdom." Evidently Solomon realized the tremendous value of wisdom. You recall that when Solomon became king over God's chosen people, the kingdom of Israel, the Lord appeared to him in a dream and says, "Ask what I shall give thee." Solomon's request is recorded in 1 Kings 3:7-9. He says, "I am but a little child: I know not how to go out or come in" ... "Give therefore thy servant an understanding heart to judge thy people, that I may discern between good and bad: for who is able to judge this thy so great a people?" I want you to notice that Solomon did not ask for riches or for long life or for victory over his enemies. Therefore God says, "Lo, I have given thee a wise and an understanding heart; so that there was none like thee before thee, neither after thee shall any arise like unto thee" (verse 12). Thus, God made Solomon the wisest man who ever lived (1 Kings 10:23). And all the earth sought to hear the wisdom of Solomon.

The real value of wisdom is expressed again and again and again in the writings of Solomon. We should especially read the books of Proverbs and Ecclesiastes to both see and appreciate the value of wisdom. The Bible teaches us that wisdom is more than knowledge. Knowledge directs a man as to what should be done, but wisdom enables him to apply his knowledge in doing the best thing, in the best way, at the best time. The wise man is the one who has learned to use his knowledge to the best advantage. Some men have the knowledge but they lack the wisdom to use it correctly. Many, many times intelligent and educated men show themselves to be lacking in wisdom by their actions or their decisions. Each of us has a need for wisdom to make the proper use of what knowledge we possess.

Where can wisdom be found? In what way does one acquire wisdom? This was a question that was asked a long time ago by Job. In Job 28:12, he says, "But where shall wisdom be found?" And after telling how it is not found in the land of the living or in the depths of the sea or in the riches of the earth, then he says, "Behold, the fear of the Lord, that is wisdom; and to depart from evil is understanding" (Job 28:28).

Writers in the Old and New Testaments give this instruction in their writings:

> James says, "If any of you lack wisdom, let him ask of God, that giveth to all men liberally, and upbraideth not; and it shall be given him" (James 1:5).
>
> Solomon says, "For the Lord giveth wisdom" (Proverbs 2:6).
>
> And the Psalmist, David, asked of God, "So teach us to number our days, that we may apply our hearts unto wisdom" (Psalm 90:12).

Some have tried to determine the beginning of wisdom as from the learning of ancient Babylon or from the ancient people of Egypt or from the philosophy of Greece or Rome, but God made Daniel and the three Hebrews with him to be ten times better than all the magicians or astrologers and all the wise men of ancient Babylon. Daniel 1:17 says, "God gave them knowledge and skill in all learning and wisdom." So wisdom is much older than the civilization of Babylon or Egypt. Wisdom existed in the very beginning, even before the earth was created or man had his existence. Wisdom in its true sense is from God.

In Colossians 2:3, Paul says, "In whom (Christ) are hid all the treasures of wisdom and knowledge." Jesus came to fully declare the wisdom of God and God's plan for our redemption (Ephesians 3:9-

10). This wisdom is to be seen in the unfolding of the eternal purpose of God in Christ and in His church.

From this foregoing study, I would suppose that all of us could be wise. I feel sure that we could. In Psalm 119:130, he says of God's word, "The entrance of thy words giveth light; it giveth understanding unto the simple." Colossians 3:16 tells us, "Let the word of Christ dwell in you richly in all wisdom." All of us can learn of the wisdom that God wants us to possess from the word of God, the Bible. We can all learn to fear God. In Psalm 111:10, we are told, **"The fear of the Lord is the beginning of wisdom."** I repeat, "The fear of the Lord is the beginning of wisdom." This is something that all of us can do, if we want to do it. And we can all obey the teachings of Jesus. The Lord says, "Therefore whosoever heareth these sayings of mine, and doeth them, I will liken him unto a wise man, which built his house upon a rock" (Matthew 7:24).

In obeying the teachings of Christ, we can repent of our sins and be baptized for the remission of our sins (Mark 16:16; Acts 2:38). In so doing, we become Christians and members of the Lord's church (Acts 11:26; 2:47). And as Christians we can pray for wisdom—remember, God "giveth to all men liberally, and upbraideth not." God wants us to be wise. He wants us to have the wisdom that is from above, that comes down from Him.

The Bible fact is this: not all men are wise. In spite of all the things God has done, and all the things that God will do, all men are not wise. Many have rejected God, even as Psalm 14:1 says, "The fool hath said in his heart, There is no God." Many have refused to accept and obey the teachings of Christ and thus become foolish before God. Jesus likened them to the foolish man who built his house upon the sand—his house, of course, would be destroyed (Matthew 7:26-27).

Many have failed to pray in faith for the wisdom that God gives. They have been too obsessed with the wisdom of this world and have been lacking in their dependence upon God; therefore, they have not prayed that God might help them be wise. Many of us are not as wise as we could be. If we were only more aware of the greatness of God's promise and of our tremendous need for God's wisdom, how wonderful it would be. We rob ourselves of God's wisdom through our own failure to lean upon the promise that God has so graciously given to us.

Many want to follow their own wisdom. This has been the history of man from the time of Eden. Satan tempted Eve by pointing out that the forbidden fruit would make her wise; all down through the centuries this has been a real temptation. Men have departed from God's wisdom and "professing themselves to be wise, they became fools" (Romans 1:22). God's warning is this, "For the wisdom of this world is foolishness with God" (1 Corinthians 3:19). It has caused men to reject God and to crucify Christ and to continue to reject the gospel of Christ. The Apostle Paul says the "preaching of the cross is to them that perish foolishness; but unto us which are saved it is the power of God. For it is written, I will destroy the wisdom of the wise, and will bring to nothing the understanding of the prudent" (1 Corinthians 1:18-19).

It would appear then that the trouble is that men often want to be so intelligent and so educated that they consider it beneath their dignity and learning to believe and to obey the word of God. The trouble is not with the Bible but within them. It should never be forgotten that:

> God **hath chosen** the foolish things of the world to confound the wise; and God **hath chosen** the weak things of the world to confound the things which are mighty; And base things of the world, and things which are despised, hath God chosen, yea, and things which are not, to bring to nought things that are: That no flesh should glory in his presence (1 Corinthians 1:27-29).

Frequently, we are reminded that so many professedly educated people reject the Bible and the simplicity of the Lord's plan of salvation and the nature of the organization of His church. But this is not difficult to understand when we remember the proneness of man to appear wise in his own eyes and in the eyes of his fellowman. It takes an humble person to be a Christian! In order to go to heaven, one must forsake the glamorous and ostentatious things of the world. He must humble himself in obedience to the simplicity of the Lord's wisdom and not his own. He must be buried with his Lord in baptism because his Lord tells him to do so; and he must worship and serve as a plain and simple Christian in the way the Lord has taught in the New Testament.

So let us be warned. The wisdom of the world will be destroyed. The wisdom of the world is as James says, "not from above, but is earthly, sensual, devilish" (James 3:15). It appeals to the natural instincts of men and to the base and animal appetites that men possess and is of the very nature of the god of this world, the devil. This wisdom is that which causes envy, strife, and confusion and every evil work. These things should be recognized. Worldly wisdom **must** be rejected lest we be destroyed by following in its ways because they only lead to eternal destruction.

Consider with me for a moment that wisdom that is from above. The scripture states in James 3:17-18 that "the wisdom that is from above is first pure, then peaceable, gentle, and easy to be entreated, full of mercy and good fruits, without partiality, and without hypocrisy. And the fruit of righteousness is sown in peace of them that make peace." This is the kind of wisdom the Lord gives. This is the kind of wise man that each one of us should want to be. The truly wise individual is pure, peaceable, gentle, easy to be entreated. He is full of mercy and good fruits, without partiality and without hypocrisy. Here is the answer to James' question: "Who is a wise man and endued with knowledge among you?" The wise man has the proof in his own life, in his own works of wisdom, the true wisdom of God—the wisdom that is from above.

This wisdom is not learned from philosophers but from Jesus. It has the rightness of the understanding of the gospel of Christ. It is the reflection, actually, of the life of Jesus. It is not the way that men ordinarily operate their temporal and business affairs or the way the policies of state or of nations are so frequently conducted. And it is certainly not in keeping with the popular practices of the fancies of the men of our day. But it is the Lord's will. It is the wisdom of God. And if we would truly be wise, and if we would desire the eternal promises of God, we must seek that heavenly wisdom. We must learn to be wise with God's wisdom and not that of man.

I would now like to sum up these thoughts. (1) The wise man accepts and believes in God. It is a fool who says there is no God. (2) The wise man fears God and keeps His commandments (Ecclesiastes 12:13). (3) The wise man rejects the wisdom of the world as that which shall be destroyed in the last great day. (4) The wise man believes and obeys the teachings of Jesus. To believe is not enough. Wisdom requires obedience, a complete and humble submission to the will of Christ. (5) The wise man demonstrates in his life the true nature of the wisdom of God. His life shows the results, the happiness, the contentment and peace of soul that the Lord gave is real—both in the life and in the dealings of the man who is wise enough to follow his Master. (6) The wise man wants to save others. Solomon says in Proverbs 11:30, "He that winneth souls is wise." The wise man wants to win others to the same joy and happiness that he shares in Christ. He wants others to have the hope of heaven and the blessings of life eternal. (7) The wise man wants to be like the wise virgins and be prepared for the coming of Christ (Matthew 25:1-13).

May God help us to want to share this wisdom of God. Will you be wise in your acceptance of Christ? Will you be wise in your obedience to His gospel? Will you be wise in preparing for the Lord's coming? Our prayer is that God will grant us the wisdom to live for Him, always seeking the wisdom that is from above so that we may so live and teach that heaven may be ours at last.

God Speaks Today

Ladies and gentlemen, once again we come to study the Lord's word and today we invite your attention to the fact that there is no greater blessing that can come to any person than the privilege of having fellowship with our Heavenly Father and our Lord Jesus Christ. When John, the apostle, began to write his first epistle, he mentioned first of all the wonderful knowledge of the Lord, the Word of Life that God had permitted him to possess. Then in verse three he stated that he wanted to share that blessing with his fellow Christians. His desire is given in these words: "That ye also may have fellowship with us: and truly our fellowship is with the Father, and with his Son Jesus Christ" (1 John 1:3).

Fellowship with God is prized highly by those who have learned its real meaning. Doctor Vincent said, "The true life in man which comes to the acceptance of Jesus as the Son of God consists of fellowship with God and with man." In further reference to that fellowship he said, "It expresses in this passage the enjoyment or realization of fellowship as compared with the mere fact of existing." We may say further that this fellowship means partnership or joint sharing in the great faith in God that is the true bond of communion with God. No doubt the reason is that God's word is the foundation of all fellowship. God has spoken to us through His word, the Bible. He had His teaching recorded so that we, today, can share these wonderful blessings. Paul, directed by the Holy Spirit, says, "Faith cometh by hearing, and hearing by the word of God" (Romans 10:17).

The first requisite is to let God speak to us through this word. This means the recognition of the Bible as the inspired revelation that God has given. The Bible must be established in our hearts as the inspired word of God. I would like for us to be reminded that God has spoken. Not only has God created us and made a revelation of both His will and His works, but He has spoken to us. The book of Hebrews begins saying, "God, having of old time spoken unto the fathers in the prophets by divers portions and in divers manners, hath at the end of these days spoken unto us in his Son" (Hebrews 1:1) from the American Revised Version. This teaching of God has been recorded for us in the New Testament. Further, when Jesus was transfigured before His disciples, they beheld His divine glory. God spoke saying of Him, "This is my beloved Son, in whom I am well pleased; hear ye him" (Matthew 17:5).

Jesus says on one occasion, "My doctrine is not mine; but his that sent me. If any man will do his will, he shall know of the doctrine, whether it be of God, or whether I speak of myself" (John 7:16-17). Again, Jesus says, "The words that I speak unto you I speak not of myself: but the Father that dwelleth in me, he doeth the works" (John 14:10). We can know that the New Testament is the true inspired word of God. The very nature of the writings, contained in all of its 27 books, is not that of ordinary men. The New Testament writers were directed in their writings by the Holy Spirit, who was sent from God. Consider these words of 1 Corinthians 2:9-10, "But as it is written, Eye hath not seen, nor ear heard, neither have entered into the heart of man, the things which God hath prepared for them that love him. But God **hath revealed them unto us** by his Spirit." Verses 12 and 13 say, "Now we have received, not the spirit of the world, but the spirit which is of God; that we might know the things that are freely given to us of God. Which things also we speak, not in the words which man's wisdom teacheth, but which the Holy Ghost teacheth." God, through the Holy Spirit, directed the chosen writers to give us His teachings. He revealed to them what to write and the Holy Spirit even selected the words which they would write the divine message for us to read. This is often called the plenary verbal inspiration of the Bible. God inspired these writers, which means that God breathed into them what He wanted them to say. He selected their words; therefore, it was **verbal** inspiration; and that inspiration was full, complete, and with His divine authority. Thus, we have before us plenary, verbal inspiration. And I think it is exceedingly important that we understand and believe that.

What is true of the New Testament is true of the 39 books of the Old Testament. The Apostle Peter says, "For the prophecy came not in old time by the will of man: but holy men of God spake as they were moved by the Holy Ghost" (2 Peter 1:21). In Acts 1:16, we read how the Holy Spirit spoke "by the mouth of David," and that prophecy was recorded in Psalm 41:9 and was fulfilled in the betrayal of our Lord. More than three hundred Old Testament prophecies concerning our Lord are pointed out as fulfilled in the virgin birth of Christ, in the very circumstances of His birth and in His life and work, and in His death, burial, resurrection and ascension to the Heavenly Father. There can be no doubt in the mind of a man who would learn that the Bible is God's message to man. It is as Jesus says, "If any man will do his will, he shall know of the doctrine, whether it be of God, or whether I speak of myself" (John 7:17). The truth is abundant and the privilege is extended to all. We can know, if we really desire to know, that the Bible is the complete and inspired message of God to man.

I think it is really quite a thrilling thing to believe, to know that God speaks to us in these last days, that He speaks to us by His Son. What is tragic is that all men will not listen to God. Over and over again in the New Testament, the words of Isaiah are repeated about how men rejected God's message. Jesus pointed to this passage in connection with those who heard Him saying, "This people's heart is waxed gross, and their ears are dull of hearing, and their eyes they have closed; lest at any time they should see with their eyes, and hear with their ears, and should understand with their heart, and should be converted, and I should heal them" (Matthew 13:15).

Why do not men listen to the Lord? Why don't we listen? If the Lord, indeed, speaks to us today, then why are we not listening to our Lord? Sometimes it is because we are more interested in the things of the world, and we permit the devil to take the word of God out of our hearts. The devil knows the power of God's word; whether we ever learn it or not, there is one thing for sure, he knows it and he believes it, and he will do all he can to keep men from believing the word of God. And with other people, it is as Jesus says, "The care of this world, and the deceitfulness of riches, choke the word, and he becometh unfruitful." With others, "when tribulation or persecution ariseth because of the word," they are offended and they no longer listen to the Lord's teachings (Matthew 13:18-22).

False teachers have deceived untold thousands; even good and honest people have been deceived by false teachers. This has been true from the very beginning when the devil himself beguiled Eve "through his subtilty" (2 Corinthians 11:3). All of us must be on guard so that our minds will not be corrupted and that we be not moved away or taken away from the simplicity that is in Christ. We must beware of false teachers.

We are imploring you, today, since God tells us that He speaks to us—He does speak to our generation ... may we implore you to let

God speak to you. Let Him speak to you in the true and pure words of the Bible. Never take my word or the word of any man regardless of the amount of confidence you may have in his integrity, regardless of how good and how influential that person may be, stand on God's foundation, the word of God. Study the Bible and be able to give chapter and verse for what you believe. Let your faith stand, not in the wisdom of men but in the power of God (1 Corinthians 2:5). Let God speak to you directly through His word, the Bible. And then let that word be the basis of your faith in God and in God's plan for your salvation. Let God's word tell you what to do to be saved. Let God's word direct you in following the example of Jesus Christ. Let God instruct you about how you can live a pure, holy, consecrated, and happy life. Let God tell you about His church that Christ established among men. Let God's word tell you, as we read in Philippians 2:13, "It is God which worketh in you both to will and to do of his good pleasure." Let His word tell you of the great and precious promises that He has in store for those who serve Him that you might be a partaker of the divine nature, "having escaped the corruption that is in the world through lust" (2 Peter 1:4).

What we are saying is—Let God have His way in your life. How often do we sing, "Thou art the Potter, I am the clay; mold me and make me, Master today?" We sing, "Lord, have your way in my life." Are we truly, genuinely convinced that that is what we want? Won't you make up your mind today to let His word become translated into your thinking, into the experiences and applications of your life? Let Christ, as the Son of the Living God, be your Saviour and your Lord. Do as Christ has taught. Believe in Him, repent of your sins, confess Him before men, and be immersed for the remission of your sins (Luke 13:3; Romans 10:10; Mark 16:16). And then the Lord will add you to His church. As a Christian, you can serve in the kingdom of God and glorify the God who made you and who has redeemed you through the Christ of Calvary. As a Christian, you can worship God in spirit and in truth, even as He has taught in His word (John 4:24). You can know the blessings of God's grace and say with Paul that God's grace is sufficient for you (2 Corinthians 12:9).

Now I want you to think—listen—think what this can mean to you. God can comfort the sorrowful, for He is the God of all comfort (2 Corinthians 1:3) and can help us all in the time when we are troubled, even as Jesus says, "Let not your heart be troubled: ye believe in God, believe also in me. In my Father's house are many mansions: if it were not so, I would have told you. I go to prepare a place for you. And if I go and prepare a place for you, I will come again, and receive you unto myself; that where I am, there ye may be also" (John 14:1-3). Such comfort and such hope can come only from God through Jesus Christ, and only the word of God can contain such exceeding great and precious promises.

To his fellow Christians in Rome, Paul writes, "The Spirit itself beareth witness with our spirit, that we are the children of God: and if children, then heirs; heirs of God, and joint-heirs with Christ; if so be that we suffer with him, that we may be also glorified together" (Romans 8:16-17). Indeed, every Christian can share this great promise of God. We can all have the witness of the Holy Spirit in our lives as we believe and obey the gospel of Christ in being born into God's family (Galatians 3:26-27). And then as children of God, we can be heirs of that home with God in heaven when this life is over. God can help you. He can help you with your burdens. He can help you with your cares. He has taught us saying, "Casting all your care upon him; for he careth for you" (1 Peter 5:7). Jesus says, "Come unto me, all ye that labour and are heavy laden, and I will give you rest. Take my yoke upon you, and learn of me; for I am meek and lowly in heart: and ye shall find rest unto your souls. For my yoke is easy, and my burden is light" (Matthew 11:28-30).

God can help you in the time of temptation. 1 Corinthians 10:13 contains the promise, "But God is faithful, who will not suffer you to be tempted above that ye are able; but will with the temptation also make a way to escape, that ye may be able to bear it." God will give you the victory over the tempter, even over the world itself (1 John 5:4). Not only this, God can make your life happy in His service. You can be a real channel of blessing through whom the knowledge of God can be passed on to those who are lost in sin. You can lead some soul to Christ and save that soul from eternal death. There is no greater happiness—hear me—there is no greater happiness in this life than that of sharing the fellowship of God and of His Son, Jesus Christ. And that joy is made complete when we really come to know and understand just how great and how good our God is in His ability to bless those who live for Him. Indeed, He is able to save to the **uttermost,** and He is able to do exceeding abundantly above all we have ever asked or ever thought. God's blessings are so many that we cannot enumerate them all. Let us exclaim with Paul, "Blessed be the God and Father of our Lord Jesus Christ, who has blessed us with all spiritual blessings in heavenly places in Christ" (Ephesians 1:3). When we attempt to count our blessings to see what all God has done for us, let us thank Him for them and use them in such a way to glorify His name. Let us trust in God and be faithful to Him in our lives at all times.

Let us remember this; "All spiritual blessings in heavenly places" are in and through our Lord Jesus Christ. It is the Christ who has "loved us, and washed us from our sins in his own blood, And hath made us"—listen to this—He has made "US kings and priests unto God and his Father; to him be glory and dominion for ever and ever. Amen" (Revelation 1:5-6). These blessings, which the Bible lays out to us, can be ours only when we let God speak to us through His word, the gospel of Christ, and tells us how to become Christians, how to live as faithful and consecrated children of God. The blessings of God are for those who obey Him. Jesus says. "Not every one that saith unto me. Lord, Lord, shall enter into the kingdom of heaven; but he that doeth the will of my Father which is in heaven" (Matthew 7:21).

The Plumbline of God

Good morning, everyone. Ladies and gentlemen, we are extremely grateful to have you in our listening audience as we come to study the Lord's word. We believe this is the day the Lord has made, and we should, as David says, "rejoice and be glad in it." Not only that—this is the Lord's Day and we are grateful that we may look forward to going to the house of the Lord. We should be glad that this can be done. What a thankful people we really ought to be that we live in this land of freedom—in this land of absolute luxury and plenty and we come unfettered in any sense of the word, free to teach the word of God, free to live it, free to contend for it—for these things we should be extremely grateful.

I would like to invite your attention today to a statement that is made in the Old Testament by a great man of God; in fact, one of the oldest prophets that we have given to us in scripture—these words were by the prophet Amos. I would like for you to listen to this quotation that we have from his book. "Behold, the Lord stood upon a wall made by a plumbline, with a plumbline in his hand. And the Lord said unto me, Amos, what seest thou? And I said, A plumbline. Then said the Lord, Behold, I will set a plumbline in the midst of my people Israel: I will not again pass by them any more" (Amos 7:7-8). These words, from the eighth century before Christ, were indeed written for our learning and our admonition. In this we are reminded that though times may change, though customs may vary, though dispensations may give way to newer and better ones, human nature remains essentially the same. The time that we are concerned with in this study is the eighth century before Christ. It was indeed a propitious and prosperous day in both Israel and Judah. The shrines of the altars at Bethel and Gilgal were crowded by prosperous worshipers; worshipers who were interpreting the word money as meaning "God with us." Prophets and priests, silenced by gifts and bribes, were catering to a people who were bent only on self gratification. The poor were oppressed according to Amos. Good times were the order of the day. They were at ease in Zion, and the glory that was Israel had indeed departed.

These were the times—the man was Amos. His home was Tekoa, a little village south of Jerusalem and west of the Dead Sea. Amos was a herdsman and a dresser of Sycamore trees. He was a poor man who made no pretentions of rank or influence. And although he made no claim of being a prophet or the son of a prophet, God chose this man to become as his very name suggests, a man with a burden.

On the occassion of the vision under consideration in Amos 7, Amos saw the Lord standing on the wall with a plumbline in His hand. He saw a wall that was so obviously out of perpendicular that it could not stand. It was headed for a fall. Amos saw the plumbline as God's testing of Israel's fidelity to His blueprint or His pattern. It was God's way of saying that it was not enough for Israel to have and to claim the house: the house must be plumb; it must be straight; it must be according to the pattern that God had showed them in the mount. After the passing of the vision, Amos, convinced that from this verdict there was simply no appeal, picked up the plumbline and went forth to preach. He marched up to Bethel and Gilgal, and he delivered a series of messages that were tremendous—a series of messages that were designed to cut to the very depth of their calloused hearts.

The truths that Amos preached are timeless truths that cannot be limited to a particular age or people. He preached that sin was sin regardless of who committed it or where. He preached that mere ritual was not pleasing to God—that God was not some vain monarch who was pleased with big gifts and empty phrases. He preached that God had utter contempt for forms of religion that neither disturb the conscience nor change one's life. He preached that the greatest peril Israel could possibly face was prosperity. As Amos drove home these points time after time, it was evident that all of his sermons were founded upon one healthy basic conviction: God is a God of law.

In Revelation 11:1-2, John sees a vision that is not unlike this one presented to Amos. John, you recall, saw a vision of the temple, the altar, and the worshipers. A reed was given to him with the command to measure the temple, the altar, and those who worshiped therein. Notice the measuring device was given to John, not made by him. The purpose of this device was the same as the plumbline of Amos. It was to determine what was approved of God and to emphasize that certain definite standards must be met by the Lord's people. In both the law that came from Sinai and the one that was to go forth from Jerusalem (Isaiah 2:2-4), we have the principle that Amos set forth in chapter 5;

that is, we must learn to hate evil and to love good. David says, "Through thy precepts I get understanding: therefore I hate every false way" (Psalm 119:104). One of the great needs of our age is to learn the fine art of hating evil.

Whether the times in which we live are the most evil ones, I do not know. I know only that in our generation we have been exposed to wars and riots, filthy people, and filthy inventions; obscenities and profanities are extremely commonplace. Indeed, we are living in times when our young do not even remember things being different from the way they are now. Some of us occupy a certain vantage point in that we can recall when those who peddled their filth must do it secretly. This is no longer true, as you well know. We can recall the times when acts of stealing, murder, and such like were not considered the sole products of one's body chemistry or his poor unfortunate environmental circumstance. Such sins, and a thousand kindred ones, were not excused under the heading of "man's temporary stumbling in the upward progress of mankind." Let me assure you today that a departure from God's word has occurred. We are experiencing in our time falls within the fall. We are experiencing plunges within the great plunge. We have lived to see the time when our children are being taught that man has no real significance, that he is no different than the rock that lies in the garden, or that he is no different than the rodent that scurries among the plants. We have lived to see the time when the criteria for right and wrong is not based upon divine revelation but rather upon the current demands of society or the wishes of the individual. We have lived to see what Amos saw.

Sin is more glamorous than it ever was. Drugs and alcohol are the subject of jokes, infidelity has become a status symbol, perversion has become an accepted life style, dirty books are called literature, and filthy shows go under the guise of realism. It is in the fullness of this time that all Christians should rise up as a mighty army and declare that all such is sin—not just sickness; that all such is sin, not just simply someone's mistake or his hangup! God hates such things! And I want to propose to you today, that to be His we must do the same.

Solomon states in Ecclesiastes 3:8 that there is a time to love and a time to hate. I submit to you, my brother that the time to both love and hate with a new intensity has arrived. Indeed, it is time to quit—it is time to quit laughing at the lewd jokes and humming the tunes and stuffing the pockets of those who are absolutely liquidating the values for which we stand! It is time to raise the old plumbline of God and say, listen world, let us tell you a few things today as the people of God. Listen world, we hate your filthy jokes, we hate your profanity and your gutter language, we hate your depraved sense of humor, your nudity, your infidelity; in short we hate any and everything that is tearing down all the Lord died to build up.

I want to remind you today, there is a cause. David says as he faces the Giant and as the people turned their backs and scurried like rodents from this man—an uncircumcised Philistine—he says, "Is there not a cause?" (1 Samuel 17:28-29). Surely, as the people of God, we should realize that there is a cause, We, like he, must become burden bearers. We, too, must be able to discern between the good and the evil. We, too, must be willing to cry aloud and spare not lest one day we awaken to see the Lord's people decimated, not from without but from within.

Amos, what seest thou? A plumbline, O Lord. Have we seen it? Are we building today as if we have ever heard about the great plumbline of God—His great word? Are we conforming to the blueprint of His will? What kind of house are we building in our generation?

In Romans 10:18-21, we notice the Jews had rejected God's simple plan of salvation that was available to everyone. When we see they had rejected that which was so obvious, the question is raised, "Have they not heard?" Since nothing had been done, it would appear that simply they did not hear. And I think this is so true today. There are so many truths that are so obvious. The old plumbline has been raised so many times that when one observes how ignored these great truths are, we are tempted to say, "Have they not heard?"

Have they not heard about modesty? Consider the number of sermons preached and articles written every year on the subject of modesty. But I can assure you, you can let the temperature rise a few degrees and the race is on to see who can expose the most of their bodies the quickest. Unfortunately, many Christians will let the world's influence in this area far exceed any consideration of what the Bible has to say. In fact, some so totally ignore the plain Bible teaching where the word modesty appears with the words "shamefacedness" and "sobriety" that they will affirm that as long as they wear whatever all others are wearing they are in no way immodest. Modesty to them is not determined by shamefacedness and sobriety but solely by what others and, in this case, what sinners are doing, Christian women and men need to study these three words very carefully because, according to Paul, our souls are at stake.

Christian mothers need to clothe their daughters, even when young, so that they will develop a sense of shamefacedness and sobriety about them. Christian fathers who understand what effect the immodest dress of wives and daughters have on other males need to use their authority given to them from heaven as the heads of families to see that Christian families are not caught up in this mad race. The Bible is so plain in regard to the importance of dress that when one considers how some Christians ignore its teaching, he tends to ask, "Have they not heard?"

Have they not heard about lasciviousness? The Bible uses another word that should be considered and that is the word "lasciviousness." Galatians 5:19-21 gives a list of sins about which the Bible says "they which do such things shall not inherit the kingdom of God." One of these sins is lasciviousness. Because this word is not commonly used today, some may fail to understand its full significance. It means tending to cause intense desire; thus, any clothing that by being too tight, too loose, too revealing, causes by its very nature lustful thoughts, is sin. Now this is not just preacher talk or puritanical philosophy. It just happens to be divine truth. Those who are guilty of lascivious actions jeopardize their soul's destiny, according to the Apostle Paul. The question that ought to be foremost in the minds of Christian women is, Is the clothing that I am wearing designed primarily to attract attention through sexual appeal? The Bible is clear on the subject of lasciviousness. But when one considers how few are affected by its teaching, he is led to ask, "Have they not heard?"

Have they not heard about lust? In our age when beauty is equated with sexual appeal, the words of Jesus sound so strange. Have you ever thought about that? "Whosoever looketh on a woman to lust after her, hath committed adultery with her already in his heart" (Matthew 5:28). The American philosophy seems to be that women should use the nature of man to attract him, to gain favor from him. The typical office joke reflects just how far the typical American man has given himself over to a life filled with lusting. Jesus makes it clear that such action by men can condemn their souls. But what about the woman who dresses in such a way that she invites lusting by others? 1 Corinthians 8:12 is a passage we need to consider. This passage shows that one can do a thing that is right and sin by doing it when it causes another to do wrong. What about the person who does a thing that is doubtful, if not sinful, and causes another to do wrong? Something is wrong with any person who can affirm that shorts, halter tops, pants, modern swim attire do not contribute to lust. What makes one think that the attire used by prostitutes does not have the same affect on men if such is worn by a "Christian"? What would the difference be? And so the question is raised, "Have they not heard?"

The question in Romans 10 is very appropriate. "Yes, verily their sound went into all the earth and their words unto the ends of the world." What we are really considering is this—with far too many people, the problem is though they have heard, they have no desire to do what the Bible says. The world has far too much influence on them; and in reference to this subject, we should raise the question, "Have you heard?"

God wants us to understand that there are certain things that are right and there are certain things that are wrong. Some things He just simply does not accept. Amos, what seest thou? A plumbline, O Lord. The question again, Have we seen it? Are we building accordingly? Have we not heard?

Honor Thy Father

Ladies and gentlemen, once again we invite your attention to a study of the Lord's word. Our Lord teaches us that we are to come and reason together upon the Holy Scriptures; and we would reason upon them in view of the time in which we live.

This past year, when I was in the country of Mexico, I saw a sign stating that ten children are born every minute of every day and every night. When one stops to contemplate the fact that in one country of the world—and this could be true in every country—ten children are born every minute, it causes us to stop and contemplate what the word of God teaches about the rearing of a child. With the birth of each one of those children born every minute, there comes the responsibility and the obligation to see that the child has the proper training and care—to see that the child is fed and clothed and taught correctly so that he or she may be what God would desire.

God has made us, as parents, responsible. Every child that is born is clean and pure and innocent. His birth was not of his own choosing. He had nothing to do with that. The parents are responsible for his existence and those parents are responsible before God to teach and to train that child to be pleasing in God's sight and to be useful in the society in which he lives. Parents shall answer to the Lord in the Day of Judgment as to whether they have reared him for good or for bad. It was to the parents that Solomon says, "Train up a child in the way he should go: and when he is old, he will not depart from it" (Proverbs 22:6). Paul writes, "And ye fathers, provoke not your children to wrath: but bring them up in the nurture and admonition of the Lord" (Ephesians 6:4). Parents must start early and "train up" the child.

His first tender recollection should be of a mother who lovingly pressed him to her bosom and the compassion of a father who sought to train him for God. Each child deserves to have the happiness and the security of a home where his life can be molded and fashioned properly. Parents cannot neglect their duties when the child is small and expect to change him when he is older. The proverb is so true,

"Just as the twig is bent, so will the tree be inclined." And as children are trained, so will they be when they are grown. For children to have the proper relation to their parents, the parents must train them. The condition of our children is largely a reflection of the condition of the home into which they are born and in which they have been reared.

The child is not to blame because he is neglected and disregarded—because his parents have left him to shift for himself and to seek his activities, interests, and companionship somewhere else. If he finds bad playmates and gets into trouble, put the blame where it belongs—upon the parents who had **no time** for that little child. If there is no bond of understanding, there can be no influence or guidance. Parents are so often sinning against their children by their failure to bear their own responsibility as parents. They fail to teach them about God. They fail to teach them about the Bible. And they fail to give them parental examples of Christian living. Of all people in this world, we need to stop and think about what the Bible has to say on this subject.

Many years ago J. Edgar Hoover wrote, while he was still in his position, "When youth commits a crime, a greater crime has already been committed in the home by the failure to instill by precept and example the fundamentals of common decency." So many children are born into homes that are not conducive to proper development or they are reared under adverse circumstances. Delinquent parents make delinquent children. And neglected boys and girls become problem children in our society. The crime rate of our country continues to increase, and the average age of criminals becomes younger every year. This condition becomes a serious reflection on the relationship that exists in homes. Almost 90 percent of American homes are plagued with the use, by one or more in the family, of alcoholic beverages. The children are reared in the environment of disregard for the importance of preserving the health and the well being of their bodies and their brains. The attendant evils of alcohol are corrupting the lives of more children every year. Almost half of the marriages are ending in divorce; and in forty percent of those divorced, every year, they have small children. It is estimated that ninety-five percent of the juvenile delinquents are the product of broken homes. The blame lies not upon these children but upon the parents.

One judge who had served many years on the bench in a juvenile court made this observation: "I have tried approximately 8,000 boys and girls under 17 years of age for violating the law and of that number there has not been a child in the court whose father or mother went to church regularly. Of that approximately 8,000, only 41 of those boys and girls went to church with regularity. My advice to any parent is, if you want to increase the possibility of your child becoming delinquent, if you want to increase the probability of your child becoming a criminal, stay away from church." The words of this judge should be a warning to parents who are letting their child grow up as a little heathen—and by that I mean without any knowledge of God, without the influence of association with Christians. That is what is happening with about twenty million young people here in the United States who are growing up without any religious training.

On any Wednesday, you may ask a room full of children, "How many of you are going to church tonight?" Only a very few hands will be raised, maybe two maybe three out of thirty children. What is even more interesting is that if you could ask the children of some people who claim to be Christians, "How many of you are going to church this Wednesday night?" and many of them are not going either.

Can we expect the children to have the proper relationship to their parents when the parents are not having the proper relationship to their children. You parents who are listening today, may I cause you to stop and to think about these matters. We need to think—and I don't say **you—WE** need to think before it is too late. These children will soon be grown, and their lives will be set in their habits and in their concepts of life. I am firmly convinced that the problems of the children of our generation are really the problems of the parents. Problem parents are making their children "problem children."

The Bible teaches that parents are to love their children. It seems odd that we would need this kind of command, yet the Bible speaks of those who are without "natural affection." May I assure you that we have reached the time when this is the case with many people. There is nothing that can take the place of love. Every child has the right to expect love from those who are responsible for his existence. There is no influence that is as strong upon a child as that of knowing the father and the mother have a real understanding love for the child. The child as a rule will respond to love, and he will reciprocate the love he receives. Every child desires to be wanted and to be loved. I have never in all my time as a preacher of the gospel or as an educator in the public schools found that to be untrue. **Every** child desires to be wanted, and he desires to be loved; and when love is not shown, the child has been robbed of one of the greatest blessings that could possibly have been his. I can assure you that you may do all manner of things to help this child, you may provide all kinds of programs, but nothing will compensate for the lack of a Christian home.

Christians, the Bible teaches, should rear their children in the "nurture and admonition of the Lord." And the Bible teaches that children are to be taught obedience. Obedience is to be first learned, not in the school or in the court, but it is to be **first** learned in the home. The Bible says, "Children, obey your parents in the Lord: for this is right. Honour thy father and mother; (which is the first commandment with promise;) That it may be well with thee, and thou mayest live long on the earth" (Ephesians 6:1-3). This command applies to US today. It is a serious matter and must not be overlooked. The parents must teach their children to obey them. When children fail to learn to obey their parents, they have little regard for the laws of society. Respect for authority in the home will create respect for authority in the school and in the community and as a citizen and toward the laws of God.

This is a duty that is older than Christianity. About 1,900 years before Christ, God said of Abraham—and I propose that this is one of the greatest things that might be said of a man who is a Christian—"For I know him, that he will command his children and his household after him" (Genesis 18:19). When Moses received the law of God at Mt. Sinai about 400 years later, the fifth of the Ten Commandments was, "Honour thy father and thy mother: that thy days may be long upon the land which the Lord thy God giveth thee" (Exodus 20:12). The penalty for the violation of this command was that the parents should take the disobedient child to the elders of the city "And all the men of his city shall stone him with stones, that he die" (Deuteronomy 21:18-21). The law of Moses was plain and the penalty upon the disobedient child was death. This fact should make us realize how important God thought it was to obey and to honor our parents.

The book of Proverbs has much teaching concerning the discipline of children by their parents. Proverbs 29:17 says, "Correct thy son, and he shall give thee rest; yea, he shall give delight unto thy soul." Proverbs 19:18 says, "Chasten thy son while there is hope, and let not thy soul spare for his crying." Again in Proverbs 13:24, we read, "He that spareth his rod hateth his son: but he that loveth him chasteneth him betimes." For parents to correct and chasten their children should be considered necessary and right.

A few years ago, psychologists were saying don't correct your child, let him develop self expression. But now most of them have seen their mistakes, and we have reaped where we have sown to the wind—we have reaped the whirlwind. We have seen children grow up with little regard for their parents, for themselves, or for society. Such attitudes toward discipline create tremendous problems in the school and in all of society. And now you can find many articles in magazines written by outstanding men and women, emphasizing the importance of teaching children obedience and respect for authority in the home.

I want to propose to you that this is God's plan, and it is right. Children owe respect to their parents. Submission to parents in the home is the first step in respect and in submission to God. I want to propose to you today as a young man or a young lady as you listen to me that there is no way you can be respectful to God and be disrespectful to your parents. There is no way that you can obey God and disobey your parents in the Lord. Good parents desire the things that are best for their children, and good children have regard for their parents. Some children talk back to their parents and are sassy and insolent and hateful and unkind. Some grossly mistreat their parents, even do them harm and injury. Other children seem to consider themselves too good or too wise or too well educated to submit to their parents. But as we grow older, we realize more and more that parents are to be honored and respected and obeyed. To disobey our parents is to disobey God's plan for us as children. The only exception would be when parents would demand the child to do **wrong** or to disobey God—and this is seldom seen. Children are to obey their parents in the Lord "for this is right."

May I emphasize, too, that we must honor our parents. The little child reflects either honor or dishonor upon his parents. The older that child grows, the more this behavior can be seen. Every boy or girl who is good, or every good man or good woman, gives honor to those who were responsible for his upbringing. And we should honor our parents when they are old. I don't know where we came up with the idea that we may honor our parents for a while and then we may stop doing so at some point in our lives. I propose to you that as long as you live you are to honor your parents in the sense that the Bible uses that term. We should not neglect them. Many a parent longs for the consideration and kindness of a son or daughter who has no thought and no time for that old father and that old mother. Because our parents may be old is no reason to neglect them or to let them suffer either want of physical care or want of our love and our affection. One of the most severe rebukes that was ever given by Jesus Christ is found in Matthew 15, and it was directed to those who had set aside God's law toward their parents because of the traditions of men. It is God's will that we honor and care for our parents even when they are old and infirm. To fail to provide for them would be to deny God's plan and to be worse, worse than an infidel (1 Timothy 5:8).

Not only can we honor our parents while they live, I want to propose to you that we can honor our parents even after they are gone. Many of us have fathers and mothers whom death has removed from our presence. But we can live today to bear them honor as long as we live and in everything we do or say. And let us never speak of them in such a way or ever live such a life as to show disrespect for them or to disregard the Lord's teaching to "honor thy father and thy mother."

I propose that the greatest honor you will **ever** bestow upon your parents— if you want to honor them—is to serve the Lord and live the Christian life. There is nothing greater than for them to know you are interested in things divine and are living a Christian life. When John writes to those who were Christians because of his influence as a teacher, he says, "I have no greater joy than to hear that my children walk in truth" (3 John 4). And I propose to you that what is true of these surely would be true of our children and our families. There is no better way to honor your parents than by being a devout Christian man or Christian woman. It was that hallowed relation of God as our Father that Jesus impressed upon His followers. Remember? He taught them to pray saying, "Our Father which art in heaven, Hallowed be thy name" (Matthew 6:9). Paul writes, "For ye are all the children of God by faith in Christ Jesus. For as many of you as have been baptized into Christ have put on Christ" (Galatians 3:26-27). To live the Christian life as a member of God's family in the church of our Lord is the best way to honor our parents and to honor our Heavenly Parent, our Father in heaven.

Let me remind you that Jesus was subject to His parents, so let us be to ours (Luke 2:51). And as Jesus was mindful of His mother, even as He died on the cross of Calvary and made provisions for her care, so let us be mindful of our parents as long as we live. Through our obedience to Christ, we will honor our God, we will honor our parents, and we will prepare to enter our Heavenly Father's eternal home. Thank you for listening.

Reconciliation

Ladies and Gentlemen, we invite your attention to the subject of reconciliation. If there is anything the Bible teaches, it teaches God has made abundant provision for our well being and our salvation. His word, the Bible, has given us a complete plan for our lives. God has taught us the greatness of His love for us, and He has demonstrated that love in sending Christ into the world.

In Romans 5:8, Paul tells us, "God commendeth his love toward us, in that, while we were yet sinners, Christ died for us." How great and how wonderful is the love that God has shown for sinful man; and God would have men to love one another. In 1 John 4:11, we read, "Beloved, if God so loved us, we ought also to love one another." Jesus says, "A new commandment I give unto you, that ye love one another; as I have loved you." He also says, "By this shall all men know that ye are my disciples, if ye have love one to another" (John 13:34-35).

It is based upon this great principle of love that we have the thought of our lesson today concerning reconciliation. The word 'reconcile' means "to cause to be friendly again, to bring back to harmony, to re-establish friendly relations between two parties who are estranged" no matter on which side the antagonism exists. Is it not true that men often need to be reconciled? There are many things that bring differences between us. Sometimes people deliberately say or do things that offend or injure their fellow men, and sometimes one may unintentionally offend his brother. The principle of love would prompt the offender to correct his error and make the necessary amends that the difference might be removed and that harmony might again prevail.

The followers of our Lord must remember that the acceptability of their worship and their service to God is dependent upon their harmony with their fellow Christians. Jesus teaches this truth in Matthew 5:23-24 when He says, "Therefore if thou bring thy gift to the altar, and rememberest that thy brother hath aught against thee; Leave there thy gift before the altar, and go thy way; first be reconciled to thy brother, and then come and offer thy gift." We could well express this thought today by saying, "When you come to worship God and there you remember that your brother has something against you, go first and be reconciled to your brother and then come to worship God." The reconciliation, or the establishment of harmony between the two estranged, must come first. Thus, the offender may offer acceptable worship to God, and only then is it possible. It is imperative that **the two be reconciled.** Jesus has plainly taught that the one who is offended is to forgive (Matthew 18:21-22).

The meaning of the word reconcile is easily understood in this passage. Possibly we have known of men who have been at variance with one another and have had sufficient regard for God's law to be reconciled, and harmony has thus been re-established between the two. Perhaps in your own experience you can recall times when you offended someone. If you have done so, may we ask, Have you corrected the matter and been reconciled to your brother? If you, my friend, are a Christian, may I especially impress you with the necessity of this responsibility? The Bible teaches that harmony and peace should prevail in all of our dealings with one another, inasmuch as is humanly possible. In Romans 12:18, Paul says, "If it be possible, as much as lieth in you, live peaceably with all men." There should be peace and harmony in our families, with our neighbors, and certainly, above all things, with our fellow Christians.

Men need to be reconciled to God. Paul says in 2 Corinthians 5:20, "Be ye reconciled to God." The word reconcile in this passage means the same as in Matthew 5:23-24. It means "to bring together again, to bring back peace and harmony, to unite again." Thus, Paul's exhortation is that men should be reunited with God. Whatever may have come between man and God must be removed. The offense **must be forgiven.** In this case, however, there is no doubt as to who the offender is. **Man** is the offender, not God. Man sinned against God and thus was separated from Him. God is the same as He was in the very beginning, and He does not change. He was there in the beginning when He made man, and He blessed him with the fullness of His presence. In the Garden of Eden, Adam was in communion with God and God's blessings were upon Adam. But Adam and Eve disobeyed God; and because of their sin, they were separated from the garden that God had provided—sin has been separating men from God since that day. There is no generation in which that has not occurred. Isaiah writes, "Behold, the Lord's hand is not shortened, that it cannot save; neither his ear heavy, that it cannot hear: But your iniquities have separated between you and your God, and your sins have hid his face from you, that he will not hear" (Isaiah 59:1-2). Again may I re-emphasize, **man is the offender.** Man has sinned against God. It is man who needs to correct his fault and be reconciled to God. This truth needs to be deeply planted in our hearts. Paul's exhortation is to each one of us today, even as to those at Corinth, **"Be ye reconciled to God."**

I want you to think for a moment of the great need for reconciliation. Isaiah says that sin separates men from God and that separation results in the condemnation of each individual sinner. Ezekiel, the prophet, says, "The soul that sinneth, it shall die" (Ezekiel 18:4, 20). The separation (and thus condemnation) is placed on the basis of **each individual.** We are not separated as a whole because of Adam's sin, nor because of the sin of our parents, nor at the time of our birth, but each man is individually separated by his own sin. The Bible says, "The soul that sinneth, it, shall die." Death is a result of sin, and the death of which the prophet wrote is spiritual death or eternal death.

Paul also teaches in Romans 6:23, "For the wages of sin is death." James, also directed by the Holy Spirit, writes in James 1:15, "And sin, when it is finished, bringeth forth death." Thus, sin not only separates the sinner from God now; but unless the sinner is reconciled to God, that sin will result in his eternal separation from God or his eternal spiritual death after this life is over. So, the need for reconciliation is universal. All men need to be reconciled to God.

In Romans 3:23 Paul says, "For all have sinned, and come short of the glory of God." Every single one of us—each individual accountable being—stands in need of God's plan for reconciliation. Not one, who is old enough and accountable, can say that he doesn't need this lesson. It is applicable to all, and each man must answer for himself. Therefore, this question should be uppermost in our minds today: **How can we be reconciled to God?**

First, I will point out that God has a plan for our reconciliation, and that plan of reconciliation is through Christ. Paul says, "God was in Christ, reconciling the world unto himself" (2 Corinthians 5:19). Verse 18 says, "And all things are of God, who hath reconciled us to himself by Jesus Christ." In Colossians, Paul writes about how God's plan is through Christ:

> Having made peace through the blood of his cross, by him to reconcile all things unto himself; by him, I say, whether they be things in earth, or things in heaven. And you, that were sometimes alienated and enemies in your mind by wicked works, yet now hath he reconciled In the body of his flesh through death, to present you holy and unblameable and unreprovable in his sight (Colossians 1:20-22).

This is the plan of God for all, both Jews and Gentiles. In Ephesians 2:16-17, Paul states, "That he might reconcile both unto God in one body by the cross, having slain the enmity thereby: And came and preached peace to you which were afar off, and to them that were nigh." No man, it is evident, can be reconciled to God except through Jesus Christ. The death of Christ on the cross of Calvary was necessary to make possible our reconciliation. Thus, Christ has become the one and only great high priest, "a merciful and faithful high priest in things pertaining to God, to make reconciliation for the sins of the people" (Hebrews 2:17).

Peter writes concerning how Christ bore our sins "in his own body on the tree, that we, being dead to sins, should live unto righteousness: by whose stripes ye were healed" (1 Peter 2:24). Paul writes, "We pray you in Christ's stead, be ye reconciled to God. For he hath made him to be sin for us, who knew no sin; that we might be made the righteousness of God in Him" (2 Corinthians 5:20-21).

The gospel teaches us the plan of God. It teaches us how to be reconciled to God. Paul speaks of it, in fact, the totality of it. He calls it the "word of reconciliation" (2 Corinthians 5:19). By our obedience to the gospel, our sins may be remitted that we can be reconciled to God. Jesus taught His apostles saying, "Go ye into all the world, and preach the gospel to every creature. He that believeth and is baptized shall be saved; but he that believeth not shall be damned" (Mark 16:15-16). Jesus commanded men to repent, saying, "Except ye repent, ye shall all likewise perish" (Luke 13:3). The gospel tells us how "Christ died for our sins according to the scriptures; and that he was buried, and that he rose again the third day according to the scriptures" (1 Corinthians 15:3-4). As men believe in the death, burial, and resurrection of Christ, they are commanded to repent of their sins and to be baptized for the remission of their sins. The need for such, I think, is apparent. How could we be reconciled to a God in whom we do not believe? How could we be reconciled through a

Christ in whom we have no faith? How could we be saved from sins from which we are not willing to turn? How could we be cleansed from those sins which separate us from God if we are not willing to be buried with our Lord in baptism—"baptized into Jesus Christ" (Romans 6:3-4)—for the purpose of coming into contact with His blood that was shed for the remission of our sins (Matthew 26:28)?

God has promised the continued forgiveness of sins to His children, saying through John, "If we walk in the light, as he is in the light, we have fellowship one with another, and the blood of Jesus Christ his Son cleanseth us from all sin" (1 John 1:7). It is by our continued obedience to the gospel and our living for Christ in our faithful work and worship to God that we continue to be reconciled to God. These steps are not too difficult to understand, and they are not too hard for us to obey. Our being reconciled to God rests upon this great fact.

Do you want to be reconciled to God? Or, to word it differently, **do we love God enough to obey Him that we can be reconciled to Him,** both for the present and for all eternity? Each person must decide for himself. May I make the question as personal as I know how: My friend, as you listen today, do you want to be reconciled to God?

> Do you really want that sin that separates you from God to be removed through your obedience to the gospel of Christ?
>
> Have you believed in Christ?
>
> Have you repented of your sins?
>
> Have you been baptized into Christ?

Remember, it is in Christ that God is reconciling the world unto Himself. "Therefore if any man be in Christ, he is a new creature: old things are passed away; behold, all things are become new" (2 Corinthians 5:17). No one else can be reconciled for you. You must decide for yourself. You must obey God's plan that you may answer Paul's commands, "Be ye reconciled to God." God is waiting and God is ready to receive you. The cross of Christ has spanned the gulf between sinful man and a righteous God. Jesus says, "Come unto me." The decision must be your own individual decision.

Let me suggest these additional points. To be reconciled in Christ is to be a Christian. It means that you must be His follower. And to be in Christ is to be in the church. You cannot be reconciled unto God unless you are willing to be in the church that our Lord established. We must understand these conclusions. When a person is reconciled to God, it is through Christ; and to be reconciled through Christ, it must be through obedience to the "word of reconciliation," the gospel of Christ.

To obey the gospel of Christ makes a person a Christian and a member of the Lord's church, which is the family of God. As a faithful child in God's family, each Christian becomes an heir of the heavenly promises through Jesus Christ our Lord (Romans 8:17). The Lord requires of each of us faithful living—godly living—devoted service, and worship throughout our lives. So, indeed, it is as Paul would say, "We pray ye in Christ's stead, **be ye reconciled to God."**

Good for Evil

Ladies and gentlemen, we invite your attention this morning to a subject that we would simply call "good for evil." But especially, we would like to emphasize the fact that we are to overcome evil, and the Lord teaches that we shall overcome evil with good. One of the hardest lessons in life to learn is to return good for evil. We are so prone to retaliate, to get even with the one who may say or do something that either insults or injures us in any way. It would rather seem the natural thing to do to seek revenge for the wrongs that are done to us whether by word or by deed. Sometimes we are inclined to do so when actually no wrong was intended by the other person; but we feel that an injustice has been done to us, and we want to "pay him back" as the expression often goes. I would like for you to be reminded today that the Bible sets a much higher standard of life for us than that. It is a standard that will bring us great happiness both for time and for all eternity. Jesus says in Matthew 5:38-39, "Ye have heard that it hath been said, An eye for an eye, and a tooth for a tooth: But I say unto you, That ye resist not evil: but whosoever shall smite thee on thy right cheek, turn to him the other also." God has never taught the spirit or the practice of retaliation whereby we do injury for injury. Jesus used one of the most common modes of insult—that of slapping a man on the face—to illustrate how the Christian should meekly endure wrong—even a second wrong—rather than to resist evil with evil.

The life of Jesus exemplifies this teaching. Peter pointed out how we ought to follow His example "who, when he was reviled, reviled not again; when he suffered, he threatened not; but committed himself to him that judgeth righteously" (1 Peter 2:23). So often in our Lord's ministry this truth can be seen, but how plain it is during the time of His trial just before He was taken to be crucified. You recall that the Bible records that they mocked Him, and they slapped Him, and they spit upon Him, and they beat Him. And though He could have called upon His Heavenly Father for legions of angels, yet He answered not a word; but He endured the pain and the shame even to the point of death. And He left us this tremendous example that Peter says we should follow "in his steps."

I want you to think of this text that is found in the Holy Scripture:

> Dearly beloved, avenge not yourselves, but rather give place unto wrath: for it is written, Vengeance is mine; I will repay, saith the Lord. Therefore if thine enemy hunger, feed him; if he thirst, give him drink: for in so doing thou shalt heap coals of fire on his head. Be not overcome of evil, but overcome evil with good (Romans 12:19-21).

This is God's plan for us today. "Be not overcome of evil, but overcome evil with good." This was the plan for Christians in Rome 1,900 years ago. It is the plan for us today. It is the way the Lord taught that His people will conduct themselves. It is our path of overcoming evil.

We can overcome evil with good. When injury comes to you, don't resist it with evil, but overcome the evil by returning good in its place. The Bible teaches that evil doing is always condemned. I realize that we live in times when people are trying to find a way out and are trying to say that the end will justify whatever the means may happen to be, but I would like to point out that it has always been wrong to do evil. Our Lord is saying that it will never be right to do wrong. "The face of the Lord is against them that do evil" (1 Peter 3:12). 1 Thessalonians 5:22 says, "Abstain from every form of evil" (American Standard Version). In Romans 12:17, we have this admonition: "Recompense to no man" ... NO MAN ... "evil for evil." We are not to do wrong even if we think that through wrong doing, good may result. It will never be right to do wrong. In Romans 3:8, we read how some say, "Let us do evil, that good may come" but the Apostle Paul says of them, "whose damnation is just." So no matter what the motive may be that would prompt us to do evil, the evil doing is always condemned. We should hold before us the fact that evil is sin "and sin, when it is finished, bringeth forth death" (James 1:15). In Romans 6:23, Paul says, "For the wages of sin is death." And the death of which the apostle speaks is death for the soul ... eternal death ... if, indeed, sin be not repented of and forgiven. Let us never do evil for the sake of evil, nor evil in return for evil, nor evil that good may come. But let us strive to do good at all times; and when others do evil to us, let us do good to them in return for evil and so overcome. We will overpower evil with good. There is a continuous war that wages in this world between the forces of right and the forces of wrong. This situation has been true for thousands and thousands of years. There is a war that exists between good and evil within your very breast at this moment.

I would like for us to be reminded that God is good. In Psalm 100:5, "For the Lord is good; his mercy is everlasting; and his truth endureth to all generations." All the works of God partake of His nature. When in the beginning God created all things we are told again and again how God looked upon each part of His creation and "God saw that it was good" (Genesis 1). "God created man in his own image" (Genesis 1:27); and God wants man to carry on His work for good by doing good and being good under every circumstance. God is good, but it is equally true that Satan is evil. He is the one who brought evil into the world; his forces are always at work. He is the enemy of all that is righteous and all that is good. The devil's influence is ever great, and it is tremendously powerful so much so that Paul says, "When I would do good, evil is present with me" (Romans 7:21). Therefore, we must remember to be as Peter says:

> Be sober, be vigilant; because your adversary the devil, as a roaring lion, walketh about, seeking whom he may devour: Whom resist stedfast in the faith, knowing that the same afflictions are accomplished in your brethren that are in the world (1 Peter 5:8-9).

Good must be triumphant, and good will be victorious; of that fact there is no doubt. God will help us to be victorious in doing good. "For the eyes of the Lord are over the righteous, and his ears are open unto their prayers" (1 Peter 3:12). His strength and His help will be ours as by obedient faith we serve Him. John says, "This is the victory that overcometh the world, even our faith" (1 John 5:4).

It takes courage to do good. Whether it is you as an adult out on the job or in the office or on the farm, or whether it be you as a young person in school or on your job—whatever the case may be—it takes a great amount of courage to do good. More courage is demonstrated in standing against evil than in following the course of least resistance and letting evil overcome us. It takes a strong person—it takes a concerned, convicted person—to stand in this day for that which is good.

The Bible teaches us that the forces of evil outnumber those of good on many occasions. And it takes great moral courage to say with

Jonathan of so long ago: "There is no restraint to the Lord to save by many or by few" (1 Samuel 14:6). As the Lord gave the courageous Jonathan victory over the Philistines, so He can give us the victory over evil in whatever form it may present itself. The question for us is, Do we have the courage to trust in God, the One who can make good overcome evil? David, a man without sword or armour, went out against the giant, Goliath, who had defied the people of God. You remember that as a shepherd lad with his sling and five smoothe stones and a heart full of faith in the great Jehovah, he went out against Goliath. He says, "I come to thee in the name of the Lord of hosts, the God of the armies of Israel, whom thou hast defied." I think this proclamation is beautiful. He says further, "The battle is the Lord's" (1 Samuel 17:45-47). The Bible simply concludes that God gave deliverance to Israel that day. It's a great day—it's a delivering day—when any person, young or old, decides he will have the courage that God supplies and will stand up and say to the world that this is right and this is wrong and I will stand for the right and not tolerate the wrong.

The Christian is not armed with any implement of war, not even David's sling, but with the Christian's armour. His sword is the "sword of the Spirit, which is the word of God" (Ephesians 6:13-18). His battle is against evil on every hand, against principalities, against powers, against spiritual wickedness in high places. The Lord is at our side as we strive to overcome evil by doing good. Returning good for evil calls for the very best qualities we have; I think we are all aware of that. It is easy to salute those who love us. It is easy to love the loveable. It is easy to do things when there are no problems; but there are times when it seems that life tumbles in and we come against some strong forces and influences and we are faced with this matter of returning good when plainly evil has been done to us.

Not only must we believe in the ultimate triumph of good and the condemnation of all kinds of evil and that God can give us the victory but we must put into practice the necessary Christian qualities to reach that end. These are things that are very practical—things that we must deal with TODAY. Let's consider some of these. First of all, if we are going to face the onslaught of the world and have a great deal of Christian courage and we are going to overcome evil with good, WE MUST HAVE LOVE. We must have more than the standard to love them which love us, Jesus says, "LOVE YOUR ENEMIES." Please notice this is not a suggestion. Our Lord is not indicating that it is something that would be good for us on certain occasions. He is simply saying:

> Love your enemies, bless them that curse you, do good to them that hate you, and pray for them which dispitefully use you, and persecute you; That ye may be the children of your Father which is in heaven (Matthew 5:44-45).

Now you will notice this is not simply a negative thing. Our Lord did not simply say, "Love your enemies," He says "Bless them that curse you." He didn't say turn your back on these individuals and say, "I can live without them; I'll try to forget it." He says be positive—"Bless them that curse you." And when you find an individual that hates you for being what you are as a Christian and for standing for what is right, you shouldn't simply go your way and let him go his. He says "Do good" ... DO GOOD—something POSITIVE to be done ... "to them that hate you, and pray for them which despitefully use you, and persecute you." This is going to take a new brand of love from that which most of us possess. Our love must be strong; but by loving men, we can accomplish these things. Even our enemies have souls that need to be saved. We should love them and by expressing that love in our actions in return for their mistreatment we may—we just may—be able to cause them to turn to God for their salvation.

Not only must we have love, we must learn to forgive others. When they do wrong to us, we must be ready and able to forgive. I will assure you that many have never learned this lesson. Jesus says our own forgiveness is based upon our forgiving others. He says, "If ye forgive men their trespasses, your heavenly Father will also forgive you: But if you forgive men not their trespasses, neither will your Father forgive your trespasses" (Matthew 6:14-15). It is just that simple, and it is just that difficult. This is not impossible as some would have you believe by the lives they live. Each one of us CAN forgive. We may not do so; but the fact is, we have the capability of doing it if we really want to. The only reason we are going to really want to is that we have a love for the "Wrong Doer"—not a love for his wrong doing but a love for the "Wrong Doer," that we may bring him to Christ.

I want you to think of the example of Jesus. Our Lord was not one who simply lays out some theoretical statements—some ideological things—and says here is what you really ought to do and here is the manifesto of the kingdom of God, but He was one who sets us a living example of these things. Even after they had nailed our Lord to the cross, He prays, "Father, forgive them; for they know not what they do" (Luke 23:34). Men have not been that evil to you or to me. If I am mistaken, please let me know; but I think I can safely say that you have not been so treated. I will assure you that people have not been that evil to me. Can we pray for those who do us wrong? Our injuries are so small compared to what they did to our Lord. Stephen's prayer for his persecutors is very similar. They seized him and cast him out of Jerusalem and stoned him to death. When he was about to die, he called upon God saying, "Lord, lay not this sin to their charge. And when he had said this, he fell asleep" (Acts 7:60). I think I am speaking to individuals who have had wrong done to you, or at least something that you construed to be wrong, but I will assure you that no body has ever treated you in such a fashion as this. These were people who lost their lives and yet they were praying, "Father, forgive them; for they know not what they do." Why can't we forgive the smaller deeds and words of those who would injure us?

Thirdly, we must leave vengeance to God. We must learn that God knows best how to punish the wicked. He will give them the right and just punishment which they deserve. "Vengeance is mine, I will repay saith the Lord," but all too often we want to see the offender punished immediately. We want to take the matter into our own hands; so we try to return injury for injury and wrong for wrong, and we fight fire with fire. We are not willing to wait for God to accomplish His justice nor are we willing to recognize for others the nature of God that has meant our very salvation. God "is longsuffering to USWARD," the Bible says, "not willing that any should perish, but that all should come to repentance" (2 Peter 3:9). And, brother, believe me, today we need somebody to be long suffering to us; for without His grace and without His mercy, we would be nothing. We would simply be without God and without hope in the world. God "is not willing that any should perish, but that ALL"—not just us—"but that ALL should come to repentance" (2 Peter 3:9). God's long suffering has meant our salvation, if indeed we are Christians. And His longsuffering toward the one who has wronged us may mean his salvation some day, especially so if we are willing to do our part in trying to overcome evil with good.

Have you ever thought about the fact that if a person has wronged you, you stand in a tremendous position that you have never had before? You stand in a position to reach out to the soul of that man as a Christian and with a Christian power and a Christian influence that you never possessed before. Have you ever thought of it in that light? When someone does you a wrong of some kind, let God take care of the punishment. We don't need to jot it down in our book so we will be sure and remember it, or simply to bide our time until we can pay him back. We must learn to forgive through love and leave the result to the Lord. Please remember He says, "Vengeance is MINE." God will take care of it. What a terrible mess we make, what a horrible web we weave when we try to take the Lord's place in bringing vengeance upon some soul. Our Lord will do what is right and He will do what is best. We may do neither.

The Bible teaches us that we must not only have love and be willing to forgive others and leave vengeance to God, but it also teaches that we must return good for evil. Do you know why? One of the best reasons in the world is that He says such action will make us like God. The scripture says, "He maketh his sun to rise on the evil and the good, and sendeth rain on the just and on the unjust" (Matthew 5:45). We should consider God's disposition toward us. If He gave us according to what we deserve, we would have been cut off a long time ago, wouldn't we? Even now, would not the abundance of His blessings be withheld from us? Would to God that we would never see the day that God would give us what we deserve. For we are weak and sinful creatures and we should think about doing good to both the good and the evil.

We should return good for good; and we should return good for evil. This is a new concept in this world of ours—both when it was introduced and even until this very moment. This is one of the great needed lessons of our generation. We need it every day we live. We don't just need this on Sunday morning. We need it on Monday morning and Monday night and every moment of our lives. The world needs it so there will be more kindness and love instead of bitterness and hate and war. The church needs this lesson so we may overcome the evil in the world and show greater love to one another. Think of the blessings it would bring. Think of the peace it would bring to our own soul. Think of the forgiveness of our own sins. Think how the practice of this teaching would break down the evils in the hearts of men, and love and tenderness and compassion would rein in the dealings we have one with another. Think of the happiness for our souls when they are filled with love and good instead of hate and evil.

Remember, our eternal destiny rests upon our recognition of and our obedience to this great command of God. Eternal souls are to be considered.

Paul reminds us that "the goodness of God leadeth thee to repentance" (Romans 2:4). If the goodness of God is what led US to repentance, is it not true then that our goodness, through Christ, may cause them to consider the goodness of God and thus lead THEM to repentance?

Are you a Christian, my friend? Have you considered what all God has done for you? Have you counted the blessings you receive from Him every day that you live? Are you aware of how much He has loved you and how Christ died for you on Calvary? Have you loved Him enough to obey His gospel? Jesus says, "He that believeth and is baptized shall be saved" (Mark 16:16). Have you done that? Have you obeyed Him in these commands? Are you living for Christ every day and every hour? Are you worshiping and serving Him with all the devotion of your life? Is Christ the pattern for your life and His word the means by which you are fashioning your life? Surely these are things we ought to consider. Every day we live we stand nearer the valley of the shadow of death and thus nearer the judgment bar of God. Think about it. What a grand concept and what a lovely thing that we can be a part of this great principle that is at work in the world of returning good for evil.

Faithfulness

Good morning, everyone. Today we would like to study with you on the necessity of being faithful. There are many challenging statements in the Bible; one of these is found in the second chapter of Revelation. It is a part of the message of the Spirit to the church at Smyrna. "Be thou faithful unto death, and I will give thee a crown of life" (Revelation 2:10). I think it would be best for us to observe the setting of these words. John the Revelator gives the message of the Spirit to this church saying:

> I know thy works, and tribulation, and poverty, (but thou art rich) and I know the blasphemy of them which say they are Jews, and are not, but are the synagogue of Satan. Fear none of those things which thou shalt suffer: behold, the devil shall cast some of you into prison, that ye may be tried; and ye shall have tribulation ten days: be thou faithful unto death, and I will give thee a crown of life. He that hath an ear, let him hear what the spirit saith unto the churches; He that overcometh shall not be hurt of the second death (Revelation 2:9-11).

The desire of the Spirit was for the Christians at Smyrna to be faithful. They had many, many things to hinder them. They had tribulation and poverty and blasphemy and sufferings and were faced with even more of these things plus being cast into prison. In view of these hindrances, comes that exhortation, "Be thou faithful unto death." I want you to notice the extent of the faithfulness that is desired of both those ancient Christians and of you and me today. The words are "be thou faithful UNTO death." It means, be faithful even to the extent of or even to the point of death. Even though we must give our own lives and die in order to be faithful, that is what should be. No matter how severe our trials, we are encouraged to be faithful. Sometimes this passage has been misread, and the word "until" has been supplied in the place of "unto," making the passage read, "be thou faithful until death." But the word in the text is "unto," meaning—be faithful to the Lord, even though you must die as a result of your faithfulness.

Other passages of scripture declare the consistent and continuous faith that a Christian should possess. Jesus says, "but he that endureth unto the end shall be saved" (Matthew 10:22). The exhortation Paul gives in 1 Corinthians 15:58 is, "Therefore, my beloved brethren, be ye steadfast, unmovable, always abounding in the work of the Lord, forasmuch as ye know that your labor is not in vain in the Lord." The words of our Master in regard to the man who had used his talents properly are found in Matthew 25:21. Christ the Judge declares: "Well done, thou good and faithful servant: thou hast been faithful over a few things, I will make thee ruler over many things: enter thou into the joy of thy lord." These passages illustrate the many exhortations to faithfulness that are given in the New Testament. They are written to Christians of our day, even as to those of centuries past. Each child of God is encouraged to be faithful every day of his life—to endure whatever trials he may encounter and then even to the extent or to the point of death itself.

Let us consider the example of Jesus. "Though he were a Son, yet learned he obedience by the things which he suffered" (Hebrews 5:8). Christ was faithful to the Heavenly Father. Philippians 2:8 declares, "He humbled himself, and became obedient unto death, even the death of the cross." The Lord prayed in the Garden of Gethsemane, saying, "Father, if thou be willing, remove this cup from me: nevertheless, not my will, but thine, be done" (Luke 22:42). Thus, Christ drank the cup of suffering and was faithful even unto death. Are we better than our Master? He suffered untold things at the hand of His enemies; He endured hardships in obedience to the Father, and then He suffered death itself upon Calvary. Can we be faithful to the Christ, even as He was faithful to the Father? Men of our day often allow little hinderances and little criticisms and persecutions—the most negligible things—to cause them to be unfaithful. Certainly we should this day be ashamed to be careless or negligent or unfaithful in the service of our Lord. We should never complain about how hard it is for us to be faithful when we consider the price He paid for us.

I would like for you to think today, for your encouragement and for the exhortation, of others who suffered. Stephen was the first to die for his faith in Christ. In Acts 7, they stoned him to death because he was faithful. In Acts 12:2, we read how Herod killed James the brother of John with a sword. This was the Apostle James, the son of Zebedee. He died a martyr's death because of his faith in Christ. One by one the other apostles, except John, were put to death as martyrs because of their faith. Let me ask the question: Are we better than they? If they could suffer even unto death, can't we be faithful under the ordinary circumstances of our lives today as we endeavor to live for Christ?

It was in this same city of Smyrna, to which the message of our text was written, that a man by the name of Polycarp lived. He was a disciple of John, who wrote the book of Revelation, as we understand it. Tradition says that he served as a bishop in the church of Smyrna. He knew the need for faithfulness to Christ. It is said he established a school in which he spent much of his time training men to be teachers of God's word. But his enemies, the enemies of the cause of Christ, sought to put him to death even as they had so many others. Eusebius, the church historian, tells us how they bound him to the stake and then asked him to recant and revile Christ and they would release him. But when they asked him to recant and revile Christ, Polycarp replied, "Eighty and six years have I served Him, and He never did me wrong. How can I now blaspheme my King that has saved me?" His enemies threatened him with fire, I understand, and Polycarp answered, "You threaten fire that burns for a moment and is extinguished; for you know nothing of the judgment to come and the fire of eternal punishment reserved for the wicked. But, why do you delay? Bring what you wish." Clasping his hands behind him, he prayed as his executioners kindled the fire that was to take his life. Polycarp was only one of multiplied thousands of early Christians who died because of their faith in Christ as the Son of God.

Why were those Christians ... answer me this ... why were THOSE Christians willing to suffer and to die and today we have people who are not even willing to do one thing? Not one word of persecution would they take. The only answer I know is—because they had faith in Christ. They believed in Him as the Son of God. They believed the teachings of Christ; they accepted the promises of eternal life as given by our Lord. Their faith was strong enough to cause them to endure suffering and sacrifices and even to die rather than to be in any way untrue to the Lord who had saved them—who had given them the hope of eternal life.

Many times today people are impressed by the examples of a faith shown in the lives of Bible characters and they marvel at the devotion of the early Christians, but they fail to think of the need of these same principles in the lives of people today—even in your life and in mine.

Let's make this lesson a very up-to-date thing today. Let's make a personal application of it to our own lives. Let's ask these two questions and then find an understandable application. First of all: "What is faith?" Faith may be defined as dependence on the truthfulness of another; as trust in God; as reliance upon the truth of the word of God and the facts and the promises contained therein. To put it plainly, faith is the acceptance of the Bible as the Divine Revelation. Romans 10:17 says, "So then faith cometh by hearing, and hearing by the word of God." Faith in the Bible and in the God of the Bible is more than just a consideration of its teachings and an assent to its truths. It is rather a living principle—listen to me—a living principle that moves the one possessing it to trust in God, to rely upon the Bible promises, and to obey the commands the Bible contains for men today. Thus, James says, "Faith without works is dead" (James 2:17-20). Again, "For as the body without the spirit is dead, so faith without works is dead also" (James 2:26). Many people recognize the truthfulness of the Bible, but they have never learned to trust in its teaching and to obey its commands. They are very much like the statement in James 2:19: "Thou believest that there is one God; thou doest well: the devils also believe, and tremble." We see the importance of faith as a moving force that would lead us to obedience to Christ or we will be no better than the devils who believe ... and tremble.

The second question, "Can we be sure of the truthfulness of the Bible?" I believe today that we can be sure that the Bible is true. There is every form of evidence to support it—both from internal evidence and external evidence. The proof of its truthfulness and accuracy has increased more and more with the years. The discoveries of archeologists as they have unearthed records of the people of the times described in the Bible have correlated every minute detail of things once disputed and thought by critics to be untrue. The findings of science have shown the Bible's statements, once doubted by many, as true and scientifically correct. The facts recorded in the New Testament concerning the life and the work of Christ and His apostles can be verified even from the writings of their enemies. The internal unity of the Bible, the fulfillment of its prophecies, and the accuracy of its record all give their proof of the inspiration of the Holy Spirit who guided the men who wrote its sixty-six books.

The influence of the gospel of Christ upon the lives of men should be proof of the value and the truthfulness of its teaching. The teachings of Christ have changed the lives of men and of nations where ever they have been taught. Lives once filled with sin and doubt have become strong and upright. Men who before were blind to the feelings and the needs of their fellowmen have been filled with mercy and compassion and love.

Faith in God's word has caused men to recognize the dignity and the true value of their own lives and of the lives of those about them. It is the truth of God that brings peace, happiness, and consideration for others. It is faith in God's word that changes men. What greater proof could one desire than this? It really takes little intelligence to follow blindly the assertions of the atheist or the infidel, but the man who uses the intelligence that God has given him can understand the truthfulness and the trustworthiness of the Bible. So, don't let the sarcasm and the ridicule of the enemies of truth cause you to doubt what God has given you. Don't let them rob you of the joy, happiness, comfort, and hope that real genuine faith can give to you.

I want you to think with me for just a moment how essential faith really is. The Bible declares, "But without faith it is impossible to please him: For he that cometh to God must believe that he is, and that he is a rewarder of them that diligently seek him" (Hebrews 11:6). Jesus says, "He that believeth not is condemned already, because he hath not believed in the name of the only begotten Son of God" (John 3:18). Therefore, we must have faith or we will be condemned. It is believe ... or perish. There is no other way. We must decide for ourselves whether we will have faith in God or be lost and be as Paul says "having no hope, and without God in the world" (Ephesians 2:12). So consider what faith can mean to you. Faith is the founding principle of true religion. It is the basis of all our relationship to God and the life on the other side of death. I promise you, it can change your life. It can give you hope instead of despair, it can give you comfort in the dark and trying circumstances that confront you now or will confront you in the future. It can make your life useful to God and others. It can show you how to worship God. It can sustain you in the hour of death and span the valley of the shadow of death. Faith in God's word will let you see the light of heaven's beauty. It can give you the star of hope that will guide you all the way through life, even until you enter that Eternal City.

Faith will lead you to become a Christian. The Bible outlines five steps that are necessary: (1) to hear the gospel of Christ, (2) to have faith in Christ, (3) to repent of your sins, (4) to confess the faith that you have in Christ, and (5) to be buried with your Lord in baptism for the remission of your sins. Thus, by the grace of God you can be saved, and you can begin to live for Christ in a new life dedicated to His service. Faith will not only lead you to become a Christian, faith will cause you to worship God. In Acts 2, we are told how those who had gladly received the word and were baptized continued steadfastly in the apostles' doctrine, and fellowship, in breaking of bread and in prayers.

It is faith that will make your life more like Jesus. The love, the compassion, the purity, the service, the fruitfulness, and the faithfulness of Jesus will all become a part of your life. The mind of Christ, the spirit of Christ, will fill and control the thoughts and the actions of your life. As a part of His body, the church of Jesus Christ, you will have continuous fellowship with Him as your Saviour (1 John 1:7).

Lastly, faith in Christ means faithfulness in all things. Faith, the strong and unfaltering faith that our Lord wants you to possess, will lead you to faithfulness in all the commands that He has given. Nothing will be permitted to intervene or deter or hinder you from placing His service first (Matthew 6:33). Whatever the trials or the difficulties that may come, whatever they are, they will be the means by which faith in Christ will become more precious (James 1:2-4). I promise you that they will refine and purify your life and draw you nearer to Him who suffered death for you. They will help you to learn the promise of God who says, "Be thou faithful unto death, and I will give thee a crown of life."

May we impress upon you this need for faith in the Bible and the need for faithfulness in your life as a Christian? The faith that God wants you to possess will cause you always to be true to Him in every Christian activity, in every part of your life, and at any cost—even "unto death."

Naaman

Ladies and gentlemen, once again we invite your attention to the Holy Scripture. One of the most interesting and remarkable stories of the Old Testament is found in 2 Kings 5. It is the story of the healing of Naaman of his leprosy. Open your Bible and read again this great narrative. The facts here given are not found in any other place in the Holy Scripture. Jesus referred to Naaman in Luke 4:27 saying, "And many lepers were in Israel in the time of Elisha the prophet; and none of them was cleansed, saving Naaman the Syrian." This Old Testament story is of value to us today to help us in understanding the nature of the God that we serve.

Paul says, "For whatsoever things were written aforetime were written for our learning, that we through patience and comfort of the scriptures might have hope" (Romans 15:4). I think it is always interesting to turn back to see those things that were written for us. We should always remember one basic little rule: all of the scripture ... all of the scripture … is written for us. Not all the scripture was written TO us, but I am persuaded that all of it was written FOR us. And as we turn back to those things that were written for our learning and our adominition, we have this story. By seeing the power of God exercised by this prophet of the Old Testament, we can better understand what God can do for us in the New Testament plan of salvation. The simple story of Naaman is fascinating to the child, and it contains many important lessons for all of us, regardless of our age.

First, I would like for you to notice Naaman himself. He was captain of the host of the king of Syria. We would say that he was the general over the armies of the king of Syria. Syria at that time was a mighty nation that was located to the northeast of the land of Palestine. Naaman's position was an important one. He was a great man with his master, the King. He was held in high esteem, and the Bible says he was honorable. He was elevated to his place as one who deserved honor, respect, and regard. It was by him the Lord had granted deliverance unto the Syrians because he had led them to victory over their enemies. Naaman was also a mighty man of valor, meaning that he was brave, courageous, and heroic. What could a man in his position desire more? He held this high office; he had the favor of the king; he had honor in victory; he was a man of great distinction. No doubt the people of the whole kingdom looked upon him as one of the greatest of the realm and had pride in him as their great leader.

But the scripture says, “But he was a leper.” Therefore, all of his success could not mean happiness. For somewhere upon his body was that loathsome and most humiliating disease of leprosy from which there was no cure. Gradually it would spread and afflict the whole body of this mighty soldier. How terrible an affliction it was can be seen and realized only by a study of the nature of leprosy. Often the affected parts of the skin became wrinkled and scaley and then broke into running sores, and the dead flesh began to fall off the remaining portions. The joints became swollen and stiff, and the leper lived in continuous, extreme pain and suffering. So dreaded was the disease that God directed His people to separate the lepers and have no contact with them. As they begged for help, they stood far off and cried, “unclean, unclean” (Leviticus 13:45).

What could all of Naaman’s attainments mean to him when his body was so afflicted with such an incurable disease—one that would gradually bring him more suffering and inevitably ... death. He would be willing to do almost anything or go almost any place to rid his body of this most painful disease. Just like men today who are faced with such physical distress, he was ready to go to any extreme for the healing of his body. He was desperate, and his condition seemed hopeless. He knew not where to turn or what to do. AH! But the scripture says there was a little maid from Israel there.

The Syrians had gone out by companies and had brought away captive out of the land of Israel a little maid, and she waited on Naaman’s wife. She was from among the people of God and was a captive maid, a slave in a distant land. But she knew God, and she knew the prophet of God. She had faith in God’s power to save: He was the one whom she served. You recall that she said to her mistress, Naaman’s wife, “Would God **my** Lord were with the prophet that is in Samaria! for he would recover him of his leprosy,” Had this little maid not had the upbringing of godly people, Naaman would have died with his leprosy. Had she not spoken of the faith she had, he would not have received help. So often we fail in this hour of golden opportunity, but she used hers. She was but a child, but she was faithful to her God, and the Syrians believed her. “And one went in and told his lord, saying, Thus and thus said the maid that is of the land of Israel." So her message was known by the king of Syria, and he wanted to help the captain of his armies, but he didn't understand fully. He said:

> Go to, go, and I will send a letter unto the king of Israel. And he departed, and took with him ten talents of silver, and six thousand pieces of gold, and ten changes of raiment. And he brought the letter to the king of Israel, saying, Now when this letter is come unto thee, behold, I have therewith sent Naaman my servant to thee, that thou mayest recover him of his leprosy (2 Kings 5:5-6).

The little maid had spoken concerning the prophet, not the king of Israel. But the king of Syria and Naaman did not understand God's ways.

> And it came to pass," the Bible says, "when the king of Israel had read the letter, that he rent his clothes, and said, Am I God, to kill and make alive, that this man doth send unto me to recover a man of his leprosy? wherefore consider, I pray you, and see how he seeketh a quarrel against me (2 Kings 5:7).

However, when Elisha, the prophet, heard of these things, he sent unto the king saying, "… let him come now to me, and he shall know that there is a prophet in Israel. So Naaman came with his horses and with his chariot, and stood at the door of the house of Elisha" (2 Kings 5:8-9).

Now, Naaman was mistaken about many, many things. First of all, may I point out, that he went to the wrong place? God had chosen to show His power in humble circumstances, not in the palace of the king. The prophet, not the king, possessed the power of God to heal him of his leprosy. Secondly, Naaman wanted a display. He carried many gifts. The talents of silver alone were worth at least $40,000, I understand. And the six thousand pieces of gold were valued even more, besides the expensive changes of raiment. The way of God, however, is not one of a display of material wealth. The gift of God can never be purchased with money. Neither Naaman nor his royal master knew that healing was the gift of God—and that the gift of God cannot be bought with money. Many people today have never learned this lesson. Thirdly, Naaman was mistaken, not only about going to the wrong place and wanting to make a display, but the main thing is Naaman wanted HIS way. He had already reasoned how this situation would occur. He said, "He will surely come out to me, and stand, and call on the name of the Lord his God, and strike his hand over the place, and recover the leper." Now Naaman was an idolatrous man. He didn't know that the true God had His own way and that it was the way of humility, not of pride. Isaiah spoke of the difference in God's ways and man's ways saying, "For my thoughts are not your thoughts, neither are your ways my ways, saith the Lord. For as the heavens are higher than the earth, so are my ways higher than your ways, and my thoughts than your thoughts" (Isaiah 55:8-9). In the New Testament, the Apostle Paul puts it like this:

> But God hath chosen ... notice the past tense ... God HATH CHOSEN the foolish things of the world to confound the wise; and God HATH CHOSEN the weak of the world to confound the things which are mighty; And base things of the world, and things which are despised, hath God chosen, yea, and things which are not, to bring to naught the things that are" (1 Corinthians 1:27-28).

WHY? Why did God choose the "foolish things? "That no flesh should glory in his presence (1 Corinthians 1:29).

Naaman had to learn to recognize the way of God. God's way is one of obedience and one of submission and of humility. Think how different it was to what Naaman expected. Elisha didn't go out to this man who thought himself so important. Rather, Elisha sent a messenger out unto him saying, "Go and wash in Jordan seven times, and thy flesh shall come again to thee, and thou shalt be clean." Just like that!! And Naaman was angry. So often people get angry at the simple commands of God and especially when they can't have their own way. And Naaman said, "Are not Abana and Pharpar, rivers of Damascus, better than all the waters of Israel? May I not wash in them, and be clean?" They were clear sparkling rivers that flowed from a copious and pure fountain above Damascus. And the Jordan was a muddy and unsightly stream." And the Bible says, "so he turned and went away in a rage" (2 Kings 5:12).

But anger at God doesn't do any good. It will not cleanse. It will not save. No man's greatness or power or honor or position or rank or nationality or valor will avail before God. God is no respecter of persons. All men alive must obey Him. This is the point: there is only one thing that avails with God, and it is faith and obedience to His will. All men must obey Him to be healed or to be saved. Peter says, "Of a truth I perceive that God is no respecter of persons: But in every nation he that feareth him, and worketh righteousness, is accepted with him" (Acts 10:34-35).

Naaman had to learn this lesson. He had to learn to obey God. Therefore, we read:

> His servants came near, and spake unto him, and said, My father, if the prophet had bid thee do some great thing, wouldest thou not have done it? How much rather then, when he saith to thee, Wash, and be clean? (2 Kings 5:13).

Now this is a hard lesson for Naaman. It is a hard lesson not only for Naaman, but it is hard for us to learn. God does not ask the impossible of men. He never has. His commands are all simple and easy and can be obeyed. His power is not dependent upon big display or large cathedrals or classic creeds or lengthy liturgies and ceremonies. And how wonderful it would be if men would come to recognize that God's way is plain and understandable and just as simple as His commands here through this prophet. What is the conmand? "Wash and be clean" ... that is all! That is how simple the command was. Men must learn to obey God, and Naaman found that he was no exception. It doesn't matter to God who you are or what you possess or what you are expecting. Finally, Naaman was convinced, you recall, and he went down and dipped himself seven times in Jordan, according to the saying of the man of God. And his flesh came again like the flesh of a little child, and he was clean. Naaman had to obey God fully. He dipped seven times, and THEN he was cleansed. Once or twice or even more did not bring the cleansing. But when he had fully obeyed the saying of the prophet of God, he was clean.

Don't you suppose that Naaman looked at his flesh each time after he had dipped to see if he was clean? I don't know that, but I have often wondered if he didn't look down to see the leper's scales still there. He dipped the second time and looked down and the scales were still there. And the third time ... and the fourth time ... every time expecting a cleansing. But like the blind man of John 9 whom Jesus sent to the pool of Siloam who says, "I went and washed and I received my sight," the healing was divine; he was healed when he washed his eyes. So Naaman found that when he washed and had dipped the seventh time he was cleansed from his leprosy. And the result was that Naaman was a happy man. "He returned to the man of God, he and all of his company, and came, and stood before him: and he said, Behold, now I know that there is no God in all the earth, but in Israel: now therefore, I pray thee, take a blessing of thy servant" (2 Kings 5:15). He urged Elisha to take gifts from him, but Elisha refused. And Naaman took some of the dirt of the ground and carried it back to Syria with him.

I want to make this observation: Naaman's cleansing is a beautiful example for us today. His hopeless condition is a picture of the sinner's condition before God. Sin upon a man's soul is like leprosy upon the body. It can be healed only by God. Sin's contagion grows and consumes and eventually brings death. The prophet Ezekiel says, "The soul that sinneth, it shall die" (Ezekiel 18:20). James says, "And sin when it is finished bringeth forth death" (James 1:15). Paul, guided by the same Holy Spirit, says, "For the wages of sin is death" (Romans 6:23). All men are sinners, "for all have sinned and come short of the glory of God" (Romans 3:23). Therefore all of us—listen—all of us, as sinners, are in the condition of need for the saving of our souls. We need healing for our souls, or we will die eternally.

Secondly, may I point out that Naaman's healing was from God? Our salvation is from God: we cannot save our souls. Christ is the great physician. He came to seek and to save the lost (Luke 19:10). He can cleanse us of our sins. We can be saved by the grace of God, but we must recognize that the power is divine and the salvation is not of our merit. We can only do our part: that is, we can do what God teaches.

Thirdly, Naaman obeyed, and he was cleansed. So also we must obey God in order to be saved. In Romans 6:17-18, Paul writes concerning the Romans' obedience: "But God be thanked, that ye were the servants of sin, but ye have obeyed from the heart that form of doctrine which was delivered you. Being THEN"—please notice this—we obey from the heart that form of doctrine ... "being THEN made free from sin, ye became the servants of righteousness." It must be observed that the Romans were made free when they obeyed the form of doctrine—it is equally true today.

Naaman's obedience was simple. He dipped seven times in the Jordan River. Now surely that was not too difficult, and he was able to do just that and be cleansed. And also notice that the obedience of the

Romans was just as simple and as plain as Naaman's. The form of doctrine that God gave to them in Romans 6 was the form of the death, burial, and resurrection of Christ. How could they obey this form? In verse 2, we are told how they died to sin; and in verses 3 and 4, we are told they were baptized into Christ's death. Paul says "therefore we are buried with Him by baptism into death; that like as Christ was raised up from the dead by the glory of the Father, even so we also should walk in newness of life." Now picture this plan in your mind: (1) a death to sin in quitting the practice of sin. (2) a burial in water like Christ was buried for us, and (3) a being raised from the waters of baptism to walk a new life in Christ. This was and is now God's plan. Many other scriptures, of course, could be quoted to show and substantiate this plan.

May I add this point, also? Naaman's cleansing was not from the water but from God. So the cleansing of our soul from sin is not from the water of baptism itself but from God. Nevertheless, Naaman had to follow through with the instruction when he was told to wash to be clean. He had to dip seven times in the River of Jordan to be free, and I propose to you this day that men have to be baptized to be saved. Peter, in 1 Peter 3:21, compares our salvation to the saving of Noah: "the like figure whereunto even baptism doth also now save us." Notice this point carefully. Baptism saves us from sin as we obey God, just as Naaman was cleansed from leprosy when he obeyed God.

The conclusion then is inescapable. We must obey God by being baptized in water in order to be saved from our sins. Many people today react to this command as Naaman first did to the prophet's command. He went away angry. I just wonder, if there is someone listening to me today who is bothered when I quote 1 Peter 3, the words of the Apostle Peter—by the way, they are not mine, they are the Holy Spirit's—"baptism doth also now save us." Does this statement make you angry, that someone is reminding you of the apostle's words? ... and like Naaman of old do we go away saying "May I not do this and may I not do that?" I just want to have the attitude of that servant and say, "If the Lord had asked me to do some great thing, would I not do it? How much rather then would I believe Him when He says, wash and be clean." The Lord expects us to obey His word. And He doesn't give it to us as an option!

I saw the story just recently of a customer who, while shopping in the bargain basement of a store, came to an item that was marked 98¢.

Thinking this price was entirely too high, the customer erased this price and wrote 49¢. He came to another one marked 89¢ and he simply wrote over it 59¢. The customer did this with several articles. At last he came down before the checker with a cart filled with marked down items and the checker began to check. Noticing the changed prices, he remarked, “I am sorry that we priced these items too high for you, I hope the prices you marked on them suits you, for it suits us perfectly.” Now maybe you are ready to say that this is absurd! No clerk in the world would do such a thing.

And I agree with you one hundred percent but the point is that there are thousands and thousands of people who will stand before the Lord in the Day of Judgment with a long list of marked down activities. Instead of regular attendance, they will bring Him irregular attendance (Hebrews 10:25). Instead of liberal giving, they will bring before Him giving that was very sparing (2 Corinthians 9:6). Instead of a steadfast and unmoveable life, they will bring to Him one that was simply indifferent and slothful. Instead of complete obedience, they will bring only partial obedience. Baptism for the remission of sins will be passed over as one of the conditions of pardon ... it will be marked down. Do you honestly think that the Lord will say in the judgment, “I am sorry that I made the requirements of heaven too high for you. What you have done suits me perfectly; pass right on through the gates. Heaven is yours!”

Now if you think this will happen, then I want you to read Matthew 7:21 where He says, “Not everyone that saith unto me Lord, Lord will enter the kingdom of heaven; but he that doeth the will ... .” We must DO IT, and it must be the will of the Father in heaven, or we simply will not enter there. And I trust today that we have learned this lesson of Naaman and listened again to this old, old story, and that you will, today, make up your mind that “I will obey my God, I will be cleansed from my sin.” You don’t have to go to the River Jordan: you can do it right here today. You can obey God TODAY. You can become a Christian, you can be baptized TODAY. Just as the New Testament teaches you to do. Then you can live a Christian life and serve God in all faithfulness as long as you live, giving the Lord the full value of all these marvelous things. We thank you for listening.

Decisions

Ladies and gentlemen, once again we have the privilege of coming into your home to study with you the word of God and for that we are exceedingly grateful. It is a real privilege to live in a country where we have the freedom simply to open up our hearts and our Bibles and declare what we believe with all of our heart to be the word of God.

We are grateful to have you in our audience today and we would invite your attention to the subject that we would simply call "The Importance of Decision Making." From the day the prophets spoke of "multitudes, multitudes in the valley of decision" (Joel 3:14) down to this very present moment, decisions have been extremely important.

When God made man, He gave him the power to think, to reason, and to decide. Man is greater than lower forms of God's creation, first of all, because of the eternal nature of man's soul—he was made in the image of God and he was made for companionship with God and for His service. Secondly, man's superiority is seen in his intellect. God made him with a will so he could exercise the power of decision, choosing which course he would follow and how he would use the abilities and opportunities before him.

Some men develop their ability to make decisions better than others; they have keener insight and stronger wills. They can decide what they should do and apply themselves to the accomplishing of the task. Mr. Hazlitt, the English author, once wrote that there is nothing more to be esteemed than a manly firmness and decision of character. I like a person who knows his own mind and sticks to it—who sees at once what, in given circumstances, is to be done and does it.

Decisions are very personal things. I could not talk to you today about anything more personal than your decisions. Each individual must learn to make his own. For each one must bear the responsibility and the consequences of his decisions—be they right or wrong. Many years ago I read a poem that had two especially impressive lines that say, "You are the one who has to decide, whether you will do it or toss it aside." And through the years I have thought of these words so often. So many decisions have to be made alone as to what you will do and what you will toss aside. You may seek help and you may seek counsel, but eventually the burden of decision must rest upon you. You must decide for YOURSELF, and YOU must be prepared to reap the benefits or pay the penalty of the choice you make. God's word clearly teaches this great point.

There are different kinds of decisions. (1) Some are wrong, either within themselves or in the end to which they lead and the consequences that follow them. (2) Some are right, either because the thing chosen is right or the course of action is upright and honest; or the final result shows the wisdom of the choice. (3) Indecision is actually one type of reaction to decisions. It is often very costly. In being undecided, one may show a weakness of character, let the right thing pass without acceptance. The ability to say yes or no and say it definitely and with certainty may make the difference between happiness or wretchedness both in time and in eternity.

But how should one make decisions? We are all aware that we do make them and must make them; but we wonder how we should make them. It is evident that, first of all, we need to get the facts at hand. We need to acquaint ourselves with what is right and what is wrong—with the advantages and disadvantages of both. Secondly, we need to think it through. Snap judgments may lead to regret, even though we may not realize it at the time. Consider the alternatives. And we must look at more than just the present. The easy course may be unwise. It takes great courage, doesn't it, to say no to something that is appealing or popular or pleasant even when you know it is not best. It is the weak and lazy person who is carried with the current and who fails to look ahead to see the direction in which he is being carried.

And thirdly, we need to seek divine wisdom to guide us. God has promised to help His children. His word teaches that "if any of you lack wisdom, let him ask of God, that giveth to all men liberally, and upbraideth not; and it shall be given him" (James 1:5). Call upon God in prayer. Let Him help you see and understand what is best and right: God knows the end from the beginning. Each one of us needs this wisdom from above. We need divine guidance that comes from a closer walk with God and an understanding of His word. If we follow these three simple rules of getting the facts at hand, of thinking things through, and of seeking wisdom from God in making our decisions, we can be right with God and we can find true happiness.

We must not minimize decisions. The one that you think has little consequence may be really important, and it may change the whole course of your life. If you can take care of the little choices each day, you will be able to make the large ones when they come. But the real index of character often lies in the little choices. Learn to measure each act of your life each day that you live by asking these questions:

Is it right?
Will it do me good?
Will it do others good?
What is the end to which it leads?
Will it please God and make me more like Him?
How will it appear in the day of eternal judgment?

So let us be warned against a wrong decision about the existence of God. David says, "The fool hath said in his heart, There is no God" (Psalm 14:1). His existence and presence and power are manifested in so many ways. "The heavens declare the glory of God" (Psalm 19:1). The marvelous works of nature proclaim His existence; but many who recognize that God IS, ignore Him in their lives. They are so obsessed by the routine and the business of life that they leave out God. They have no time to read His word, no time to serve Him, no time to worship Him, no time for the church that He gave to men for their spiritual blessing and enrichment. They have not learned that "a man's life consisteth not in the abundance of the things which he possesseth" (Luke 12:15). And in seeking after material gain, they have chosen to leave God out of their lives and to deny themselves of the pleasures and joys of God's service.

It is also foolish for us to ignore the fact that sin is always wrong. It will never be right to do wrong. The Bible defines sin saying, "All unrighteousness is sin" (1 John 5:17). God's word teaches the right way to live; and when men choose to violate it, they sin against God. Again we are told "sin is the transgression of the law"—that is, the law of God (1 John 3:4). "Whosoever transgresseth, and abideth not in the doctrine of Christ, hath not God" (2 John 9). It is sin to choose to do what God has not taught, and what He has not authorized either in manner of life or in worship to God or in His service.

God teaches us—listen—God teaches us the value of truth and warns us "lie not one to another" (Colossians 3:9). To speak that which is untrue violates God's law of righteousness. To choose to misrepresent a matter or to become a party to tale bearing would be sinful and should be carefully guarded against.

Honesty is always right. God says, "thou shalt not steal" (Exodus 20:15). To fail to regard the principles of honesty would be wrong no matter what the circumstances might be. Sin satisfies the desires of lust and passion but it is not right with God. He has warned:

> Now the works of the flesh are manifest, which are these; Adultery, fornication, uncleanness, lasciviousness, idolatry, witchcraft, hatred, variance, emulations, wrath, strife, seditions, heresies, envyings, murders, drunkenness, revellings, and such like: of the which I tell you before, as I have also told you in time past, that they which do such things shall not inherit the kingdom of God (Galatians 5:19-21).

In the very next chapter, Galatians 6:7-8, we read, "Be not deceived; God is not mocked: for whatsoever a man soweth, that shall he also reap. For he that soweth to his flesh shall of the flesh reap corruption; but he that soweth to the Spirit shall of the Spirit reap life everlasting."

Wrong decisions are often made on the basis of how popular an evil practice is or whether we can get by with it. But some things are basically wrong and they should never be practiced no matter who does them or how common they may be, even if the whole world does them. If they are wrong, they will never be right for us to do.

You recall that Satan made the temptation in Eden appear appealing. He caused Eve to think the forbidden fruit was good for food, that it was pleasant to the eyes, and that it was a tree to be desired to make one wise, (Genesis 3:6). She decided to yield to the temptation, thus sinning, and then she gave to her husband, Adam, and he sinned; therefore, death came into the world. Since then, wrong decisions have been bringing spiritual death upon all. Ezekiel warns, "the soul that sinneth, it shall die" (Ezekiel 18:4). And we should never forget this fact. In every decision we make today, let us remember this guiding principle "the soul that sinneth, it shall die."

So we must make decisions for right. We must obey God—obedience is always right. Solomon says, "Let us hear the conclusion of the whole matter: Fear God, and keep his commandments: for this is the whole duty of man. For God shall bring every work into judgment, with every secret thing, whether it be good, or whether it be evil" (Ecclesiastes 12:13-14). Place God first in your life. Jesus says, "But seek ye first the kingdom of God and His righteousness" (Matthew 6:33). Your choice of service to God should be the most important decision of your life. The young person should "remember now thy Creator in the days of thy youth, while the evil days come not, nor the years draw nigh, when thou shalt say, I have no pleasure in them" (Ecclesiastes 12:1). Throughout our lives, our greatest desire should be to please God by keeping His commandments.

Some are torn—I suppose at times all of us are torn—between two opinions. We have all come up to the place where we have had to decide whether we will serve God or whether we will not serve Him. You remember in the Old Testament, we have the story about how some were hesitating between the service of God and idolatry. God's prophet Elijah says, "How long halt ye between two opinions? if the Lord be God, follow him: but if Baal, then follow him" (1 Kings 18:21). "If the Lord be God, follow him" … I like that. "And if it be Baal ... follow him." In other words, do not halt between these two things. Make a decision! Notice, if God is God, you should then look into it, get the facts. Determine: if God is God ... serve Him. If Baal is God ... serve him. Get the facts, but do not halt between the two.

You remember, of course, that Elijah went on to show the superiority of God over the 450 false prophets of Baal and their sacrifice, you recall, was not consumed. But the Lord consumed the sacrifice of Elijah in a grand and impressive manner. Jehovah was shown to be the true God and that they should serve Him.

We must remember at all times that God will stand—God will stand in the face of opposition. He stood then against the prophets of Baal, and He has stood against the railings of men through the past. Though they crucified His Son, God raised Him from the tomb. Though they put Him in the earth, God raised Him to heaven and placed Him at His own right hand. The church of our Lord stood against the persecutions and the trials that were heaped upon it and God's name triumphed over all. So make your decision for God. Decide for Christ. He says, "come unto me, all ye that labor and are heavy laden" (Matthew 11:28). You must make this decision: I will go to Him or I will not go to Him. I want you to remember that Jesus Christ loved you, He died upon Calvary for your salvation, and He teaches you "he that believeth and is baptized shall be saved; but he that believeth not shall be damned" (Mark 16:16). And you must decide whether you want to accept Jesus and obey Him or whether you will continue in sin and be lost for all eternity. You must make your decision for the church, which is the kingdom of God; and Jesus says, "seek ye first the kingdom of God, and his righteousness; and all these things shall be added unto you" (Matthew 6:33).

It is so evident that the world is filled with error. Satan's kingdom is powerful. Sectarianism is all around us, but we are pleading with you not to be satisfied with the doctrines and organizations of man. We are pleading with you to make your decision for the New Testament church. Read your New Testament. Learn about the simplicity that is in Christ—the simplicity of the church that Jesus established—and lay aside the ways of men to serve the Lord. These are the decisions that you need to make. In obedience to the gospel of Christ, repent of your sins, be buried with Christ in baptism for the remission of your sins, thus being baptized into Christ and into His church (Romans 6:1-7). Make your decision to live right, to live as a Christian. Satan will always be on hand to tempt you (1 Peter 5:8), but the scripture declares that "God is faithful, who will not suffer you to be tempted above that ye are able; but will with the temptation also make a way to escape, that ye may be able to bear it" (1 Corinthians 10:13).

So be upright, be honest, be truthful, be faithful, and be pure in your everyday life. There is no place in the Christian life for questionable practices and doubtful deeds. It will never be right to do wrong. So beware this day of indecision. Beware of halting between two opinions. Indecision has caused many a person to die outside of Christ. Many have been almost persuaded but could never make up their minds and so lived without Christ and died without God and without hope in the world. Your indecision could cost you heaven, my friend, and it is extremely important that you understand that.

Indecision hinders one from doing his duty to God. It keeps him from doing right. It gives Satan and his forces the advantage, and it will cause one to really and actually be against Christ. Jesus says, "He that is not with me is against me" (Matthew 12:30). Won't you this day make your decision to live for the Lord. Stand no longer in the valley of indecision, but come out as we sometimes sing, "Open wide thine arms of love. Lord, I'm coming home."

The Sin Against the Holy Spirit

Good morning, everyone. One more time we are allowed the privilege of coming to you with a study from God's word. Today we approach a study that has been a source of concern to great numbers of people all down through the ages and over which there has been a great deal of speculation. Our subject for today is "What is the sin against the Holy Ghost?" Do you think people commit this sin today? Before we answer, let us turn and read what Jesus had to say on this subject.

> Then was brought unto him one possessed of the devil, blind, and dumb: and he healed him, insomuch that the blind and dumb both spake and saw. And all the people were amazed, and said, Is not this the son of David? But when the Pharisees heard it, they said, This fellow doth not cast out devils, but by Beelzebub the prince of devils. And Jesus knew their thoughts, and said unto them, Every kingdom divided against itself is brought to desolation; and every city or house divided against itself shall not stand: And if Satan cast out Satan, he is divided against himself; how then shall his kingdom stand? And if I by Beelzebub cast out devils, by whom do your children cast them out? therefore they shall be your judges. But if I cast out devils by the Spirit of God, then the kingdom of God is come unto you. Or else how can one enter into a strong man's house, and spoil his goods, except he first bind the strong man? and then will he spoil his house. He that is not with me is against me; and he that gathereth not with me scattereth abroad. Wherefore I say unto you, All manner of sin and blasphemy shall be forgiven unto men: but the blasphemy against the Holy Ghost shall not be forgiven unto men. And whosoever speaketh a word against the Son of man, it shall be forgiven him: but whosoever speaketh against the Holy Ghost, it shall not be forgiven him, neither in this world, neither in the world to come (Matthew 12:22-32).

The word "blasphemy" as used here in Matthew is the one with which we are most concerned. I might also add that Mark's account of this conversation adds these words of explanation: "Because they said, He hath an unclean spirit" (Mark 3:30). The word "blaspheme" means "to speak to hurt or to speak against." In other words, it means to speak irreverently or with evil intent. There is always the idea of hurt or injury in blasphemy.

The question has been raised and discussed quite at length by scholars as to why all manner of sin would be forgiven except for this particular one. Did Jesus mean that it was of such a nature that God Himself would refuse forgiveness? Or did He mean that one whose heart was so hardened and perverse simply was beyond the bounds of true pentitence? It certainly seems that the heart of one so utterly wicked and degenerate that it would blaspheme the Holy Spirit might be unable to repent. Since God cannot forgive an unrepented sin, there would be no way provided for the salvation of one who was found in such an impentitent state.

It's a fearful thing for man to reject the truth of God. To pervert God's truth is to pervert the words supplied by God's Holy Spirit. In speaking of the divine origin of the scripture, Peter says "holy men of God spake as they were moved by the Holy Ghost" (2 Peter 1:21).

The Apostle Paul also affirms that the apostles' teaching was not "in the words which man's wisdom teacheth, but which the Holy Ghost teacheth" (1 Corinthians 2:13). The Holy Spirit then, gave us our Bible through the agency of prophets and apostles, divinely inspired for that purpose. For one to reject the teaching of the New Testament, then, would be to reject the Holy Spirit. If one dies in this condition, surely he is lost. James admonishes us to "receive with meekness the engrafted word, which is able to save your souls" (James 1:21). To speak **evil** then, of the word of God is to blaspheme the word of the Holy Spirit.

In the scripture, we read that the Pharisees were accusing Christ of casting out demons or devils by the spirit of the devil. This was primarily blasphemy against Christ. For it was attributing to Him an intimate association with evil spirits. It actually constituted a malignant rejection of Christ Himself, meanwhile attributing to Him a wicked purpose against the clearest evidence to the contrary. Now if this was not blasphemy against the Spirit itself, it was the nearest thing to it and served as the occasion to call forth His dire warning concerning this sin.

When we apply the sin of the Pharisees against Christ or the Holy Spirit, we have an accurate definition of this sin. It is, therefore, a willful and persistent rejection of the Spirit of God in its pleading with men through the word. The sin of despising the Holy Spirit is clearly set forth in the Hebrew letter. Let's read it together:

> For it is impossible for those who were once enlightened, and have tasted of the heavenly gift, and were made partakers of the Holy Ghost, And have tasted the good word of God, and the powers of the world to come, If they shall fall away, to renew them again unto repentance; seeing they crucify to themselves the Son of God afresh, and put him to an open shame (Hebrews 6:4-6).

Now this scripture is dealing with the Christian who falls away and becomes an apostate. One who at one time had received the Holy Ghost and had tasted of the heavenly gift but now rejects that salvation that Christ procured, thus in effect crucifying the Son of God afresh and putting Him to an open shame.

This sin, again, is referred to in Chapter 10 of the Hebrew letter wherein we read:

> For if we sin wilfully after that we have received the knowledge of the truth, there remaineth no more sacrifice for sins, But a certain fearful looking for of judgment and fiery indignation, which shall devour the adversaries. He that despised Moses' law died without mercy under two or three witnesses: Of how much sorer punishment, suppose ye, shall he be thought worthy, who hath trodden under foot the Son of God, and hath counted the blood of the covenant, wherewith he was sanctified, an unholy thing, and hath done despite into the Spirit of grace? For we know him that hath said, Vengence belongeth unto me, I will repay (or recompense), saith the Lord. And again, the Lord shall judge his people. It is a fearful thing to fall into the hands of the living God (Hebrews 10:26-31).

This passage again describes the Christian who falls to such a low level of sin that he turns and tramples under foot the Son of God and casts a reproach upon the precious blood by which at one time he was sanctified.

But someone might say that such a thing would seem very unlikely. How could one who had at one time been saved ever fall to such a degree? Let me say, first of all, that if such a thing is possible, it seems most unlikely that the Holy Spirit would have used up so much space in warning against something that couldn't ever happen. Friends, God does not waste words. The warning is to be heeded. The scripture states that we should take heed lest we fall. But how could this ever come about? It usually does not come about at all—certainly not all at once.

There are many sins against the Holy Spirit that man may commit in finally reaching the point of no return, for he blasphemes the third person of the Godhead and thus forfeits eternally his hope of salvation. For example, men may lust against the Spirit. In Galatians, we find these words:

> This I say then, Walk in the Spirit, and ye shall not fulfill the lust of the flesh. For the flesh lusteth against the Spirit, and the Spirit against the flesh: and these are contrary the one to the other: so that you cannot do the things that you would" (Galatians 5:16-17).

Now when we allow our animal passions to take possession of our bodies and thus engage in things unlawful in God's sight, we lust against the Holy Spirit.

Secondly, the Bible teaches that man may resist the Holy Spirit. This sin, Stephen the first Christian martyr charged his accusers with as he says, "Ye stiffnecked and uncircumcised in heart and ears, ye do always resist the Holy Ghost: as your fathers did, so do ye. Which of the prophets have not your fathers persecuted?" (Acts 7:51-52). Their fathers had rejected the inspired messages of the prophets and thus by so doing had resisted the Holy Ghost who was in the prophets. And now they were doing the very same thing in rejecting the inspired message of Stephen who had received the miraculous measure of the Spirit through the laying on of the apostles' hands in Acts 6:5-8.

But again, man may not only do these things but also the Bible teaches he may grieve the Holy Spirit. Paul gives a clear warning to the Ephesian brethren against such: he admonishes them to "grieve not the Holy Spirit of God, in whom ye were sealed unto the day of redemption" (Ephesians 4:30) (ASV). Now this sin may be committed by means of falsehood, wrath, anger, railings, clamor, corrupt speech, gross idleness, and other sins.

But again, we read of some who lied to the Holy Spirit. Any person who claims to be what he knows he is not and strives for recognition in the church, lies to the Holy Spirit. See the case of Ananias and Sapphira in Acts 5. Not only this situation, but also it is possible to do despite to the Holy Spirit.

Those who ignore the weekly worship period and the observance of the Lord's Supper do despite to the Spirit—that is, they insult Him. Such is a serious offense before God. In Hebrews 10:23-29, notice that passage again. It would appear that any of those sins, if persisted in, might finally result in the final and utter quenching of the Holy Spirit. In 1 Thessalonians 5:19 Paul writes, "Quench not the Spirit." You know when a fire is quenched, it is put out. No longer can it be revived. When one sins to the extent that he chokes out the Spirit in his life, he has committed the unpardonable sin. After this, the Spirit no longer pleads with him, not because God is unconcerned, but because he, himself, has put out the fire by a willful and persistent rejection of God's Holy Spirit. He has committed the sin unto death the Apostle John speaks of from which there is no recovery. Yes, it is entirely possible to commit this sin today. But the warm, comforting thing to know is this: the person who is anxious and fearful, truly anxious and concerned about such a sin has probably not committed it. He may have sinned mightily, he may have grieved the Spirit, he may have lied to the Spirit, he may have lusted against the Spirit, and in ignorance he may have even insulted the Spirit of God, but I guarantee you, as long as there is the longing in his heart for truth and righteousness, thanks be to a merciful God, he has not yet quenched the Spirit. If he, with broken heart, returns to God through His Holy Son, peace again will dwell in his heart. The unforgivable sin is the unrepented sin.

Let no man linger, but hasten, as the Book would say and as the grand old song would say, "Hasten to the eternal Rock of Ages, while mercy still lingers." Today as you listen to my voice, it is our plea that you will obey the gospel of God that God's Holy Spirit has given to you. As Paul insists, it is His power to save. And if today, if you are not a Christian, today is the day to quench not the Spirit of God. Listen to the teaching of the word of God, believe it, repent of your sins, confess the Holy Christ today, and be baptized for the forgiveness of your sins. Peter says in Acts 2:38, one should repent and be baptized in Jesus' name for the remission of his sins, and he shall receive the gift of the Holy Spirit.

If you are listening to me today and some of these things have been true in your life, why don't you, this day, if you are backslidden from the fold of God, why don't you do as the Lord admonished the church that they should repent and return to their first love. That you can do today. But if you persist in rejecting that which you know to be right and just simply go on and on and on, one thing we should recall: God says, "My spirit will not always strive with man" (Genesis 6:3).

The Thief on the Cross

Good morning, everyone. We are grateful for the opportunity of coming into your home today to study with you the gospel of Christ. This morning we would like to invite your attention to a study regarding the thief on the cross. Many, many sermons have been preached about the thief on the cross. Indeed, he has become—as some have said—the most popular person in town during the course of any Bible studies or gospel preaching. But I would like to view with you some of the beauties that surround the story and the account of the thief on the cross. So many times we become embroiled in various controversies, and indeed there are some, but we sometimes become so embroiled that we fail to see the beauty. As the smoke of battle sometimes veils the beauty of God's landscape, so the dust of controversy can hide, not only the beauty, but the very meaning and lesson of a passage of scripture. If ever one of the most beautiful and wonderful scriptural lessons has been obscured in the clash and the strife of tongues, it is that most tender, touching, and wondrous story of the thief on the cross.

Some, interested in eliminating baptism, have sited this incident as a case of salvation without baptism. And that, of course, roused up others who both zealously and rightfully have shown that this is no illustrative case for us—not only because the thief was fastened to the cross and could not have been baptized, which has always seemed to me to be one consideration, but that all this occurred on yonder side of the Covenant before the maker of the Testament had died (Hebrews 9:17-18)—over yonder before the new order was ushered in by the resurrection and the coming of the Spirit on Pentecost. You are aware, I am sure, that some have attempted, Uzzah like, to help the Lord out of a difficulty by denying that the thief on the cross was even saved. On the other hand, I have found those who are interested in putting over the soul-sleeping doctrine. They have undertaken to torture the Saviour's holy words into agreement with their peculiar scheme of things. It would evidently never do to let the Lord Jesus tell the thief that he would be with Him that very day—in paradise—because that would ruin their whole theory. And in the eyes of a real Voltaire, a sectarian theory is more precious any day than a mere passage of scripture. So they proceed to examine, as they say, the troublesome passage and arrive at the foregone conclusion that said passage does not at all mean what it says and does not furnish even the least shred of evidence that such a thing as a man's going after death to Paradise and see the Saviour there could ever be. There are those who would insist that it is not possible for this incident to have occurred.

They raise questions like, "What is Paradise anyway? A garden!" Now who could ever think of such a thing as spirits of departed ones going to a "garden?" That is evidently "highly figurative," to quote one, and none of that could be taken literally and so on and so on. Or we listen as people do injustice to the utterance of the Lord Jesus by changing the punctuation, making nonsense of it, all the while attempting to save their precious theory. Thus, the statement: "Verily, I say unto thee today, Shalt thou be with me in Paradise?" is turned into a question. Those who believe this change say that the Saviour solemnly informed the dying thief that he was telling him something today—not yesterday or tomorrow—and then tells him nothing after all, but merely asks him a meaningless question. This is the sort of thing that makes honest people turn away from religious controversy very weary and very sick at heart.

I would like for us, this morning, to look past all the fog. Let's forget all of this for a while and put it completely out of our thoughts and let us take a simple look at the wonderful story of the thief on the cross. Let's behold the scene.

On Calvary are three crosses. On the tree in the midst, the Son of God and on either side a thief is crucified. The chief priests and scribes, dehumanized with their false religion, were mocking and reviling the royal Sufferer. The rabble joined in with them, you recall—also the soldiers. And, is it possible? ... even one of the thieves took up the reproach and says tauntingly, "Art not thou the Christ? Save thyself and us." The other thief, in the meanwhile, saw and heard. What he saw and what he heard impressed him yet more and more. He began to sense the truth of the situation. Both Matthew and Mark say the thieves who were crucified with Him cast on him the same reproach or as one states, "cast it into his teeth." Either, at first both of the thieves reproached Him and one began to realize the truth and turned about or else Matthew and Mark's statements are general, not noticing the details. The former explanation is, of course, probably the more correct one. He had witnessed the quiet majesty of the Man on the middle cross. Perhaps like Pilate (Mark 15:10), he discerned the motive of the mocking priests and scribes. Perhaps he knew something of their sort of religion, and their very hate and venom made him more attentive toward this man. On what charge, after all, did they crucify the man on the middle cross? That He claimed to be the Christ, the Son of God, the King of Israel? It might be just true that He was all of that. That prayer for His enemies, "Father, forgive them for they know not what they do." Did ever any man pray such for his tormentors? "For they know not what they do" (Luke 23:34). Is it not a strangely merciful consideration that while He suffers the worst from their hate and meanness, He allows for the one mitigating circumstance and prays for forgiveness on their behalf because of their ignorance.

This man on the middle cross is different from all men. Could He, indeed, be the Christ? We know not what thoughts surged through the heavy, agonized soul and brain of that dying criminal when his partner in crime and doom says, "Art not thou the Christ? save thyself and us" (Luke 23:39) (ASV). He raised his voice in protest: "Dost not thou fear God, seeing thou art in the same condemnation? And we indeed justly; for we receive the due reward of our deeds: but this man hath done nothing amiss" (Luke 23:40-41). Please notice with me the appeal of the Crucified One. The crowning word, looking to the Man in the midst, he says, "Lord, remember me when thou comest into thy kingdom" (Luke 23:42). It was a brief prayer, but better and more honest than many a long one. The Lord's response was immediate. He says, "Verily I say unto thee, To day shalt thou be with me in paradise" (Luke 23:43). Paradise, the garden of God—Paradise! What a lovely word in the ears of the tortured man. A word yet more than a word—it was a place full of promise and rest and release and relief from all pain. It gave a hope of happiness in a pure, unsullied place—a place where all eyes will shine with innocence while the sunlight of heaven itself still lingers upon the world. Paradise—a place not lost, as the poet has said, because of the Man on the middle cross. Because of Him, there is hope of Paradise today.

Please notice the words, "This day shalt thou be with me ... ." One might cry out with this poor soul, "Lord, how can it be?" One cannot doubt the word of Jesus at such a time and such a place. We simply cry out, "What great compassion; what a wondrous life!" We simply see loving kindness that is absolutely boundless and free. For me, such a promise? Someone has said it is not sin that humbles us most, but grace. And the older I grow and the more I study the word, the more I am persuaded that that is so true. It is not sin that humbles us most, but the great, tremendous, sovereign grace of God.

The thief's body hung on the tree but his soul was at Jesus' feet. Indeed, we sometimes sing "The dying thief rejoiced to see that fountain in his day. There may I, though vile as he, wash all my sins away."

Let's take a little closer look now and behold the principle of this entire matter. If there was ever an exhibition of the grace of God, it is here. "Not by works of righteousness which we have done, but according to his mercy he saved us" (Titus 3:5). Here is the God that justifies the ungodly. If as some say, "In the last hour, the panorama of the past life is unfolded before the inward eye." How terrible must the vision have been to that dying thief. Scenes of crime and lust, of bloodshed and vile revelry, were passing before his mind. Conscience was tormenting with the memory of opportunity he had spurned time after time; of worse than wasted days and years, of deeds that could never be righted; and now no chance of ever doing better or making good. The hands and the feet that might have done service to God and man are now fastened to the wood with crude spikes. The film of death is drawing over his eyes. The tongue that might have praised Him, cleaves in fiery thirst to the roof of his mouth. It was the case of one who could plead no right or goodness and who could not in any wise pay for it by offer of future service that God was pleased to make known the length and the breadth and the heighth and the depth of His free grace and His forgiving love in Christ.

But there is one thing that was there—a broken and a contrite heart. Let's take a closer look. Let's note the revelation in the thief's last words. "Dost not thou fear God," he says to his fellow, "seeing thou art in the same condemnation? And we indeed justly; for we receive the due reward of our deeds: but this man hath done nothing amiss" (Luke 23:40-41). Please notice, here is the vindication of law and justice and here also is outright confession. The punishment, terrible as it is, is just in his own eyes. He fears God, bows before the authority of His moral government, and takes his place as a condemned—a justly condemned—sinner. He makes no plea for himself, no excuse. He acknowledges his sin and the righteousness of his condemnation. And I think this is a point of exceeding importance, God cannot forgive if this is disregarded. Please read Jeremiah 2:35.

But "a broken and a contrite heart, O God, thou wilt not despise," David says in Psalm 51:17.

The thief's speech revealed repentance toward God from a heart that is humbled and chastened and penitent. But there is more than that. Turning to the Lord, he says, "Lord, remember me when thou comest into thy kingdom" (Luke 23:42). It is vain for us to sit here today and wonder how the thief came by such a remarkable faith. Upon distressed and penitent souls, the truth sometimes bursts suddenly without conscious, logical process. But the thief had heard—of this there is no doubt—faith does come by hearing the word of God. The thief had heard, and he had seen much. After all, the accusation over that thorn crowned head read, "Jesus of Nazareth, King of the Jews." And surely He is King, though He seems to be now dying miserably on the cross. He doesn't belong there. This cannot be the end of Him. Perhaps the thief had heard more than we know. But however it be, his faith leaped boldly forward. "Thy victory, Lord, is bound to come, thy triumph shall not fail. Somewhere, sometime, somehow Thou wilt come into Thine own, and in that day, Lord, remember me."

In this appeal, lay his trust in Christ's power and His mercy. This—listen—this was faith! Where faith is there grace operates. "Therefore it is of faith, that it might be by grace; to the end the promise might be sure to all the seed" (Romans 4:16). Here, as when Moses lifted up the serpent in the wilderness, was one who looked to the Son of Man as He was lifted up—he looked and was made whole. "God so loved the world, that he gave his only begotten Son, that whosoever believeth in him should not perish" (John 3:16). Here then is the picture of the grace of Christ, luminous with the glory of heaven, though set in the blackest of dark framing. And that is still the pattern of His dealing with us even today under the New Covenant. Though the new order has since gone into effect, it is still the same way of faith and grace. We are saved by grace, through faith; it is the gift of God, just as free and loving and gracious as it was that day for the dying thief and on the same principle and on no other.

Though in His loving wisdom, our Lord has now placed baptism before the sinner as the step in which faith is manifested and accepted and becomes effective to the remission of our sins, it is not as though a work of merit or worthiness were imposed as a condition of salvation. It is still—hear me—it is still a pure grace through faith, faith that is manifested in the obedience of faith. Nor was this plan given that man might feel emboldened to defer salvation to the dying hours. The man who attempts such calculations will find that God is not mocked. But I believe today that it is written that any man who will now come, though his sins be as scarlet and red as crimson, though golden years may be forever lost and no hope remains, may cast himself upon the Saviour who gave Himself for our sins that through Him he may find the free and full forgiveness and an entrance forever into the very paradise of God!

We thank to you, today, for listening. We simply wanted to share with you some of the beauties that surround the story and, in fact, is the story of the thief on the cross.

The Conversion of Saul

Your attention, this morning, is invited to a study in Acts chapter 9. Actually the study begins in Acts 7:58 with an introduction by Luke, "The witnesses laid down their clothes at a young man's feet, whose name was Saul." "And Saul was consenting unto his death" (Acts 8:1). Such is Luke's way of introducing the person of Saul to the narrative of the spread of Christianity throughout the then-known world. In Acts 8:3, the scripture declares, "But Saul laid waste the church, entering into every house, and dragging men and women committed them to prison." (ASV) No stronger or more determined enemy of the church was there than the young man Saul. And when converted to the Lord Jesus Christ, there was no stronger advocate, no more courageous defender of the faith, no finer example to be found among the followers of Christ. When we come to chapter nine of Acts, it is natural that we will give attention to the conversion of Saul, for it is the principle event of this chapter. In verses 1 through 31, we find a recording of those things related to Saul's change from persecutor to preacher, and the remainder of the chapter is preparatory to the events of chapter ten and eleven wherein the Apostle Peter is the central figure in carrying the gospel to the household of Cornelius.

In our lesson today, let us look at the man, Saul, and consider the record of his change. Three places in the book of Acts we find details of this most striking event in the life of Saul of Tarsus. In chapter nine, we have the historic setting just as Luke records it when it happened. Twice later we have Luke's record of Paul's own account as he speaks in defense of his serving Christ as Lord. In chapters 22 and 26, we have these two speeches in which details of the conversion of Saul, who became Paul, are prominently featured. It is right and proper, then, to draw upon all three of these sources for details of our lesson this morning, with the account in chapter 9 as our basic outline.

Here is a marvelous occurrence, the turning or the conversion, of a man. "And Saul, yet breathing out threatenings and slaughter against the disciples of the Lord, went unto the high priest, And desired of him letters to Damascus to the synagogues, that if he found any of this way, whether men or women, he might bring them bound unto

Jerusalem" (Acts 9:1-2). The ancient city of Damascus, I understand, was some one hundred fifty miles north east of Jerusalem. And Saul's going there indicates the expectation of finding disciples of the "way" as it is here designated. This method of identifying the Christian faith is common in the book of Acts:

> But when some were hardened and disobedient, speaking evil of the Way before the multitude, he departed from them (Acts 19:9) (ASV).

In the same chapter, still referring to Paul in Ephesus, the text reads: "And about that time there arose no small stir concerning the Way" (verse 23) (ASV). In his defense speech on the stairs in Acts 22:4, Paul says, "And I persecuted this way unto the death, binding and delivering into prisons both men and women."

Before Governor Felix in Acts 24, Paul uses this same language:

> But this I confess unto thee, that after the Way which they call a sect, so serve I the God of our fathers, believing all things which are according to the law, and which are written in the prophets; having hope toward God, which these also themselves look for (Acts 24:14-15) (ASV).

Not a "sect," but "which they call a sect," says Paul. And Luke uses this common term in describing Felix's attitude after the defense of Paul: "But Felix, having more exact knowledge concerning the Way, deferred them, saying, When Lysias the chief captain shall come down, I will determine your matter" (Acts 24:22) (ASV). Jesus on that dark night of betrayal had comforted the apostles with these words, "I am the way, the truth, and the life: no man cometh unto the Father, but by me" (John 14:6). Isaiah had prophesied of the way of the Lord in Isaiah 40:3, as had other prophets of Israel. So it was in opposition to the way that Saul of Tarsus was making the journey to Damascus:

> And it came to pass, that, as I made my journey, and drew nigh unto Damascus, about noon, suddenly there shone from heaven a great light out round about me. And I fell unto the ground, and heard a voice saying unto me, Saul, Saul, why persecutest thou me? (Acts 22:6-7) (ASV).

Such circumstances would be most overwhelming. And the natural question that one would ask is asked by Saul, "Who art thou Lord? And he said unto me, I am Jesus whom thou persecutest ... . Arise, and go into Damascus; and there it shall be told thee of all things which are appointed for thee to do" (Acts 22:8-10) (ASV). That Paul received the gospel, which he preached, from the Lord Himself is quite clear. In Galatians 1:11-12, "I make known to you, brethren, as touching the gospel which was preached by me, that it is not after man. For neither did I receive it from man, nor was I taught it, but it came to me through revelation of Jesus Christ" (ASV).

That the conversion of Saul of Tarsus was unique was quite clear. Paul writes in Galatians:

> Ye have heard of my manner of life in time past in the Jews' religion, how that beyond measure I persecuted the church of God, and made havoc of it: and I advanced in the Jews' religion beyond many of mine own age among my countryman, being more exceedingly zealous for the traditions of my fathers. But when it was the good pleasure of God, who separated me, even from my mother's womb, and called me through his grace, to reveal his Son in me, that I might preach him among the Gentiles; straightway I conferred not with flesh and blood: neither went I up to Jerusalem to them that were apostles before me: but I went away into Arabia; and again I returned unto Damascus (Galatians 1:13-17) (ASV).

Now this is Paul's explanation of the purpose of the appearance of the Lord to him on the Damascus road. And certainly it carries us on beyond the events of chapter nine with which we are now particularly concerned. But they do explain for us the reason for the miraculous intervention and the purpose of God for Saul: later under the name Paul, he preached the unsearchable riches of Christ to the Gentile world.

So the appearance of the Lord on the Damascus road was not to save Saul from his sins. It convinced Saul that he should change; but it was only after three days without sight, time spent neither eating nor drinking but in prayer, that a disciple at Damascus, having been instructed of the Lord, came to Saul and told him what he was to do. Saul had heard the voice of Jesus and had seen the light; but even though his eyes were open, he saw nothing. They led him by the hand

and brought him into Damascus. The reputation of Saul had preceded him to Damascus, you recall. And the disciple, Ananias, had heard of many concerning this man—how much evil he had done to the saints who were at Jerusalem. Nevertheless, when he was told to do so, Ananias arose and went to the street called Straight and enquired for Saul of Tarsus. Laying his hands on him, he says:

> Brother Saul, the Lord, even Jesus, that appeared unto thee in the way as thou camest, hath sent me, that thou mayest receive thy sight, and be filled with the Holy Ghost. And immediately there fell from his eyes as it had been scales: and he received sight forthwith, and arose, and was baptized. And when he had received meat, he was strengthened (Acts 9:17-19).

In Paul's own words in Acts 22, he explains what happened to him on the Damascus Road as well as when he was led into the city of Damascus. In this passage, he quotes the words of Ananias about his commission to preach the gospel to all men: "Now why tarriest thou? arise, and be baptized, and wash away thy sins, calling on his name" (Acts 22:16) (ASV). Then, Paul was told he would be sent to the Gentiles to preach. Notice, he was penitent and believing for three days; and having spent this time praying, he was yet in his sins. After all of these things that he had done, he had seen the Lord, he had believed, prayed and fasted; yet he was told to arise and be baptized and wash away his sins, calling on the name of the Lord.

The genuine effect of this experience is reflected in the completeness of the change that was effected in the life of Saul of Tarsus. To Agrippa, in Acts 26 Paul later declares, "Wherefore, O king Agrippa, I was not disobedient unto the heavenly vision: but declared both to them of Damascus first and Jerusalem and throughout all the country of Judaea, and also to the Gentiles, that they should repent and turn to God, doing works worthy of repentance" (Acts 26:19-20) (ASV). Here is Paul's statement of obedience. In the record we have of his service in the cause of Christ in Acts chapters 13 through 28 and the books he has wrote to the churches of the Lord and to individuals, there is abundant testimony to the conversion of Saul, who became Paul, the apostle to the Gentile nations. Saul stopped persecuting the "way." He left the ranks of Judaism. He changed his way of life. He changed his associates, and he began to preach the gospel of Christ. You do recall that he suffered greatly for his change.

But the record we have of his turning to Christ should inspire all who are zealously searching for the truth. It should inspire us to follow his example. In fact, he declares in 1 Corinthians 11:1, "Be ye imitators of me, even as I also am of Christ" (ASV). Saul's conversion teaches us that one may think he is right with every fiber of his being and still be absolutely wrong. Men today often teach that "whatever a man thinks is right, is right." How many times have we heard someone say if you think it is all right, it's all right, or if one is honest and sincere, then whatever he is doing is correct. But this simply is not the case. It was not true in the case of Saul of Tarsus. Paul says in Acts 26:

> I verily thought with myself, that I ought to do many things contrary to the name of Jesus of Nazareth. Which thing I also did in Jerusalem: and many of the saints did I shut up in prison, having received authority from the chief priests; and when they were put to death, I gave my voice against them (Acts 26:9-10).

These are Paul's own words of what he thought he ought to do, but he was so very, very wrong at that time. His conscience was clear. In Acts 23:1, we have these words, "Men and brethren, I have lived in all good conscience before God until this day." This passage, too, makes it quite evident that one may live in a good conscience so far as doing what he has been taught to do and be entirely wrong.

How can we today follow the example of Saul of Tarsus given in Acts 9? We should not expect to see the miraculous light and the presence of Jesus on the Damascus way because this experience was for Saul for a particular mission he was to accomplish with the Gentiles. We can see the light, however, for the word tells us that Jesus says, "I am the light of the world: he that followeth me shall not walk in darkness, but shall have the light of life" (John 8:12). Paul points out where we learn about Jesus: "So faith cometh by hearing, and hearing by the word of God" (Romans 10:17). He also says:

> But what saith it? The word is nigh thee, even in thy mouth, and in thy heart: that is, the word of faith, which we preach; That if thou shalt confess with thy mouth the Lord Jesus, and shalt believe in thine heart that God hath raised him from the dead, thou shalt be saved. For with the heart man believeth unto righteousness; and with the mouth confession is made unto salvation" (Romans 10:8-10).

Peter defines a good conscience for us in these words as he speaks of Noah and his family, that is, of eight souls who were saved by water "which also after a true likeness doth now save you, even baptism, not the putting away of the filth of the flesh, but the interrogation (that is, the answer) of a good conscience toward God, through the resurrection of Jesus Christ" (1 Peter 3:21) (ASV). And like Saul, we should obey the Lord Jesus Christ regardless of what it would cause in our lives; and like Paul we should remain faithful to our Lord after baptism, living a life of service even until death.

We thank you today for listening. We ask you to be listening again next Lord's Day as we study a lesson from the word of God.

Worship

Good morning, everyone. Our lesson today is based upon the premise that man is by nature a creature of worship. From the earliest of man's existence, he has endeavored to worship. The oldest records that we have of even pagan nations would suggest to us that man is ever up-reaching and out-reaching for some power higher than himself. It may have been the wrong kind of worship. It may have been ignorant worship. It may have been coldly intellectual, but the fact remains that in ages past, men have always sought outside help ... they have sought to worship that which they believe to be God. It may be, as we suggest, the wrong thing as is the case in Exodus chapter 32, when Moses returned from communing with God and found the people worshiping the golden calf; or it may be the right things as was the case with Abraham who worshiped the one true God. But regardless of what it is, man will worship. I propose to you that man will worship something regardless of how cold or how cruel or how useless it may be. This necessitates, I think, the importance of discovering what worship is and what constitutes true worship.

We thus begin then with the question, "What is worship?" True worship is more than the performance of certain acts. To specifically define worship would be pretty hard indeed. We may be sure, however, that it does not only include praise but also embraces the direct acknowledgment of God's nature, of His attributes, and of His commands by the deeds that we perform. In short, true worship is reverence for and obedience to God and all of His commandments. But just what are the characteristics of true worship? Let's turn this morning to the New Testament and find the things that are specified as characteristics of those who are the true worshipers of God. The basis of true worship is given to us in John 4 where Jesus says:

> Ye worship ye know not what: we know what we worship: for salvation is of the Jews. But the hour cometh, and now is, when the true worshippers shall worship the Father in spirit and in truth: for the Father seeketh such to worship him. God is a Spirit: and they that worship him must worship him in spirit and in truth (John 4:22-24).

Now from this passage we can see that there are three basic characteristics or ingredients of true worship. Consider them please. (1) There is the right object, and that is our God. (2) There must be the right motive, and He expresses that as spirit. (3) There must be the right way, and that is truth. So we are involved with three things: God, spirit, and truth.

Consider with me first of all the right object of our worship and that is our Father, our God. The fact that a man is a worshiping being many times results in the wrong object being worshiped. Man can make a god of almost anything, and I think this fact has never been more apparent than the time in which we live. Money, pleasure, entertainment, and a thousand other things often become the object of man's worship. Worship of this type is contrary to God's will, God's desire. In Exodus, we read these words:

> Thou shalt have no other gods before me. Thou shalt not make unto thee any graven image, or any likeness of anything that is in heaven above, or that is in the earth beneath, or that is in the water under the earth. Thou shalt not bow down thyself to them, nor serve them: for I the Lord thy God am a jealous God, visiting the iniquity of the fathers upon the children unto the third and fourth generation of them that hate me (Exodus 20:3-5).

Again we read in Mark 12:28-30: "And one of the scribes came, and having heard them reasoning together, and perceiving that he had answered them well, asked him, Which is the first commandment of all?" You remember that Jesus answers him, "The first of all the commandments is, Hear, O Israel; The Lord our God is one Lord: And thou shalt love the Lord thy God with all thy heart, and with all thy soul, and with all thy mind, and with all thy strength: this is the first commandment." From the preceding passages, it is quite evident that God expects us to worship Him and Him only. He is a jealous God, and He requires exclusive devotion. God isn't going to share you with anybody; and you are not going to share God with just anybody. We must never be guilty of creating an image of some type and worshiping that image, for this would be rank idolatry. It would be hard to conceive of a Creator worshiping His creation, but we the creation worship God, the Creator. This is the proper order. In Revelation 22:9, there is some good advice for us: "Then saith he unto me, See thou do it not: for I am thy fellowservant, and of thy brethren the prophets, and of them which keep the sayings of this book: worship God." Here we just simply have the flat statement in two words, "worship God."

Consider with me next the right motive. Are we worshiping God in spirit? To worship God in spirit according to John 4 is to worship with the proper attitude and to be in the correct frame of mind. We as individuals are the only ones who really know whether or not we are worshiping in the spirit. In 1 Corinthians 11:28, the apostle says, "But let a man examine himself, and so let him eat of that bread, and drink of that cup." We must ever inventory ourselves to see if we are in the proper attitude. There is one thing sure. It is certain that we cannot praise and reverence God if we are thinking about what we have done in the past or what we are planning to do in the future or crowding it out with ten thousand other things. Our attention must be given solely to the things we are doing and the purpose for which they are being done.

Let's thirdly consider the right way. Since we understand the right object and this is God; and the right motive and this is in spirit; then the right way Jesus says is in truth. "And ye shall know the truth, and the truth shall make you free" (John 8:32). But we raise the question as Pilate did so long ago, "What is truth?" In John 17:17. Jesus says, "Sanctify them thru thy truth: thy word is truth." So we see that the word of God is truth, the truth makes us free, and we are all to worship Him in truth. It should be evident then that to worship God in truth is to worship Him according to His word. To affirm that there is true worship, we are simply implying that there is also a false worship. I would like for us to study this point before we finish today. If there is such a thing as a true worshiper, then there are people who are false worshipers. The Bible talks to us about some things that constitute false or vain worship.

Number One, The scripture speaks to us of ignorant worship. In Acts 17:23, the Apostle Paul makes these remarks to the Athenians, "For as I passed by, and beheld your devotions, I found an altar with this inscription, TO THE UNKNOWN GOD. Whom therefore ye ignorantly worship, him declare I unto you." In Romans, he describes the condition of another group. He says:

> Brethren, my heart's desire and prayer to God for Israel is, that they might be saved. For I bear them record that they have a

> zeal of God, but not according to knowledge. For they being ignorant of God's righteousness, and going about to establish their own righteousness, have not submitted themselves unto the righteousness of God (Romans 10:1-3).

I propose to you today that the Bible teaches that there is no excuse for ignorance. There is no excuse for ignorance when we have in our homes today a Bible. Nevertheless, we find that many, many people worship God in ignorance today simply because we do not read the Bible for ourselves. We need to understand God's righteousness. If we don't, we, like those in Romans 10, will go about to establish our own righteousness and thus be lost. So there is such a thing as ignorant worship.

Secondly, the Bible teaches there is such a thing as vain worship. In Matthew 15:9, Jesus says, "But in vain they do worship me, teaching for doctrines the commands of men." Please notice then if we put anything into the worship that is a commandment of men, then we have vain worship.

When we talk about vain worship, we are discussing that which means "to no avail." So if we worship God using for our doctrines the commandments of men, we have a worship that is to no avail. It is just as if we had never worshiped God at all if we worship Him according to human tradition. I understand the Bible to teach that we don't have to change the worship to a great extent to ruin it. But only a small addition or subtraction on our part can render it vain. Even though man may think that his ideas are better than God's, we must always remember the Lord says, "For my thoughts are not your thoughts,"— please notice—"neither are your ways my ways saith the Lord." But He says here is the way it is—"For as the heavens are higher than the earth, so are my ways higher than your ways, and my thoughts than your thoughts" (Isaiah 55:8-9).

Thirdly, the Bible speaks to us of will worship. In Colossians 2:21-23 we read, "(Touch not; taste not; handle not; which all are to perish with the using;) after the commandments and doctrines of men. Which things have indeed a shew of wisdom in will worship, and humility, and neglecting of the body; but not in any honour to the satisfying of the flesh." Will worship is worship fashioned after our own will. "Not in any honour," Paul says, "to the satisfying of the flesh." It is that which is self chosen. To obey God in all His commandments is true worship and everything else is a form of will worship. I would like to mention in closing the items of true worship.

We as Christians assemble every first day of the week for the purpose of worshiping God. As a body of believers we observe several acts of worship. We wish to notice them according to the scripture as follows:

(1) We gather to sing (Ephesians 5:19; Colossians 3:16). We are admonished to sing and make melody in our hearts.

(2) The Bible teaches that when we assemble, prayer is in order. 1 Thessalonians 5:17 teaches us to pray without ceasing. God tells us in Isaiah 56:7 that His house shall be called a house of prayer.

(3) We should teach. In 1 Corinthians 14 and 1 Timothy 2:11-12, we find some of the divine regulations that govern the teaching of the church assembly.

(4) We commune when we assemble if we worship in spirit and in truth. We read in Matthew 26:26-29, Mark 14:22-25, and Luke 22:19-20 of the institution of the Lord's Supper. We also read in 1 Corinthians 11:23-29 that Paul delivered the same institution to the church there in the very same way. In observing the Lord's Supper as Jesus did, we use, according to the scripture, one loaf of unleavened bread and one cup containing the fruit of the vine.

(5) We give as we have been prospered. In 1 Corinthians 16:1-2, we find the divine pattern or the divine regulation concerning our contribution.

Our plea today, in view of our subject, is this: the aforementioned items of worship become important to you because the Bible teaches them. These items of worship are observed each Lord's Day at the Third Street Church of Christ here in Lubbock, Texas. We try to observe them just as the apostles and early disciples did. We reject man-made practices such as instrumental music, the Sunday school system, and individual cups in the Lord's Supper. Not because we wish to be different but because we wish to follow the Bible in everything we do. Why don't you please investigate the church of

Jesus Christ that worships according to the Bible pattern? Our desire, I repeat, is not to be different or contrary, but to completely restore New Testament Christianity but above all things to worship God in spirit and in truth. Won't you join us today? Remember, it does make a difference how you worship God.

The Misunderstood Church

Good morning, everyone. Once again we invite your attention to a study of the Lord's word, and this morning we are inviting your attention to the subject, "Understanding the Lord's Church." The greatest organization in all the world is the church of our Lord. It is great because it was built by the Son of God. Jesus says, "And upon this rock I will build my church; and the gates of hell shall not prevail against it" (Matthew 16:18). And the Lord Jesus Christ did establish His church, as is recorded in the second chapter of the book of Acts. Christ had been exalted to the right hand of the Father. God had made Him "both Lord and Christ," (verse 36). It was on that day that about three thousand people gladly received the preaching concerning Christ and were baptized. Furthermore, verse 47 says, "The Lord added to the church daily such as should be saved." The importance of the church can be seen when we realize that Christ is the head of the church. In Ephesians 1:22-23, we are told that God gave Christ "to be head over all things to the church, which is his body, the fulness of him that filleth all in all." Thus, the church has a divine Builder and a divine Head. Further, Christ is the Saviour of the church. In Ephesians 5:23, we read that "Christ is the head of the church: and he is the saviour of the body." And in verses 25 and 27, "Christ also loved the church, and gave himself for it; That he might sanctify and cleanse it with the washing of water by the word, That he might present it to himself a glorious church, not having spot, or wrinkle, or any such thing; but that it should be holy and without blemish."

To these thoughts, we add Paul's statement in Acts 20:28, that it is the church that He, Jesus, "hath purchased with his own blood." After reading these scriptures how could anyone doubt the importance of the Lord's church? It was built by Him. He is the Head and the Saviour of the church. He loved the church enough to die that it might be established. He purchased it "with his own blood"; and He wants it to be "a glorious church."

But, often times people treat the Lord's church with little concern. Some ignore the teaching of the New Testament pertaining to the greatest kingdom the world has ever known. Others are not interested enough to learn the true value and the nature of the Lord's church. This attitude is nothing new; down through all centuries men have passed by matters of greatest importance for trivia. It is no marvel that men should show so little interest in understanding the church. Yet, when we consider that our own salvation and the salvation of the whole world depends on the recognition of the Lord's church, the need for thought, consideration, and proper understanding of it, all stand before us as absolutely imperative.

But, some misunderstand. The people of Christ's time often did not understand Him nor did they grasp the true nature and the importance of His work. Matthew 16:13 records that Jesus asked His disciples, "Whom do men say that I the Son of man am?" The answers were many and different. "And they said, Some say that thou art John the Baptist: some, Elias; and others, Jeremias, or one of the prophets." How little the people understood concerning Christ is most evident. Even though these were all great characters, Christ was far greater than any of them. They were but servants proclaiming and preparing for the coming Son of God. The people should have understood and should have recognized God's Son but the fact is they didn't. Even so it is today, concerning the church that our Lord established.

The Lord's church is absolutely misunderstood by the majority of people. If you were to take a poll of people about their understanding or misunderstanding of the New Testament church today, the answers would be more varied than those given to Jesus when He asked, "Whom do men say that I the Son of man am?" If you were to take your pencil and sit down to write your conceptions of the church, listing some salient points, what would you write? What would be your first point? What is your understanding of the Church of Christ? You may have heard about it—you may have heard something good or something bad, depending on what someone may think about some member of the church. In some way you have formed a conception of the Church of Christ. But, what do you understand about the church? Have you investigated for yourself? Have you really searched the scripture to see what the Bible has to say about the Church of Christ? Or, have you been relying on what you what you have heard?

I want you to think for a moment about Paul's experience. When Paul was taken prisoner to Rome, we read in Acts 28 how he desired to explain his circumstances to the Jews who were in Rome. They were of his own nationality, and they are the ones to whom God had given the promise of the coming of Christ. As the descendants of Abraham, they were looking forward to the coming of Christ, to the establishment of the kingdom of God, and to the fulfillment of the prophecies contained in scripture.

Now to these Jews, Paul says, "For the hope of Israel I am bound with this chain" (verse 20). Indeed, as Christ had come into the world as the seed of Abraham and the descendant of David, so Christ was the "hope of Israel." Paul was bound as a prisoner because of his faith in Christ. I want you to notice their reply. They say, "We desire to hear of thee what thou thinkest: for as concerning this sect, we know that everywhere it is spoken against" (verse 22). Now this was a typical statement. "We know that everywhere it is spoken against." The Jews of Rome were not acquainted with Paul. They knew little about the church the Lord had established. They called it "this sect," classifying it in their own thinking as a heresy, something in violation of God's teaching, rather than the fulfillment of God's promise. They thus expressed their own prejudice and not the true nature of the church. There were Christians in Rome but these Jews had not taken the time to investigate their teaching and to determine the truth of their claim. They had followed the easy course of labeling it as a sect or a heresy, and they were certain of one thing: "We know that everywhere it is spoken against." These Jews passed over the truth because of the criticism of others. They did not know and did not try to find out for themselves. They listened to others who just simply said, "Why, there's nothing good about this; this is the sect that is everywhere spoken against." Instead of trying to find out for themselves, they allowed these criticisms to turn their minds against the Church of Christ.

According to this passage, however, they appointed a day for Paul to speak to them, and he reasoned with them "from morning till evening." He "expounded and testified the kingdom of God, persuading them concerning Jesus, both out of the law of Moses, and out of the Prophets." And what was the result? Look at verse 24: "Some believed the things which were spoken, and some believed not." Even Paul, the great preacher, even Paul, teaching for a whole day, could not remove the misconceptions and the prejudice from some of their hearts.

And so it is today. Many people look upon the Church of Christ as a sect. They consider it as some heresy that has come from some man or group of men. Possibly it is classed as one of the many sectarian groups—one of many differing and conflicting teachings in matters of religion. To many people, the Church of Christ is just another denomination among the two hundred fifty other bodies of denominations. But, may we reason with you from the scripture and may we point you to the truth of God's word? The Church of Christ, as revealed in the New Testament, is not some organization originated by men. CHRIST established the church. It is HIS body. It is the kingdom of God. It is the family of God, with God as the Heavenly Father and Christ as His Son. It is a divine organism, bearing the name and the nature of the church that began on earth 1,900 years ago, as recorded in Acts 2. It bears the name of Christ; we call it the Church of Christ because it belongs to Him ... for He purchased it "with His own blood" (Romans 16:16; Acts 20:28).

The Church of Christ proclaims the teachings of Jesus as set forth in the New Testament. The gospel of Christ is God's power to save; and that is the message Christians, as members of the Lord's church, must proclaim to all the world (Mark 16:15-16). So may we plead with you to open your Bible and read for yourself? It is our desire to teach God's word faithfully. You must study to show, as the Bible says, yourself "approved unto God, a workman that needeth not to be ashamed, rightly dividing the word of truth" (2 Timothy 2:15).

Let God's word, specifically the New Testament, be the basis of your understanding, the standard for your decisions, and the light to guide you in accepting Christ and His church. Don't let misunderstandings keep you from Christ. The Jews at Rome had listened to the criticism of others; therefore, they said of Christ's way, "we know that everywhere it is spoken against." And many people today are kept from an understanding of Christ and of His church by the criticism and the denunciation of people who do not know what they are saying.

In Matthew 13, we have recorded the Parable of the Sower. Jesus says the seed sown was the "word of God" (Luke 8:11). Of some of those who heard, He says, "When anyone heareth the word of the kingdom, and understandeth it not, then cometh the wicked one, and catcheth away that which is sown in his heart. This is he which received seed by the wayside" (Matthew 13:19). The devil realizes the power of the word of God; now WE may not, but the devil knows how powerful it is. He does not want men to know or to understand God's word. The devil is always on hand, through his servants, to snatch the word of God out of the hearts of men, lest they should understand and believe and obey the truth and be saved.

The Lord's word CAN be understood. Paul says, "Wherefore be ye not unwise, but understanding what the will of the Lord is" (Ephesians 5:17). The Lord's will can be understood. In 2 Corinthians 11:3, Paul expresses the fear that men would "be corrupted from the simplicity that is in Christ."

The plan of our Lord has been given to us in the New Testament. The church has been revealed in understandable and simple language, but men have corrupted the Lord's plan and have deceived the minds of countless numbers of their fellowmen. May we give you this example? In Ephesians 4:4-7, we read: "There is one body, and one Spirit, even as ye are called in one hope of your calling; One Lord, one faith, one baptism, One God and Father of all, who is above all, and through all, and in you all."

Now these seven "ones" given by the Apostle Paul are very plain. They show the unity of the spirit that the Lord intended for His church, but men have corrupted all seven of them. They have ignored the Lord's teaching that there is one body, the church; they teach many churches and that you may join the church of your choice. However, the Lord's church is one body, directed by the one Holy Spirit, possessing one hope, having one Lord as Head, filled with one faith, into which men are baptized by one baptism, that of a burial with Christ in water for the remission of sins (Romans 6:4). God is one, the Father of all those who are born into His family, the church (Galatians 3:26-27). May we let all these seven points become very clear in our understanding.

In conclusion, the Lord's church, as revealed in the New Testament, can be and must be understood if we are to be saved. The Church of Christ does exist among men today. May we point you to the Lord's organization as the Lord's plan for the salvation of lost souls of men and women?

Let us recognize that there is one God and one Lord Jesus Christ as taught by one Holy Spirit in the New Testament. Let us possess the one faith that comes by hearing the word of God (Romans 10:17). Let us be baptized with the one baptism that the Lord has taught for us, therefore being baptized into the one body, the church of our Lord, the body of which He is the Saviour, and the Head. And then by faithful consecrated Christian living in obedience to our Lord and Master, we at last can share that one great hope of eternal life through Jesus Christ our Lord. God's grace is sufficient, and the Lord's plan is plain enough. Our prayer is that we may have the wisdom to accept it and to be saved.

Singing & Instrumental Music

Good morning, everyone. One more time we are concerned with a study of God's word. Our study today is concerning praising the Lord in song. The Bible teaches us to praise the Lord. Both in the Old Testament and in the New Testament we are told how God would have us to praise Him. In Psalm 117, we read, "O praise the Lord, all ye nations: praise him, all ye people. For his merciful kindness is great toward us: and the truth of the Lord endureth forever. Praise ye the Lord." In Psalm 138:2, it is written, "I will worship toward thy holy temple, and praise thy name for thy loving kindness and for thy truth: for thou hast magnified thy word above all thy name."

When the Apostle Paul writes to the Roman Christians concerning the salvation that can be enjoyed by the Gentiles through Christ just as the Jews do, he says in Romans 15:9-11, "And that the Gentiles might glorify God for his mercy; as it is written, For this cause I will confess to thee among the Gentiles, and sing unto thy name. And again he saith, Rejoice, ye Gentiles, with His people. And again. Praise the Lord, all ye Gentiles; and laud him, all ye people." We can praise the Lord today; and we not only can, we should.

Jehovah, our God, is worthy of all of our praise. In Revelation chapter 4, we are told of a scene that occurred in heaven. In verses 10 and 11 are these words, "The four and twenty elders fall down before him that sat on the throne, and worship him that liveth for ever and ever, and cast their crowns before the throne, saying, Thou art worthy, O Lord, to receive glory and honor and power: for thou hast created all things, and for thy pleasure they are and were created." And as these in heaven esteemed the Lord worthy to receive glory and honor and power, so should we give Him our praise here on earth.

The Christian is the one who has this privilege, and it is a wonderful privilege, to be able to praise God. He is the God who made us. The Apostle Paul says, "For in Him we live, and move, and have our being" (Acts 17:28). All of the good things that we have, come from

Him. James says, "Every good gift and every perfect gift is from above, and cometh down from the Father of lights" (James 1:17).

And think how God loved us and gave His Son to die for us (John 3:16). May we never forget how "God commendeth His love toward us, in that, while we were yet sinners, Christ died for us" (Romans 5:8). God has been so great and so good and so wonderful toward us. How could we possibly neglect to thank Him and to praise Him? The prayers that we offer, the songs that we sing, and the lives that we live every day should reflect our praise and our thanksgiving to Him as our Heavenly Father.

Especially today, we want to think of the praise that is to be given to God in singing. Let us establish in our thinking how singing is an important part in the Christians worship in the church of the Lord. In Hebrews 2:12, the apostle says, "I will declare thy name unto my brethren, in the midst of the church will I sing praise unto thee." From this comment we observe that (1) God is to be praised, (2) He is to be praised in the midst of the church, and (3) the praise may be expressed in song as he says, "I will sing praise unto thee." So we are quite aware then that singing praise is a part of Christian worship.

There are five things that we are taught in the New Testament that comprise the worship in the church of the Lord. Two of these were to be observed on the Lord's Day, the first day of the week. In Acts 20:7 we have these words: "And upon the first day of the week, when the disciples came together to break bread ... " that is—to eat the Lord's Supper. Second, in 1 Corinthians 16:2, we are told, that "Upon the first day of the week let everyone of you lay by him in store, as God has prospered him," that is, to the Christian, his weekly giving or contribution or offering to the Lord of the bounty with which the Lord has prospered him.

The other three items of worship are not limited by New Testament teaching or example to just the Lord's Day. We have examples of the Christians worshiping God in prayer and in the teaching of God's word and in singing praises to God. These three things were parts of the Christian worship as they came together at different times through out the week as well as on the Lord's Day. All of these matters may be clearly established by a study of the New Testament; and they may be established from the writings even of the early Christians.

Let's notice these passages in regard to singing:

> Let the word of Christ dwell in you richly in all wisdom; teaching and admonishing one another in psalms and hymns and spiritual songs, singing with grace in your hearts to the Lord (Colossians 3:16).
>
> Speaking to yourselves in psalms and hymns and spiritual songs, singing and making melody in your heart to the Lord (Ephesians 5:19).
>
> I will sing with the spirit, and I will sing with the understanding also (1 Corinthians 14:15).
>
> In the midst of the church (or congregation) will I sing praise unto thee (Hebrews 2:12).

Now this is God's plan for worship as given in the New Testament for His people. (1) We are to praise God in singing psalms and hymns and spiritual songs. (2) The singing is to be with grace in your hearts to the Lord. (3) It is singing and making melody in your heart to the Lord. (4) It is to be done with the spirit and with the understanding also. (5) In the midst of the church then we will sing praise unto God.

The act is singing in praise to God: it is in worship to God. The melody to accompany the singing is the melody in the heart of the worshiper as he sings with grace in his heart to the Lord. The singing, please notice, is to be "with the spirit" that is—sincerely as an act of worship or an act of the spirit. "With the understanding" that is—to use the understanding, knowing, and realizing what is being done. God's plan in the New Testament is singing.

In every passage in the New Testament where reference is made to this act of worship it is always, without exception, singing. The Lord's plan is quite plain. It is always vocal music as the expression of the praise of melody from the heart. And may we make this observation, had the Lord wanted Christians to use mechanical instruments of music, such as the piano or the organ or wind instruments, surely He would have so designated it in His word. But in no place in the New Testament do we have any instruction or any authority or any example whatsoever by which the Christian may use mechanical instruments of music in the church in worship to God.

The Lord, has taught us as Christians to sing and to make the melody where? In the heart! To Him! We should be satisfied to follow the Lord's plan to praise Him in singing. There is no one who should know how He wants to be praised quite as well as the Lord; and He has told us how in His word. I propose to you today that there is no instrument as great as what God has given to man, the human heart and the human voice.

Notice these principles that are laid down by the Lord himself in the book of John:

> The hour cometh, and now is, when the true worshippers shall worship the Father in spirit and in truth; for the Father seeketh such to worship him. God is a Spirit: and they that worship him must worship him in spirit and in truth (John 4:23-24).

Please notice, the Lord has designated two major principles to govern acceptable worship. These must be respected by those who worship God today: (1) To worship God in spirit and (2) to worship God in truth. Let's think about the meaning of these terms. First of all, to worship God in spirit means to worship Him with the spirit. That is—it is spiritual worship, and it is to be done sincerely without any false pretension—really putting the whole spirit of the worshiper into the worship as designated by God's Holy Spirit. Secondly, to worship God in truth means simply in the right manner, according to the truth or in the bounds of truth or just as God teaches in His truth.

Jesus defines truth saying in John 17:17 "Thy word is truth." The New Testament contains God's truth as it is expressed, in the will of Christ for us today. Jesus sent the Holy Spirit as the "Spirit of truth" to guide the apostles into all truth (John 16:13). Later the Apostle Peter writes, saying, "According as His divine power hath given unto us all things that pertain unto life and godliness, through the knowledge of Him that hath called us to glory and virtue" (2 Peter 1:3). Thus, the truth of God is fully revealed to us in the New Testament and to worship God in truth is to do so according to the truth expressed in the New Testament.

The kind of music, therefore, for the church today in worship to God (with those guidelines) is simply vocal music, singing—and that is congregational singing. The songs that you hear on this program each Lord's Day are accompanied with heart melody. There is no mechanical instrument of music used. No organ, no piano, or any such thing. And if you attend our worship as we gather to praise God you will find the same is true there, also. We are not trying to be different. We are simply endeavoring to follow the New Testament pattern: to sing and make "melody in your heart to the Lord."

We know this is right in God's sight because the New Testament so teaches. The churches of Christ use vocal music, congregational singing, in their worship. Every Christian has the privilege of praising God in each spiritual song and in each hymn and in each psalm that is sung in worship to God. Each Christian is exhorted to sing and to make melody in his heart to the very best of his ability. I propose to you that this is his duty as a Christian. When one neglects to do so, he misses a part of the blessings that God has intended for him in Christian worship. And may we emphasize that as members of the church of Jesus Christ, according to the Lord's word, we must believe in music in the worship, but that music is to be vocal music, accompanied with the melody in the heart of the worshiper and not mechanical instruments of music.

Is it ever safe to go beyond the word of God? In 2 John 9, we read according to the American Standard Version, "Whosoever goeth onward and abideth not in the teaching of Christ, hath not God: he that abideth in the teaching, the same hath both the Father and the Son." As long, therefore, as we abide in the Lord's teaching we can know that this is right and that we will have God's blessings; but anytime we go beyond what our Lord has taught, it is said we simply "have not God." That is—God is not with us. Now let us apply this teaching to worship. God has taught us to sing; but when we go beyond God's plan of worship in the church and introduce that which God has not authorized, can we expect God's blessings and God's approval? Would not the introducing of mechanical instruments of music in the worship be a violation of this scripture? (2 John 9). Think seriously today. Please ponder this statement and this passage very carefully. I think it deserves all the consideration and attention that we can give it.

There are many other passages that one may bring to bear upon this point. In Galatians 1:7-9, the apostle warns against the preaching or believing of a perverted gospel. When we add to God's plan, we pervert or change what God has given. The matter of adding to God's word is condemned in Revelation 22:18-19. Also, the apostle teaches the Corinthians so that they might learn not to go beyond the things that are written (1 Corinthians 4:6). These passages should be warnings to us today, and we should be exceedingly careful not to disregard the wisdom and the authority of God's word in the worship that we give to Him.

But someone might ask, "When were mechanical instruments of music introduced into Christian worship?" I would like to answer that question very frankly: they came after the New Testament was written. Men had instruments of music, but Christians did not use them in worship until during that period when men had drifted away from the Bible's teaching.

Chambers Encyclopedia, volume 7, page 112, says, "The organ is said to have been first introduced into church music by Pope Vitalian I in 666 A.D." *The Catholic Encyclopedia* says, "Pope Vitalian is related to have first introduced organs into some of the churches of Western Europe about 670 A.D." (volume 12, page 668). But it was not until much later, possibly the thirteenth century, when the organ came into general use in religious worship. Even then, as it is today, such a practice did not meet with universal approval. I think this is common knowledge with those who are true Bible students of the Reformation. Most of these people, as you know, were opposed to such practices.

Martin Luther once said, "The organ is the ensign of Baal." John Wesley was a lover of music and wrote many songs; but when asked about instruments of music in the chapels of worship, he said, "I have no objection to instruments of music in our chapels provided they are neither seen nor heard." John Calvin wrote, "It is no less than the introducing of burning of incense and returning to the old law." Charles Spurgeon wrote, "I would as soon pray to God with machinery as to sing to God with it." And he would not tolerate its use where he preached. Adam Clark, in his commentary on Amos 6:5, said, "Music as a science I esteem and admire but instruments of music in the house of God I abominate and abhor. This is the abuse of music and I register my protest against all such corruptions in the worship of the author of Christianity" (volume 4, page 684). J. W. McGarvey once wrote, "We cannot adopt the practice without abandoning the only ground upon which a restoration of New Testament Christianity can be accomplished."

These quotations are given you that you may know that what I am telling you is not just the idea of one man or one group of men, or something of recent origin. They point you to the teaching of God's word and as these principles have been recognized and taught in the generations of the past, so should they be today. As the New Testament was given to govern the lives of those who became followers of Christ, these principles should direct the worship and the work of the church today.

I realize there are many objections that can be raised to this teaching, and I would like to discuss one or two with you. First of all, some would say, "Instruments of music can be used in the home, why not in the worship?" I would answer that the church and the home are quite different. There are many things that can be done in the home, such as eating a common meal, that is not permissible in the worship of the church (1 Corinthians 11:22). Yet others would say, "The majority of people use mechanical instruments of music, so why can't we?" I would answer that our standard must be God's word, not the thinking of the crowds; in fact, the majority is usually wrong so far as God is concerned (Matthew 7:13-14). You remember that God warned Israel, "Thou shalt not follow a multitude to do evil" (Exodus 23:2). We should remember that we are worshiping to please God not the multitudes about us. God's teaching should be the basis of our action.

It is often said that "we should use instruments of music in worship because we need an aid to help us to sing." I would say this—God's plan is sufficient. Do you think for a moment that God has asked of us that which we cannot do? Or we cannot give? If God had thought such was necessary, He could very easily have so ordered it in His word. Let us obey God!

Sometimes the question is raised, "Won't there be instruments of music in heaven? Doesn't the Bible say somewhere that there are instruments of music in heaven?" Read carefully Revelation 14:2-3, and you will notice it says "the voice I heard was AS the voice of harpers harping with their harps." The whole passage is a figurative expression, and this part is no exception and has no bearing whatsoever on the worship that God has ordered in the church today.

There are, of course, many other objections that could be considered, but I would like to point you to this one thought—simply do what the Bible says and no more. May our aim always be to obey God's word and to live and to worship as much like the Bible teaches as we possibly can. Let us praise the Lord in song, singing and making melody in our hearts to Him.

We have given these truths to you today, with the prayer that they might lead some of you who listen to have a deeper regard for God's word and to help you walk a little nearer to God and to worship Him a little more acceptably than you ever have.

Salvation and Election

Good morning, everyone. One more time we have the privilege of coming into your home to study with you the word of God. Today we would like to invite your attention to the subject, "Salvation and Election." These are two things that are taught in the word of God, and they are in no sense contradictory to each other. I would like for you to study with me this question; "Did God choose and elect man's salvation or damnation before he was born into the world?" I believe this is an important question, and it's one that may well involve the destiny of your soul. Here is a quotation that should cause every man and every woman to think seriously upon this question: "By the decree of God, some men and angels are predestined into everlasting life, and others fore-ordained to everlasting death. Their number is so certain and definite that it cannot be increased or diminished." I would like to assure you, as my friends, this quotation is not from the Bible but from a religious creed or confession of faith of which man is the author.

We come, then, to the question of Adam's sin: Was the sin of Adam unavoidable? If God unchangeably foreordained whatever shall come to pass, then, of course, he has foreordained exactly the person who shall be saved and exactly the person who shall be lost. Actually this theory makes God a monstrosity of injustice without reason or without mercy. Here's an example: Adam sinned against God and was punished for doing so; yet God made Adam and placed him under law. Adam violated that law. He ate of the fruit that God had commanded him not to eat. Now if God foreordains whatever comes to pass, then, He foreordained that Adam should eat the fruit and that places Adam in a most peculiar position. The law that he must observe said he shall not eat of the forbidden fruit; yet the unchangeable ordination or decree is that he MUST eat the fruit. The law said he should not eat. The unchangeable decree—if such theory were true—declared he must eat—that is, he must eat and violate the law or not eat and change God's unchangeable decree. It was impossible for Adam to change God's unchangeable decree, we are told; therefore, it was a necessity for him to eat and violate God's law.

Can you imagine such injustice of an all-wise and merciful God. He placed Adam in the garden, foreordained and elected that he must eat the fruit yet gave him a law forbidding him to eat any of the fruit ... and then punished him for disobeying the law and eating the fruit—which he couldn't avoid in the first place. I must say to you today, that such a theory, although advocated by many, many honest and sincere folk, is without scriptural authority and is contrary to both human and divine wisdom.

Let's consider the word "elect" as it is used in the Bible. First, observe what the word means. The word elect simply means, "to choose." The elect of God, therefore, are God's chosen. That does not mean that God foreordained and elected that a certain and fixed number should be saved or lost. Biblical history reveals the fact that God at different times had elected or chosen people, persons, families, and nations for the benefit of His creatures on earth, but their final and ultimate happiness and salvation were not secured upon the basis of God's election of them without the exercise of their own choice or volition. On the contrary, God's elect are admonished to "work out your own salvation with fear and trembling" (Philippians 2:12). In many cases the elect of God have sinned and fallen far from the grace of God even to the point of forfeiting the positions to which they were elected.

I would like to point out very vividly that man CAN and he MAY disobey. In Leviticus 10:1-2, we have a case of disobedience. Nadab and Abihu, the sons of Aaron, "offered strange fire before the Lord, which he commanded them not. And there went out fire from the Lord, and devoured them, and they died before the Lord." In the theory of unconditional election and reprobation—if they were true—to which class did Nadab and Abihu belong? Now think about it. Did God elect them of the non-elect and appoint them as priests to officiate in the tabernacle having already fore-ordained and elected their destruction and having pre-determined to kill them for their choice of disobedience yet it was a choice they could not avoid because they were pre-elected by God to do so. Or ... on the other hand, were Nadab and Abihu foreordained and elected by God to go to heaven, and yet God killed them for their wickedness, which they could not avoid, because it was unchangeable and foreordained that they should commit that sin? Did God elect them priests, foreordained that they should sin against Him, then kill them and take them to heaven because they were foreordained to disobey? Such, I will assure you, is not the election and foreordination of the God of heaven.

Every man is a free moral agent. That is, he may choose to obey God and be saved or he may choose to disobey God and be lost. There will not be one soul in hell who did not choose to go there. If it is your choice to go to hell, then you may go. You may turn aside; you may ignore every plea for salvation; you may ignore the entreating of the love of God; you may resist the power of the gospel of Jesus Christ; you may trample under your feet the church of the living God; you may trample under your feet every Christian's prayer and worthy endeavor for your salvation. In spite of the church, in spite of the gospel, in spite of every Christian influence, you may choose to go to hell. But remember God will not send you there. He does not elect that any should be lost. If you are lost, it will be because THAT WAS YOUR CHOICE.

The elect of God under the Jewish law could forfeit the blessings and the promises of God. In studying the history of Israel, we find that some of them committed just about every crime and sin in the book. If such murderers, idolaters, fornicators, and the like were fit subjects for heaven, then we must conclude that election and not character and faith entitles one to the crown of life.

I would like to submit to you today the fact that the Bible teaches that all Christians are priests unto God. Now the Jewish age was a typical age. The church in the wilderness was in a way a type of the church of the living God. Moses, the Jewish law giver, was in a sense a type of Christ, our law giver. Aaron, the Jewish high priest, was a type of Christ, our high priest. And all the Jewish common priests were types of Christians in this age; all Christians being priests of God. In 1 Peter 2:5, the apostle writes, "Ye also, as lively stones, are built up a spiritual house, a holy priesthood, to offer up spiritual sacrifices, acceptable to God by Jesus Christ." Furthermore, in verse 9 of the same chapter, Peter declares, "But ye are a chosen generation, a royal priesthood, an holy nation, a peculiar people." It is a fact that the elective priesthood under the Jewish law had to be faithful to God or forfeit their election and inherent rights as priests. Surely, we today as common priests of Christ in the church of our Lord must be faithful to the discharge of our duties and our responsibilities or we too shall forfeit our election.

I am simply preaching today what the Bible states—that Christians may fall. After telling us that God was displeased with many in the wilderness—they were overthrown in the wilderness—the Apostle Paul tells Christians today as well as the church in Corinth:

> These things were our examples, to the intent we should not lust after evil things, as they also lusted. Neither be ye idolaters, as were some of them, as it is written, The people sat down to eat and drink, and rose up to play. Neither let us commit fornication, as some of them committed, and fell in one day three and twenty thousand. Neither let us tempt Christ, as some of them also tempted, and were destroyed of serpents. Neither murmur ye, as some of them also murmured, and were destroyed of the destroyer. Now all these things happened unto them for ensamples: and they are written for our admonition, upon whom the ends of the world are come. Wherefore let him that thinketh he standeth take heed lest he fall (1 Corinthians 10:6-12).

Paul himself declared that he should bring his body into subjection or he too would be rejected (1 Corinthians 9:27). This warning is definite and positive proof, submitted by the inspired Apostle Paul, that the number of the elect—the chosen of God in the church of God in Corinth—could be greatly diminished by their unfaithfulness as Christians. He tells them of the overthrow of many of the Jews, and he specifically enumerates certain sins that caused them to fall. Then he makes the application to you and to me as Christians, saying, "These things happened unto them for ensamples:" (to us), "and they are written for our admonition." He concludes, "Wherefore let him that thinketh he standeth take heed lest he fall." I want to say to you today that if the elect of God were predetermined before the foundation of the world, and the number could not be diminished or increased, then why all this warning of the Holy Spirit through the Apostle Paul? Furthermore, if some of the elect were elected to be the non-elect, that is—be lost—then who is responsible for their being lost? Think about it. Since they could not avoid being lost, it having been predetermined that they should be lost, then would not God be responsible for the non-elect being lost? There could be no other logical conclusion. Listen—I assure you that God will not send one soul to hell. Man is not pre-elected to be saved or lost. Every man must choose his own destiny, and everyone who will go to hell will go there of his own choice and his own volition.

The Bible tells us that branches are going to be burned. Listen to the Lord. He declares:

> I am the vine, ye are the branches: He that abideth in me, and I in him, the same bringeth forth much fruit: for without me you can do nothing. If a man abide not in me, he is cast forth as a branch, and is withered; and men gather them, and cast them into the fire, and they are burned (John 15:5-6).

I ask you honestly, why should the Lord charge men to "abide in Him" if they could not do otherwise but "abide in Him?" If the saved of God are eternally saved—elected to be saved and cannot be lost—then why did our Lord declare that "if a man abide not in me, he is cast forth as a branch, and is withered; and men gather them, and cast them into the fire, and they are burned." Listen to it again, Jesus says, "If a man abide not in me, he is cast forth as a branch, and is withered; and men gather them, and cast them into the fire, and they are burned." The branch, which Jesus says is "a man," had to be on the vine, "Christ," before he could be cast from it. The MAN, having been cast forth from Christ, is passed into hell and is burned. There simply couldn't be—could there—there couldn't be any plainer or more positive refutation of the idea of unconditional election and impossibility of apostasy than this declaration of our Master in John the fifteenth chapter? A man may be cut off from Christ, cast into hell, and be burned, our Lord affirms.

This theory of unconditional election rejects the atonement of the blood of Jesus Christ. If God, before the foundation of the world, unconditionally ordained exactly the number to be saved and exactly the number to be lost, then the atoning blood of Jesus could not under any circumstances reach the lost. Furthermore, if the saved were pre-elected to be saved, and could not be lost, then the blood of Jesus could not make their salvation any more secure. If the saved must be saved, and the lost must be lost, then the death of our Lord and the sacrifice of His blood were totally unnecessary.

Such a conclusion is contrary to the teaching of God's word. In Hebrews chapter 2, verse 9, we read, "But we see Jesus, who was made a little lower than the angels for the suffering of death, crowned with glory and honour; that he by the grace of God should taste death for every man." I say unto you—Where is the person who would dare add to the word of God? Who would willingly add the word "elect" and make the passage read, "Jesus tasted death for every ELECT man." The Holy Spirit didn't say that. He says Jesus tasted death for EVERY MAN, regardless of who he is ... elect or non-elect ... whatever the case may be. Man cannot afford to add to the word of God upon this subject or for that matter, on any other Bible subject. The consequences are too severe. Listen to what they are:

> For I testify unto every man that heareth the words of the prophecy of this book, If any man shall add unto these things, God shall add unto him the plagues that are written in this book. And if any man shall take away from the words of the book of this prophecy, God shall take away his part out of the book of life, and out of the holy city, and from the things which are written in this book (Revelation 22:18-19).

The Bible teaches us that we are to make our "calling and election sure." Surely we need to heed the admonition of the Apostle Peter in this respect. "Wherefore the rather, brethren, give diligence to make your calling and election sure" (2 Peter 1:10). Please notice we must make this election "SURE." Obviously it is not sure unless we do the things pleasing unto God. The apostle declares, "If ye do these things, ye shall never fall." But on the other hand, the alternative is ... if we DO NOT do these things we SHALL fall.

You must choose your own destiny today. What do you choose? Yes, I believe that God's people are elected or chosen to be saved. Paul declares that "God hath from the beginning chosen you to salvation through sanctification of the Spirit and belief of the truth" (2 Thessalonians 2:13). Men are chosen to salvation through sanctification and obedience to God's word. In His prayer Jesus says, "Sanctify them through thy truth, thy word is truth" (John 17:17). Man has the choice of obeying or disobeying the truth. God will force him to do neither. Every man must choose his own destiny.

We plead with you today. In fact, the churches of Christ throughout the world plead with you to choose Jesus Christ as your Saviour. By that we mean with a genuine faith and a true repentance to confess your faith in the Master today and be immersed in His name for the remission of your sins and the Lord will add you to the church. And then follow the divine pattern of Christianity as revealed in the New Testament, every day living a Christian life, thus making your "calling and election sure." This is our plea today in Jesus' name.

By Bread Alone

Ladies and gentlemen, we are pleased to be in your home or in your automobile or wherever you are this morning to bring you the gospel of Jesus Christ.

Our subject today is concerned with the statement Jesus made when He says, “Man shall not live by bread alone, but by every word that proceedeth out of the mouth of God” (Matthew 4:4). We are especially concerned, not only with the statement but with the events that brought this statement to pass. In Matthew 3, we read about the teaching and the work of John the Baptist and how Jesus came to the River Jordan to be baptized of John, saying, “Thus it becometh us to fulfill all righteousness.” Then, God acknowledged Christ as His Son when “he saw the Spirit of God descending like a dove, and lighting upon him: and lo a voice from heaven, saying. This is my beloved Son, in whom I am well pleased” (Matthew 3:13-17).

As we begin Matthew 4, we learn Jesus “was led of the Spirit into the wilderness to be tempted of the devil.” As one states, “He was driven by the Spirit into the wilderness to be tempted.” It is interesting to think of where this place may have been. Brother J. W. McGarvey describes the wilderness as “that section that sets back of Jericho and extends thence along the western shore of the Dead Sea. The northern end of the region is in full view from the Jordan as one looks westward, and a more desolate and forbidden landscape it would be hard to find. It is vain to locate the temptation in any particular part of it. Jesus may have wandered about over nearly all of it.”

The Bible teaches God does not tempt men (James 1:13) nor did He tempt His own Son; however, He does permit men to be tempted. James says, “My brethren, count it all joy when you fall into divers temptations; Knowing this, that the trying of your faith worketh patience. But let patience have her perfect work, that ye may be perfect and entire, wanting nothing” (James 1:2-4). Verse 12 reads, “Blessed is the man that endureth temptation: for when he is tried, he shall receive the crown of life, which the Lord hath promised to them that love him.”

The writer of Hebrews confirms that Jesus was tempted, even though He was the Son of God: "For in that he himself hath suffered being tempted, he is able to succour them that are tempted" (Hebrews 2:18). And, by overcoming, He became our example in overcoming our temptations. Also, His temptations helped Him understand our temptations. "For we have not an high priest which cannot be touched with the feeling of our infirmities; but was in all points tempted like as we are, yet without sin. Let us therefore come boldly unto the throne of grace, that we may obtain mercy, and find grace to help in time of need" (Hebrews 4:15-16). And, we have this assurance: "God is faithful, who will not suffer you to be tempted above that ye are able; but will with the temptation also make a way to escape, that ye may be able to bear it" (1 Corinthians 10:13).

Being familiar with Jesus' temptations helps us in our own struggles. Jesus first temptation in Matthew 4 is after He fasted in the wilderness for forty days and forty nights, and "he was afterward an hungered. And when the tempter came to him, he said, If thou be the Son of God, command that these stones be made bread" (Matthew 4:3). It was a natural temptation. He had the power to change the stones to bread! Later, He demonstrated that power by changing water into wine at Cana (John 2:1-11), by feeding five thousand with five loaves and two fishes (Matthew 14:15-21), and by feeding four thousand with seven loaves and a few little fishes after which they took up seven baskets full of the broken meat that was left over (Matthew 15:32-38). He could still the tempest of the sea, raise the dead, and heal the sick. Satan was well acquainted with Jesus' power. In this case, Jesus answered Satan, "It is written, Man shall not live by bread alone, but by every word that proceedeth out of the mouth of God" (Matthew 4:4). Notice Jesus defended Himself with the **scripture of God.** He says, **"It is written"** and quoted Deuteronomy 8:3.

Satan had caused Adam and Eve to sin, in part, by telling to them that the forbidden fruit was good for food (Genesis 3:6). Through the hunger of Israel, Satan had led the nation of Israel to murmur and complain against God and to desire to return to Egypt (Exodus 16:1-9). Now, he tries the same means of temptation with Jesus, but He answered, "It is written," thus using the word of God as His defense, His rock, and His sword of defense. So, today God's word becomes our sword and our shield to "quench all the fiery darts of the wicked" (Ephesians 6:16). God's word can be our stay in times of trouble and temptation. Jesus overcame by using the scriptures and so can we.

"Man shall not live by bread alone." Bread was important to life then, and it is important today. Food is satisfying to hunger, and it gives health to the body; but bread is not the most important thing in life. It is not the giver or the source of life. You see, God gives and sustains life. He fed Israel with supernatural food—manna in the morning and quail in the evening for forty years in the wilderness—that they might know Him as the giver and sustainer of life. When you think about that case, it makes you know that indeed, "Man shall not live by bread alone." He will live by whatever means his Creator chooses for him to live. If He chooses him to live by manna, he can live by manna. But, notice that He makes the point for us spiritually: we will live by every word that proceeds out of the mouth of God.

Jesus taught His disciples to pray, "Give us this day our daily bread" (Matthew 6:11). Truly, our daily bread comes from God Who provides for all men. "He maketh his sun to rise on the evil and on the good, and sendeth rain on the just and on the unjust" (Matthew 5:45). Can He not provide, therefore, for the needs of those who love and serve Him? His provision was good enough in the days long ago. David writes, "I have been young, and now am old; yet have I not seen the righteous forsaken, nor his seed begging bread" (Psalm 37:25). God is able to provide that which is best for His children. Our petition should be that of Proverbs 30:8-9: "Give me neither poverty nor riches; feed me with food convenient for me: Lest I be full, and deny thee, and say, Who is the Lord? or lest I be poor, and steal, and take the name of my God in vain." God knows what is best for us. He can provide our daily bread; and if we seek first His kingdom and His righteousness, He can add the material things we need (Matthew 6:33).

The Lord's temptation was an appeal to place **His physical needs first**—to use His divine power to provide for His selfish needs. Thus, He would have heeded the command of Satan instead of trusting in the provision of God. It is at this point we learn that "testing" is not "trusting." The devil says, "If thou be the Son of God, command that these stones be made bread." The idea was to cast doubt on His divinity—"If you are ... ."—and on the provision of God. As James McKnight writes in his commentary about this passage, "In this temptation, Jesus was solicited to doubt the evidence of His mission that had lately been given in the presence of the multitude, and to distrust the divine power which the devil would have Him think was not sufficient to sustain Him without food."

Which is to be first—the will of God or the provisions of the body? The word of God or satisfying hunger? Which shall be obeyed? Which shall be the master? Jesus places the emphasis on God's will. "Man shall not live by bread alone, but **by every word that proceedeth out of the mouth of God.**" God's will is to come first.

Upon another occasion, Jesus says, "My meat is to do the will of him that sent me, and to finish his work" (John 4:34). Again, He says, "For I came down from heaven, not to do mine own will, but the will of him that sent me" (John 6:38). So, at the close of His life on this earth, He prayed, "I have glorified thee on the earth: I have finished the work which thou gavest me to do" (John 17:4). He taught His disciples He was the bread of life: "I am the living bread which came down from heaven: if any man eat of this bread, he shall live for ever: and the bread that I will give is my flesh, which I will give for the life of the world" (John 6:51). Again:

> Verily, verily, I say unto you, Except ye eat the flesh of the Son of man, and drink his blood, ye have no life in you. Whoso eateth my flesh and drinketh my blood, hath eternal life; and I will raise him up at the last day. For my flesh is meat indeed, and my blood is drink indeed. He that eateth my flesh, and drinketh my blood, dwelleth in me, and I in him. As the living Father hath sent me, and I live by the Father: so he that eateth me, even he shall live by me. This is that bread which came down from heaven: not as your fathers did eat manna, and are dead: he that eateth of this bread shall live for ever (John 6:53-58).

Our Lord placed His body and His blood as the source of life to all who will receive Him. Each man must become a partaker of the benefits of His death—His slain body and shed blood—by faith in the fact that He gave His body and His blood for our lives and by obedience to the "form of doctrine" that is represented by His death, burial, and resurrection—a death to sin, a burial with Him in baptism, and a resurrection to live with Christ.

We read in Romans the sixth chapter how to live with Him as a partaker of the salvation provided by such a sacrifice. We invite you to turn to Romans 6 and make a thorough study of it. We can partake of Christ's body and blood by making His will our will and His life our life. He becomes our spiritual sustenance that we may live eternally. He is. He must be the point of emphasis in our lives as Christians—that we may live through Him and for Him.

Satan tempts us in so many areas in this respect—to live by and for material things, to satisfy the needs of man by satisfying our bodies. Men often strive to live by bread alone. They forget the higher will of God, which is "every word that proceedeth out of the mouth of God." Each person must make a choice: will I yield to the desires of the flesh or determine to do the will of God? Will material blessings become an end within themselves to satisfy my lusts or will I use them as a means to serve God? We have a choice. But we should remember that "no man can serve two masters: for either he will hate the one and love the other; or else he will hold to the one, and despise the other. Ye cannot serve God and mammon" (Matthew 6:24).

There is an ever present danger—regardless of the people, the time and the age—in seeking material gain. In Matthew 13:22, our Lord expresses so beautifully: that the cares of this world and the deceitfulness of riches may choke out the word of God in our lives and make us unfruitful. Paul says in 1 Timothy 6:9-10: "They that will be rich fall into temptation and a snare, and into many foolish and hurtful lusts, which drown men in destruction and perdition. For the love of money is the root of all evil: which while some coveted after, they have erred from the faith, and pierced themselves through with many sorrows."

Overemphasis on food, clothing, and material gain is causing a great deal of anxiety in the hearts of men today. Jesus warns against such things in Matthew 6:25-33. Men are laying up treasures on earth and forgetting to lay them up in heaven, according to Matthew 6:19-21. Satan is winning many a battle in this field. We live in a materialistic age—a world that is money crazy and is ignoring the word of God. Christians can easily become involved in this same course of life and forget God. The devil is trying the souls of men every day. Our nation is, by far, the richest nation on earth, and our temptation to live by bread alone is really strong.

Ask yourselves these questions: Am I living by bread alone? Is it more important than God's word? Do I neglect God to earn my bread? Am I so busy with my work and earning my livelihood that I don't study the Bible or live the Christian life or worship God? Is my job or profession more important than the church for which Christ died? Do I have time to pray? Do I minister to the needs of others with the things God has blessed me with? Am I laying up treasures in heaven by giving to the Lord's work with liberality? Am I anxious about material things or worried about the provisions of tomorrow—forgetting that God is able to provide our daily bread when we live for Him and seek first the kingdom of God?

God intends that we provide for our families (1 Timothy 5:8), but which is more important—the feeding and clothing of the bodies or providing for the souls of our children by teaching the word of God and setting a Christian example before them? Striving for bread, in many homes, means starving the soul through neglect of obedience to the word of God. Here in America our homes are threatened, the church of the Lord is in peril. Satan is leading thousands of souls on a downward path to destruction. In a more personal sense, he is at your heart's door this very day. He is at mine. He is tempting us, and we may follow the course of trying to "live by bread alone." Will you, my friend, yield to his temptation and let him become your master? Let's weigh these matters seriously—weigh them on the scales of God's revelation. Consider them in view of the fact that this old body will die, but the soul of man will never die. And where will you live in eternity? Whether you live in heaven or hell depends on your decision.

Jesus says, "For a man's life consisteth not in the abundance of the things which he possesseth" (Luke 12:15). The Lord is saying that the inventory of one's goods may not be equated with the inventory of one's soul. He is saying that to be "better off" is not necessarily to be better. He also wants us to remember that when we come to die, in the Judgment Day the provision for the soul will be the important thing.

But you must make your standard now to live by "every word that proceedeth out of the mouth of God." This should be your decision today—to obey all His commands, to become a Christian now. You must believe, repent of your sins, confess the Holy Christ, and be baptized for the remission of your sins. You must dedicate your life to Christ's service, trusting in God to give you your daily bread as you place Him first in your life and work. You must study your Bible every day, pray to God for guidance, and lean upon Him for strength. Then you will know the blessings of living for Him Who died for you and of laying up treasures in heaven, and you shall have the great assurance of having overcome Satan by using the word of God.

Sin – Our Enemy

Ladies and gentlemen, this morning we invite your attention to a discussion of the subject of sin, man's greatest enemy. Man is a creature with many enemies. He has enemies that would envy him of his material peace and prosperity and would make war in order to rob him, especially in such a wonderful country as our America. These enemies are always at work both within and without, plotting the destruction and overthrow of man's freedom.

When we think back through history, we are made to shudder and to tremble as we consider the evil forces that have destroyed man's freedom and have made men slaves and servants, both politically and religiously. As we consider these matters, we cry out to God and pray that such a thing may never happen in our country, that such enemies may never rule here in the United States of America.

Man has enemies, too, that fight against his body. Think of the thousands upon thousands of diseases that have fought against the health and well being of man's body through the years. When one disease seems about to be controlled, another disease rears its ugly head and takes its toll in communities and sometimes across the country. Men and women, dedicated to their tasks, work on in their laboratories to try to find new ways to overcome these dreaded enemies that continue to fight against man's body.

But, our greatest enemy—mankind's greatest enemy—is sin. It is sin that lies behind all of the troubles and heartaches and pains that plague the lives of mankind. It is sin that causes the wars and the destruction throughout all the earth. It is sin that brought all these other enemies to fight against each one of us. I wonder, this day, if we can really grasp—possibly not, but we shall try—really grasp the enormity of sin's effects. Have you ever stopped to consider what all this enemy has done to the world? Have you thought about how its marks are all around you on every hand? Listen to the cry of the suffering, and remember that every hospital was built because sin entered the world; and all the pain that tears at the bodies of men came into the world as the result of sin. And the silent markers in all of the cemeteries of the land give their quiet testimony that sin came and man yielded to sin; and because of sin, death reigns over man. Death is a constant reminder of the reality of the consequences of man's disobedience of God.

Consider the forms of sin so close at hand that are causing so much suffering and trouble all of the time, day in and day out. The sins of hate and envy, jealousy and pride, and falsehood, all of which are at work in every city and in every town of our land every day. You read the increasing numbers of crimes and murders and robberies, of rape and cruelties, of oppression and destruction. Year by year the statistics show their numbers just mount higher and higher in our land. Why? It is sin that is in the land. All of these are the effects of man's greatest enemy, and that great enemy is sin.

Listen to the cry of the broken hearted and consider the tragedy of the broken homes, and you will find more of sins effects. See the neglected children, often unloved and deserted, some of whom will grow up to be the delinquents who will trouble society because a sinful society has robbed them of their rightful heritage. To try to comprehend the enormous effects of sin now—to say nothing of sin's eternal effects upon man's soul—is to most of us like trying to comprehend the vast expanse of the universe or to fathom the depths of the sea. Yet, somehow, in some way, we must be brought face to face with the realization that sin is man's worst enemy.

The challenge of foreign powers to our nation continues to be met with increasing stockpiles of weapons of defense and with the forming of patterns of strategy in the event of an attack by an enemy. The challenge of disease is met by the continuous research in the world's greatest laboratories and the talents of capable scientists. But the challenge of the forces of sin go unnoticed by the rank and file of the peoples of the earth. Therefore, sin continues to gain in its destruction throughout the earth. May I beg you to come to the realization of this great fact—sin is man's worst enemy. Sin is YOUR worst enemy. It IS your enemy. It is the enemy of your body, the enemy of your home, and the enemy of your soul. It would make you suffer eternally; for "the wages of sin is death" (Romans 6:23).

Let's talk for just a few moments about the origin of this thing that is our worst enemy. Sin came into the world, as we read in the opening chapters of the Bible. God made man in His own image and placed him as a pure creature upon earth made for his dwelling place, a place that was without sin.

Man's work was to be the work of God and his pleasure, the enjoyment of God's great creation. But Satan brought sin to man by leading man to disobey God. He tempted Eve to yield to his desire and to partake of that which God had forbidden. God had given His law, and God's law was clear and understandable; and God had plainly stated the penalty in Genesis 2:17, "Thou shalt surely die." But Satan created the desire to disobey, and Adam and Eve sinned; and the result of sin began among men—death came upon the earth.

From that day to this, death has continued among men. The Bible says, "By one man sin entered into the world, and death by sin; and so death passed upon all men" (Romans 5:12). As a result of that sin, all men die. Physical death will come to all of us, even as it has to the generations of the past. Paul says, "The whole creation groaneth and travaileth in pain together until now" (Romans 8:22). From this physical death there will some day be deliverance through our Lord Jesus Christ. We read in 1 Corinthians 15:22, "For as in Adam all die, even so in Christ shall all be made alive." We can say with the apostle, "But thanks be to God, which giveth us the victory through our Lord Jesus Christ" (verse 57).

Sin is our spiritual enemy. Every man is a living soul (Genesis 2:7). Satan not only desired to destroy man physically, but he actually desired to destroy man's soul, the eternal part of man. To this end, sin has always been working from the beginning until this moment; but this destruction must be an individual matter. The prophet Ezekiel says, "The soul that sinneth, it shall die" (Ezekiel 18:20). Sin, therefore, lays its attack at the heart and the soul of each individual before God. So it is an individual matter, and I think we should do some thinking about that.

Each individual has the right and the opportunity to overcome his terrible enemy of sin. There is one great truth that we must always remember in this regard. Peter says, "Of a truth I perceive that God is no respecter of persons: But in every nation he that feareth him"—Have you ever noticed the construction—"In every nation **HE** that feareth him, and worketh righteousness, is accepted with him" (Acts 10:34-35). And to each accountable being, God has given this privilege to choose to serve God and thus to overcome sin. Each man can choose or decide for himself whether he will yield himself to be the servant of God or to be the servant of sin. Paul lays out this choice when he wrote his epistle to the Roman church. He also pointed out the end result of that service. He gives this warning:

> Know ye not, that to whom ye yield yourselves servants to obey, his servants ye are to whom ye obey; whether of sin unto death, or of obedience unto righteousness? (Romans 6:16).

So what we are looking at is this: there are two forces at war, (1) the force of God, which is the force of righteousness; (2) the force of sin, which is the force of evil. God has always desired that man choose the force of righteousness.

In other words, God has always wanted to save the souls of His creation from sin. He has made every necessary provision for our salvation. He arranged the supreme sacrifice on our behalf when he planned the death of His own Son on Calvary. He has given us the perfect law of liberty in the New Testament to teach us how to obey Him and thus to be free from the burden of sin. He "hath given unto us all things that pertain unto life and godliness, through the knowledge of him that hath called us to glory and virtue" (2 Peter 1:3). He has offered man the power to overcome sin's temptation and to have the "victory that overcometh the world" (1 John 5:4).

But while it is true that God would save our souls from sin—listen—Satan would destroy us. Sin is our enemy, and it is out to destroy us totally. Sin is of "your adversary the devil, as a roaring lion, walketh about, seeking whom he may devour" (1 Peter 5:8). "Sin is the transgression of the law" (1 John 3:4); or as the American Standard Version translates it, "Sin is lawlessness." It is opposed to the law of God and has no regard for it. In 1 John 5:17, it is defined, "All unrighteousness is sin." So sin is your enemy. And it is my enemy, even as it is the enemy of God and opposed to the law of God.

I think we must remember that sin keeps men from obeying the law of God. Now God loves men. He is "longsuffering to us-ward, not willing that any should perish, but that all should come to repentance" (2 Peter 3:9).

Jesus taught men God's plan of salvation. He taught men to believe in Him, but sin has blinded the eyes of men; and men have "loved darkness rather than light, because their deeds were evil" (John 3:19). So sin is keeping people from accepting Christ, and sin is keeping people from obeying the Lord's commands. "He that believeth and is baptized shall be saved" (Mark 16:16). So it is sin that keeps men out of the church. The church is the body of Christ, as we read in Colossians 1:18.

Sometimes sin keeps men out of the Lord's body through a love for evil itself. Sometimes it is through false teaching. Sometimes it is through denominational doctrine saying it is not necessary to be a Christian after the New Testament order or that the church doesn't make any difference or that one church is as good as another. Sin has many ways to keep YOU, my friend, from becoming a New Testament Christian. If you will listen to the teaching of sin, you will never be a member of the Lord's church. Thus the divisive doctrines of men are working to keep men out of the Lord's church.

It is sin that keeps men's souls corrupt. It teaches them to lie and to steal, to hate and to kill, to gamble, to drink intoxicants, to yield to lustful desires, reveling, and dancing. And it robs men and women of their chastity and their self respect. It is sin that breaks up marriages and destroys family ties. And I will assure you the Bible teaches that it is sin that will keep us out of heaven. No sin can enter that eternal city. To the impenitent Jesus says, "Ye shall seek me, and shall die in your sins: and whither I go, ye cannot come" (John 8:21).

The blessings of that eternal home are for the redeemed who will overcome in the battle against sin. We must remember this—sin's price—sin's price is eternal. Of its followers, Jesus says, "And these shall go away into everlasting punishment" (Matthew 25:46). And again He says, "Depart from me, ye cursed, into everlasting fire, prepared for the devil and his angels" (Matthew 25:41).

And so, throughout all eternity the servants of sin will continue to pay the penalty of destruction and suffering. Not because they COULD NOT be saved but simply because they WOULD NOT be saved. Men will not heed the warning. Warning after warning has been sounded in the Bible; and we can point out the horrible effects of sin all about us and through them point to God's warning concerning eternity, but the multitudes rush on unheeding.

Will you stop to think, my friend, as you listen to this broadcast this morning, please remember—sin is your enemy. God has warned you. We are echoing the warning of God. Stop and think and repent. Obey the gospel of the Christ before it is too late. Become a New Testament Christian and work for the saving of other precious souls. Let us fight sin in every form and be faithful to the very end. God has promised us the victory through Jesus Christ our Lord.

The Lord added to the Church

There is no other book in all the world like the Bible that can express so much in so few words. The story of creation was recorded in thirty-four verses. A history of events for 2,369 years is outlined in fifty short chapters in Genesis. Four books of sixty-nine chapters give the story of the life of Christ for the span of His more than 12,000 days upon the earth. Truly, the Bible was written under the guidance of divine power. Few words are used to present many of God's truths.

That fact is true in our text in Acts 2 in Peter's sermon on the day of Pentecost and the days that immediately followed. The last part of Acts 2:47 reads: "And the Lord added to the church daily such as should be saved." The American Standard Version expresses the thought in these words, "And the Lord added to them day by day those that were saved." These few words touch upon four important matters that all of us should know: (1) The church was then in existence. (2) The Lord added people to the church. (3) The kind of people who were added to the church, and (4) The nature of the church to which they were added.

Number One: The church was then in existence. In this verse for the first time in the Bible, the church is spoken of as being in existence. John has preached, "Repent ye, for the kingdom of heaven is at hand" (Matthew 3:2). Jesus, after His baptism and temptation, began to preach, saying, "Repent, for the kingdom of heaven is at hand" (Matthew 4:17). The Lord had told His disciples, "I will build my church" (Matthew 16:18). But now for the first time, the church is taught as a reality. Jesus of Nazareth had been made both Lord and Christ, and the church began that day as recorded in Acts 2.

The matter of fact statement of Acts 2:47 should silence the erroneous teaching that the church began in Old Testament days, in the days of John the Baptist, or at some later time. This passage can supply a fact men need to understand today. The church was then in existence. It began on the day of Pentecost in A.D. 33 (Acts 2 and supported by Mr. Usher's chronology of the Bible). Further, all religious bodies professing to be of a divine origin, but which began hundreds of years later, need to re-examine and withdraw their assertions.

Number Two: The Lord added people to the church. Christ is the head of the church, as we read in Ephesians 1:22-23; and Acts 2 says the Lord Himself adds men to His church. He has not delegated this responsibility to men. The Bible teaches no other way for men to become members of His church. This statement, "The Lord added to the church daily such as should be saved" (Acts 2:47), is quite different from many present day expressions. For example, the expression so often used is—"join the church." Men may join some fraternal order, some civic organization, or some denominational body, but the Lord does the adding to His church. Men may be voted into various religious organizations, but the Bible example is, "The Lord ADDED to the church," and the decision belongs solely to the Lord as to who shall be members of His spiritual body, the church.

Number Three: The kind of people who were added to the church. The Lord added the "saved" to His church, according to Acts 2:47: "...And the Lord added to His church daily such as should be saved" or as another translation says, "...such as were being saved." Those whom the Lord added day by day to the church were the saved. Acts 2:41 teaches the same process: "Then they that gladly received his word were baptized: and the same day there were added unto them about three thousand souls." We conclude then that sinners are saved from their past sins when they obey the Lord's terms of pardon given in the gospel, and they are added to the church. As J. W. McGarvey wrote, "Primarily the term 'saved' means simply to 'make safe.' In the religious sense, it means to make safe from the consequences of sin. If man had never sinned, he could not be saved, seeing he would already be safe. But having sinned, people are saved when they are made safe from the consequences of their sins; that is, their sins are forgiven. At the moment a penitent sinner obtains pardon, he is, so far as the past is concerned, completely saved. It is in this sense that the parties in this case added to the church are called the saved."

Jesus teaches, "He that believeth and is baptized shall be saved" (Mark 16:16). And Peter says, "Repent and be baptized every one of you in the name of Jesus Christ for the remission of sins" (Acts 2:38). These verses teach that the sinner must believe in Christ, repent of his sins, and be baptized to receive remission of his sins. Ananias told the penitent, grieving Saul, "Arise, and be baptized, and wash away thy sins, calling on the name of the Lord" (Acts 22:16). Saul's obedience did not exclude the grace of God but brought him in obedience by accepting the salvation afforded by God's grace through the blood of Christ that was shed for the remission of sins (Matthew 26:28).

A proper understanding of this matter would remove the need for the question: Can a man be saved outside the church? The saved are added to the church by the Lord according to our text. And since this is true and has been true from the time the church was first established, it should be clear that all those who have been saved from their past sins have been added to the church.

Next, let us read Acts 5:14. As the church continued to increase in number, it says, "And believers were the more added to the Lord, multitudes both of men and women." First, observe that the believers were added to the Lord. The church is the body of Christ (Ephesians 1:22-23). These expressions are the same in meaning: "added to the church" and "added to the Lord." For one to be added to the church simply means he is added to the Lord's body, which is the church. The believers who were added to the Lord were the saved. They were not added, as so many teach today, upon the condition of faith alone. And they were not saved or added to the Lord the very moment they believed. These believers, who were added to the Lord, were those who had enough faith in Christ to obey His commandments. They were added when they were saved.

According to John 1:12, Christ gave the right to become sons of God to them who believe on His name, but all those who believe in Christ do not exercise that right. Only those who have enough faith in Him to cause them to obey His commandments and to be born again really become the sons of God (John 1:13). Jesus says in John 3:5 that "except a man be born of water and of the Spirit, he cannot enter into the kingdom of God." The conclusion then is inevitable. The salvation of the sinner requires faith in Christ as the Son of God, and that faith in Christ must be sufficient to cause him to obey the Lord's command to be baptized for the remission of his sins. And his very obedience of being buried with Christ in baptism by which he is saved is the obedience by which he is born into God's family, the church. He is thus added to the church of our Lord.

Number Four: The nature of the church. The saved were added to the church. The definite article "the" is used to designate the church.

It is singular in nature, for the church of our Lord is ONE. Surely we cannot escape the conclusion: The Lord established one church. The Lord's church is described as one body in Ephesians 4:4. Christ is the saviour of the body, the church, as we read in Ephesians 5:23. He purchased the church with His own blood on Calvary (Acts 20:28). The simplicity of this oneness of the church stands in contrast to the divided condition of the religious world today. The Lord's teaching in the New Testament is that the church is to be "one body." Sectarian and denominational organizations are not taught in the Bible. Such conceptions of religion must be learned from the commandments and the doctrines of men. I think that probably the greatest thing we could urge today is to say, "Let us go back to the Bible." Let us teach the Lord's plan for our salvation with a united faith in the Bible as the word of God. Let us teach men to repent even as our Master says, "Except ye repent, ye shall all likewise perish" (Luke 13:3). Let us tell men that Jesus says, "He that believeth and is baptized shall be saved" (Mark 16:16).

These are the Lord's teachings. Let us tell them to lost sinners so that they may know what to do to be saved from their sins. Let us tell the world that the Lord added the saved to His church, which is His body. And let us proclaim the unity of the Lord's body to the divided religious world. Let us call upon men to forsake the creeds that are causing confusion and division. And may we learn the prayer of our Lord for His disciples as He prayed "that they all may be one; as thou, Father, art in me, and I in thee, that they also may be one in us: that the world may believe that thou has sent me" (John 17:21). Let us make up our minds today that we will do all we can do to restore the Lord's church. It can be done through the preaching of the gospel of Christ as it is found in the New Testament. Let us call upon men to live for Christ. Let us tell them about heaven and warn them about the punishments of hell. Let us fill our lives with the love for Christ and for one another that will prepare us for an eternal life in heaven. Let us be Christians—humble, faithful, godly, and consecrated Christians who are described as "they continued steadfastly in the apostles' doctrine and fellowship, and in breaking of bread and in prayers" (Acts 2:42). And in so doing we can convince the lost world of the real meaning of being saved through Christ and of being members of the Lord's church, united and happy in the hope of eternal life. This is our plea to all of you today.

The World

Good morning, everyone. Once again, we bring you the gospel of Jesus Christ. We come to talk to you about those things that matter most—those things that will reach into the great eternity. This morning we are discussing with you the subject of the world and our relationship to the world as a Christian. Over and over in Holy Scripture, we are exposed to the word 'world.' Jesus Christ used it in His teaching; and as we endeavor to teach the great message of the Saviour, we must use the same word, (world); but all too often there is little understanding of the meaning of that term. So, let's spend a few moments this morning considering its use in the New Testament.

First of all, we learn that the earth is spoken of as the world. In John 1:10, it is speaking of the relation of Christ to the creation: "the world was made by him." Indeed, Christ had a part with the Father in the forming of all things in the beginning. "Without him was not anything made that was made." In Colossians 1:16, we read, "For by him were all things created, that are in heaven, and that are in earth, visible and invisible." Frequently, the word world is used to designate the earth God made through Christ, the earth on which we dwell.

Again, the inhabitants of the earth are referred to as "the world" in some passages. For instance, Jesus says, "For God so loved the world, that he gave his only begotten Son, that whosoever believeth in him should not perish, but have everlasting life" (John 3:16). In this verse, I am persuaded, the Lord is thinking of all the people who live on the earth. God loved them every one and loved them enough to give His only begotten Son to die for their salvation. Jesus tells His apostles, "Go ye into all the world, and preach the gospel to every creature. He that believeth and is baptized shall be saved; but he that believeth not shall be damned" (Mark 16:15-16). Our Lord wanted all men of the earth to hear the gospel of salvation, and He wants all people today to be saved and to come to the knowledge of the truth (1 Timothy 2:4).

The material things or wealth are sometimes referred to as "the world." Jesus speaks of them in contrast with spiritual things. In Mark

8:36, He says, "For what shall it profit a man, if he shall gain the whole world, and lose his own soul?" All the material wealth of this world is small, indeed, when we consider the value of the eternal soul.

The wicked and the sinful are also sometimes referred to as "the world." Jesus says, "Love not the world, neither the things that are in the world. If any man love the world, the love of the Father is not in him. For all that is in the world, the lust of the flesh, and the lust of the eyes, and the pride of life, is not of the Father, but is of the world" (1 John 2:15-16).

Jesus came to be the Saviour of the world (John 4:42). The world was lost because of sin and wickedness. Jesus condemned the sin in the lives of men, and He spoke of the devil as the "prince of this world" (John 12:31). Because of His condemnation of sin, the world hated Him and rejected Him. You recall that our Lord came to be the "light of the world" (John 9:5). He spoke of the sin of the world as darkness. He says, "And this is the condemnation, that light has come into the world, and men loved darkness rather than light, because their deeds were evil. For every one that doeth evil hateth the light, neither cometh to the light, lest his deeds should be reproved" (John 3:19-20).

The kingdom of the devil is the kingdom of sin (Matthew 12:26). Satan is the "god of this world" of sin (2 Corinthians 4:4). He is the one who brought sin into the world. The influence of sin and its effect upon men is called **darkness** ... in contrast to the light of God and of Christ and of righteousness. Satan's power is referred to as the "power of darkness" (Colossians 1:13). The works of his citizens in the world are called "the unfruitful works of darkness" (Ephesians 5:11). Of them, Jesus says, "Ye are of your father the devil, and the lusts of your father ye will do" (John 8:44). The kingdom of the devil is the kingdom of this world. The citizens of the devil's kingdom are those who have chosen to serve the devil instead of serving the Lord.

There is also the kingdom of God. You see, in the world we have the kingdom of Satan and we have the kingdom of God, which was established by Jesus Christ according to God's purpose (Daniel 2:44). It was on the day of Pentecost, as recorded in Acts 2:36 that Peter says, "Therefore let all the house of Israel know assuredly, that God hath made that same Jesus, whom you have crucified, both Lord and Christ." The word Lord means "ruler," and Christ means "anointed." Christ became the Anointed Ruler over God's kingdom upon the earth—which was established that day. God's kingdom is the church of our Lord (Matthew 16:18-19). Paul says the Colossian Christians were "delivered from the power of darkness," which is the devil's kingdom, and they were "translated into the kingdom of his dear Son," which is Lord's church.

The kingdom of the devil is the kingdom of this world of lust and sin. "The kingdom of God is ... righteousness, and peace, and joy in the Holy Ghost" (Romans 14:17). The contrast is as great as the contrast could be between God and Satan. The kingdom of this world is opposed to the kingdom of God. All people are members of one of these two kingdoms—either in the kingdom of God, of which Christ is King or in the kingdom of the world, over which Satan is the ruler. Jesus teaches plainly, "No man can serve two masters" (Matthew 6:24). He says, "He that is not with me is against me" (Matthew 12:30). There is no middle ground for us to occupy. James says, "Know ye not that the friendship of the world is enmity (or war) with God? whosoever therefore will be a friend of the world is the enemy of God" (James 4:4).

We must decide—you must decide—each one of us must evaluate his position. The man who would follow Jesus Christ must separate himself from the world. Paul had this in mind as he writes, "Wherefore come out from among them, and be ye separate, saith the Lord, and touch not the unclean thing; and I will receive you, And will be a Father unto you, and ye shall be my sons and daughters, saith the Lord Almighty" (2 Corinthians 6:17-18).

The Christian is to live as Christ lived. Peter says, "Christ also suffered for us, leaving us an example, that ye should follow his steps" (1 Peter 2:21). In following Christ, the Christian cannot live like the world lives. Paul says, "The world is crucified unto me, and I unto the world" (Galatians 6:14). The Christian must be **different** from the world. In Romans 12:2, we read, "Be not conformed to this world: but be ye transformed by the renewing of your mind, that ye may prove what is that good, and acceptable, and perfect, will of God." You must decide whether you are going to live for Christ or for Satan—whether you are going to be a member of the kingdom of Christ or remain in the kingdom of the world.

We enter God's kingdom by the new birth. Jesus says, "Except a man be born of the water and of the Spirit, he cannot enter the kingdom of

God" (John 3:5). The birth of the Spirit comes by faith in God's word, (1 Peter 1:23). The birth of water is accomplished by a burial in water in baptism for the remission of sins (Romans 6:4; Acts 2:38). Jesus says, "He that believeth and is baptized shall be saved" (Mark 16:16). Thus, when the believing penitent is baptized, he is saved. He is born again—born into God's family, and the Lord adds him to the church (Acts 2:47). Paul says, "For ye are all the children of God by faith in Christ Jesus. For as many of you" ... (how many??) ... "as many of you as have been baptized into Christ have put on Christ" (Galatians 3:26-27).

Have you been born again? Have you really been born of the water and of the Spirit? Have you been begotten by the Spirit and born or delivered of that watery grave? As you listen today, we beg you to consider this question with all the seriousness that your soul can command! Your eternal happiness depends upon your answer to this important question. Jesus placed the emphasis here, remember—"Except a man be born of water and of the Spirit, he CANNOT enter into the kingdom of God." This, of course, becomes the point of separation. When a person is born into God's kingdom, he is to put on Christ who is to be his Saviour and Lord! He is to "put on the new man which is renewed in knowledge after the image of Him that created him" (Colossians 3:10). This separation from the world is to be evident in the very nature of everyday living. It is to be shown in mercy, kindness, humbleness of mind, meekness, long-suffering, forbearance, forgiveness, and love (Colossians 3:12-13). The peace of God is to rule in his heart and the word of Christ is to dwell therein, and all things to be done in the name of the Lord Jesus, giving thanks to God and the Father by him (Colossians 3:15-17).

The separation that has come as we obey the Lord must be maintained for our own salvation (and we reach that point of separation as we are added to Christ's kingdom). It was to the followers of Christ that John says, "Love not the world." It was to Christians that James writes, "The friendship of the world is war toward God." It was to them that Paul writes, "Be ye separate." Jesus says, "He that endureth to the end shall be saved" (Matthew 10:22). This separation must be maintained not only for our own salvation but for the growth of the church. The lives of the members of the Lord's church should not be filled with the practices of sin that are found in the world. It is by godliness and purity of Christian living that Christians, or the children of God, are to lead men out of the world into the kingdom of Christ.

If church members live like the world, then those in the world will never be won to Christ. The spiritual and numerical growth of the church depends upon this great principle of divine truth. The pressures are great. You have found that to be so true. There is so much corruption and sin around us. The devil is at work at all times seeking to destroy and devour (1 Peter 5:8). Christians must always be on guard and not be overcome by the temptations that are on every hand. God can give us the victory through our Lord Jesus Christ. John says, "This is the victory that overcometh the world, even our faith" (1 John 5:4). Jesus says, "If ye were of the world, the world would love his own: but because ye are not of the world, but I have chosen you out of the world, therefore the world hateth you" (John 15:19).

The world hated Christ, and He says, "If the world hate you, ye know that it hated me before it hated you" (John 15:18). The life of the Christian is to be a continuing condemnation of the lustful practices of the world. A man of God cannot be a man of the world; and because he strives to live a pure, clean, upright and godly life, the world does not like it. This is the reason the world hates the church of our Lord today; and the more Christians become like Christ, the more they are hated by the world. Nevertheless, the Christian must keep himself "unspotted from the world" (James 1:27).

Members of the Lord's church must keep this line of distinction not only for their own salvation but also for their positive influence among those in the world. We are supposed to be the "separated of God." In the world, you will find some who live very wickedly and you will find some who live rather good lives—and they live very close lives to those of the church—but it is in the church that we ought to see the greatest line of distinction. People should be able to see by their devout Christian behavior that the church and the world are not the same. Yet, sometimes the lines are so blurred and the line of distinction is so indistinct that really many Christians and the world itself cannot tell where the line of distinction is drawn. In the words that Christians speak, in the purity of their conduct, in the honesty of their dealings, in the faithfulness of their worship, in the modesty of their dress, and in the habits of their everyday living, we should be able to see allegiance to God and faith in Jesus Christ. There should be no doubt as to which side we have chosen. Our friends and associates should be able—as they did in the time of Christ—to know that we have been with Jesus. The friends that we have should be able to tell from the way we live, by the way we treat those about us, and by the way we deal with people in matters of business that we are followers of Jesus Christ and members of the Lord's church.

It is not enough simply to go to church. It is not enough just to profess some kind of religion. I don't suppose there has ever been a time that you could die and go to hell in a more respectable fashion than you can today. You can live "some kind of life" and still leave this world, and people seem to feel that everything is lovely and everything is good—when according to this Book, that just simply is not the case! It is not enough to go to church. It is not enough just to profess some kind of religion. Christianity is to make us **like Christ**. Christianity is not something you **do** on Sunday morning. It is not something you do at any time—**it is a way of life**. Christianity involves **doing**, but it is ***a*** total concept of living that requires **total dedication.** It is to be a separation from the sinful practices of the world around us. It is to lead us to obey Christ in all things. It is to make us members of the church of our Lord. We are to lead others to glorify God and to become Christians so that they can go to heaven because of the example we have set.

Our Lord still insists, "Ye are the salt of the earth," "Ye are the light of the world," and we are that candle that is placed upon a candlestick—not under a bushel—that we may give light to all that are in the house. We have been enlightened that others may be enlightened, so others can go to heaven because of our example and because we show them the difference that exists between the church and the world. It can be done! Christ has given us the example. It requires the surrender of our lives to Jesus Christ. It means that we make Him our Saviour, the Captain of our Salvation. He becomes to us the "Rose of Sharon," the "Lily of the Valley," the "Fairest of Ten Thousand," and it will mean the joy and the happiness of heaven will be ours when we come to the end of this earthly life.

Rejoice in the Lord

In Philippians 4:4, we have the words of the Apostle Paul, "Rejoice in the Lord always: and again I say, Rejoice." Evidently the apostle believed that a Christian should be a happy person, and I am persuaded this is the Christian's privilege at all times. Every day he lives is to be a happy day. He is not to be happy just now and then or on some special occasions or at distant intervals. The joy of being a Christian is to be his every day that he lives. In fact, the text says, "Rejoice in the Lord **alway** ... ." The person who is not a Christian may not understand that. And I suspect there are many Christians who do not understand it. The person who is not a Christian may not understand because he may not see all the reasons that lie behind such an exultation. He may be looking at the wrong thing and be dependent upon the wrong source for his joy.

The Bible teaches that a Christian is to "rejoice in the Lord." His joy is not to be rooted in some exterior circumstance or time or place. His joy is to be "in the Lord." When a person's joy is dependent upon circumstances that surround him, his happiness will change as those circumstances change. And when everything is not just right, he will certainly see nothing in which to rejoice. The joy of the Christian is "in the Lord." If everything else changes, the Lord does not change. If other sources fail, the Lord does not fail. If the the surrounding circumstances are filled with trouble or pain or hardships or sorrow, the Lord is there to help and to strengthen and to sustain. There is not a moment of the Christian's life when he cannot find joy in the Lord if, indeed, his life is filled with the great faith and love that should be his at all times.

I think what I just stated is a tremendous challenge to any thinking Christian. We have so many unhappy Christians today. Not just unhappy people, but I really feel many of our brothers and sisters in Christ have many unhappy days. And many of us see nothing at all to rejoice about, and we have reached the place where to "rejoice in the Lord alway" sounds very odd and very strange to us. We are prone to say to Paul, "But you didn't live in the 20th century ... you didn't have to deal with some of the things we have to deal with today; and if you were here, you wouldn't think like that!!" I want us to think of Paul's circumstances for just a moment. At the time he wrote the Philippian letter, Paul was a prisoner in Rome. He was soon to be tried before the court of Caesar. His life had been filled with many trials and tribulations. Persecutions and hardships had befallen him on all of his journeys many of which he lists in 2 Corinthians 11:24-27. It was at Philippi that Paul and Silas were beaten with many stripes and then cast into the inner prison with their feet made fast in stocks (Acts 16:24). You recall that at midnight, Paul and Silas prayed and sang praises unto God; and God delivered them from prison. The first Philippian converts knew of the persecutions that had come to Paul. They too had adversaries; and Paul says, "For unto you it is given in the behalf of Christ, not only to believe on him, but also to suffer for his sake; Having the same conflict which ye saw in me, and now hear to be in me" (Philippians 1:29-30). So Paul's happiness was not dependent on the circumstance surrounding his life. His life was for Christ. His joy was in serving the Lord Jesus Christ, regardless of what happened to him. He says, "I know both how to be abased, and I know how to abound: every where and in all things I am instructed both to be full and to be hungry, both to abound and to suffer need. I can do all things through Christ which strengtheneth me" (Philippians 4:12-13).

Paul's joy was where he admonished ours to be—it was in the Lord. He wanted the Christians at Philippi to share that same joy. The keynote of the whole Philippian letter is one of rejoicing. Nineteen times—now you think about this—nineteen times in 104 verses of these four short chapters Paul referred to joy, to rejoicing, and to gladness over and over again. No one can read his epistle and escape the happy spirit of the aged apostle who had learned the real source of happiness, the Lord Jesus Christ. Always remember, please, that this great, wonderful, happy man was writing from a Roman dungeon and yet he says, "I can rejoice." Why? Because he was a real Christian, and he was living in the Lord.

Consider yourself today. My friend, if you are not a Christian, you have missed thus far the greatest joy in life. You have robbed yourself of the real heart of all happiness. We trust that this lesson will cause you to think upon the joy of living for Christ and that you will become a Christian so that you may be a partaker of the happiness that can be found only in the Lord. And if you are a Christian, we hope this study will cause you to consider the happiness that can be yours in your life for Christ and in your faith in the person of our Lord and what He can personally mean to you. Let's learn to rejoice in the Lord "alway."

First of all, think of what the Lord has done for us. He came to earth, laying aside the joys of heaven to live, to suffer and to die so that we might be saved. "Who his own self bare our sins in **His** body on the tree, that we, being dead to sins, should live unto righteousness: by whose stripes ye were healed" (1 Peter 2:24). And when we consider our sins and that we have all sinned and come short of the glory of God, we must know that "the wages of sin is death" (Romans 6:23). Had not Christ suffered for us, there would be no hope, no salvation. Christ came to save us from the peril of eternal death. He died that we might have life and have it abundantly. He was buried so that we might be raised. Christ had no sin. He died so that we might be made free from **our** sins. His blood was shed on Calvary's cross for the remission of our sins. We should rejoice that we have such a Saviour. We should appreciate Him enough to obey His commands. If Jesus laid down His life for us, surely we should be willing to give our lives to Him. Jesus says, "Greater love hath no man than this, that a man lay down his life for his friends. Ye are my friends, if ye do whatsoever I command you" (John 15:13-14).

When Philip taught the eunuch about Christ and the eunuch believed on Him as the Son of God, he desired at once to be baptized in obedience to Christ; and Acts 8:38 states, "they went down both into the water, both Philip and the eunuch; and he baptized him." The very next verse tells us how the eunuch went on his way doing what?—"he went on his way rejoicing." And that same joy can come to each one of us as we are willing to obey Christ so that Christ can save us from our sins.

Salvation in the Lord should be our joy. It is in Christ that Paul says, "we have redemption through his blood, the forgiveness of sins, according to the riches of his grace" (Ephesians 1:7). We can, as penitent believers in Christ, be baptized into Jesus Christ according to Romans 6:3-5. And as we are buried in baptism, we can rise to walk in that happy new life of service for Christ. No person who has not become a Christian can experience this joy. Salvation is in Christ, and the person who has not obeyed Christ is lost in sin. He cannot rejoice that his past sins are forgiven. He cannot know the blessing of God's grace in the forgiveness of his sins day by day. But the Christian has the promise as recorded in 1 John 1:7, "If we walk in the light as he is in the light, we have fellowship one with another, and the blood of Jesus Christ his Son cleanseth us from all sin." How wonderful is the assurance of God's grace to the Christian—that God through the blood of Christ will keep him cleansed from sin. How great the promise of Romans 8:1: "There is therefore now no condemnation to them which are in Christ Jesus, who walk not after the flesh, but after the Spirit." It is no marvel, then, that the Christian can always be happy when he has so great a salvation through such a wonderful Saviour as the Lord Jesus Christ.

Furthermore, we should be happy and joyful because of the spiritual blessings we have in Christ. In Ephesians 1:3, "Blessed be the God and Father of our Lord Jesus Christ, who hath blessed us with all spiritual blessings in heavenly places in Christ." You see, it is in Christ as Christians and members of the Lord's church that we can be partakers of these great spiritual blessings, and these blessings are so many that we do not have time to list all of them in this lesson. But let's think of a few of them:

First of all, as Christians, we are the children of God. John says, "Behold, what manner of love the Father hath bestowed upon us, that we should be called the sons of God" (1 John 3:1). The Christian is born into God's family as he is baptized as a penitent believer into Christ (Galatians 3:26-27). He becomes a child of God, a member of God's family, the church (1 Timothy 3:15). As a child of God, he becomes an heir of heaven (Romans 8:17).

The new birth, a birth of water and of the Spirit (John 3:3-5), brings us into covenant relationship with God and Christ. As a child of God, the Christian has all of the blessings and the privileges of the family of God. And all of the promises of God are his to enjoy.

Not only are we the children of God, but in Christ we are made kings and priests unto God. In Revelation 1:5-6, we read how Christ "washed us from our sins in his own blood, And hath made us kings and priests unto God and his Father." As kings, it is ours to reign with Him; and as priests, it is our privilege to offer worship to Him. To us, as Christians, it is a matter of joy to be privileged to worship our God. Like the Psalmist we can say, "I was glad" ... think of that ... "I was **glad** when they said unto me, Let us go into the house of the Lord"

(Psalm 122:1). We will never want to forsake the assembly of the saints (Hebrews 10:25). Every worship service will be an opportunity—not a burden. It will be a joy to worship God. We would want to "Enter into his gates with thanksgiving, and into his courts with praise: be thankful unto him, and bless his name. For the Lord is good; his mercy is everlasting; and his truth endureth to all generations" (Psalm 100:4-5).

Furthermore, there is a real joy in Christian unity and Christian fellowship. Paul says, "Fulfill ye my joy, that ye be likeminded, having the same love, being of one accord, of one mind" (Philippians 2:2). Psalm 133:1 describes this privilege by saying, "Behold, how good and how pleasant it is for brethren to dwell together in unity!" There should be no strife or bitterness or jealousy or division to mar the happiness of Christian fellowship in our Lord's body, the church. But as Christians, the bond should be so close that we can know how to share our brother's needs and to rejoice with them that rejoice and weep with them that weep (Romans 12:15). We should seek our brother's good and rejoice that we can "bear one another's burdens, and so fulfill the law of Christ" (Galatians 6:2).

There is a real joy in serving the Lord! Peter writes of the faith that makes us rejoice with "joy unspeakable and full of glory" (1 Peter 1:8). John writes, "And these things write we unto you, that your joy may be full" (1 John 1:4). James says that even when we are tried, to count it all joy (James 1:2). And even if we suffer for Christ, Peter reminds us, "But rejoice, inasmuch as ye are partakers of Christ's sufferings; that, when his glory shall be revealed, ye may be glad also with exceeding joy. If ye be reproached for the name of Christ, happy are ye; for the spirit of glory and of God resteth upon you" (1 Peter 4:13-14). Remember how the apostles rejoiced that they were counted worthy to suffer shame for His name. Think about that. How many of us would **rejoice** to be counted worthy to suffer shame for the name of Jesus today? (Acts 5:41). In Acts 2:41, we are told, "they that **gladly** received his word were baptized." They were happy that they could be saved, even through Christ whom they crucified, and their joy is seen in their steadfastness. "And they, continuing daily with one accord in the temple, and breaking bread from house to house, did eat their meat with **gladness** and singleness of heart, Praising God, and having favour with all the people" (verses 46-47). At Iconium it says, "And the disciples were filled with **joy**" (Acts 13:52).

Paul writes to the Roman Christians concerning the faith and peace and grace that is in Christ and "rejoice in hope of the glory of God" (Romans 5:2). There is a real joy in Christian sacrifice and service. Paul teaches the Philippians to shine as lights in the world "holding forth the word of life; that I may rejoice in the day of Christ, that I have not run in vain, neither laboured in vain." And then he says, "Yea, and if I be offered"—listen—"if I be offered upon the sacrifice and service of your faith, I joy, and rejoice with you all. For the same cause also do ye joy, and rejoice with me" (Philippians 2:16-18).

When our Lord suffered upon Calvary for us and became the author and finisher of our faith, we are reminded in Hebrews 12:2 that "for the joy that was set before him endured the cross, despising the shame, and is set down at the right hand of the throne of God." So for the joy that is set before us—listen—for the joy that is set before us in the hope of eternal happiness, we are to live for Christ every day of our lives. Let us rejoice in the Lord. He can save our soul from sin and from eternal death. He can give peace to our troubled heart. The Lord can support us in our trials and comfort us in our bereavement. He can walk with us and sustain us even when we walk through the valley of the shadow of death. He can raise us up to live with Him in the Father's house where there are many mansions. So it is our privilege, today, to rejoice and to be happy in the Lord. We have more sources of joy than any other people in all the world. And the Christian's joy will not fail, it will not fade. True religion is not sadness or grief or hardship. The service of our Lord is joy and gladness.

I trust that this very day you will enter into the joy of your Lord. I trust that this day you will enter into His courts with praise and with thanksgiving and with joy, that some day you may hear the Lord say, "Well done, thou good and faithful servant: I will make thee ruler over many things: enter thou into the" ... what? ... "into the **joy** of thy lord." (Matthew 25:21) So there is a real joy, today, in Christian living!

We thank you for listening.

Beyond the Law

Ladies and gentlemen, we invite your attention to the gospel of Jesus Christ and to a subject that we will title "Beyond the Law." Our Lord Jesus Christ gave the greatest commandment the world has ever known. He went beyond the commandments that had been given prior to that time, and He told His disciples "a new commandment I give unto you." The old Mosaic law that was given to the Jews contained hundreds of commandments, but the Lord went beyond them all to give a new commandment to His disciples who were then present and to all the disciples in the centuries to follow. In John 13:34, we have these words, "A new commandment I give unto you, That ye love one another; as I have loved you, that ye also love one another."

When we look at this commandment and Jesus' statement "a new commandment I give unto you," we are prone to raise the question. What is new about it? The old Mosaic law had taught love. In Deuteronomy 6:5, it is written, "Thou shalt love the Lord thy God with all thine heart, and with all thy soul, and with all thy might." Leviticus 19:18 teaches "Thou shalt love thy neighbor as thyself." Jesus points out these teachings in reply to the lawyer who asks him, "Master which is the great commandment in the law?" And Jesus says to him:

> Thou shalt love the Lord thy God with all thy heart, and with all thy soul, and with all thy mind. This is the first and great commandment. And the second is like unto it, Thou shalt love thy neighbor as thyself. On these two commandments hang all the law and the prophets (Matthew 22:36-40).

So the teaching of love was not new. For 1,500 years, the law had taught love. The new part of the commandment of our Lord was found in those words, "As I have loved YOU, that ye also love one another." Such love as the Saviour taught was new. It was so intense and so great; it was the greatest love that man had ever known. It passed beyond the law of Moses; in fact, it passed beyond all law. Jesus teaches how extensive that love is when He says, "As I have loved YOU." This teaching was new. The Lord's measure of love is, "As I have loved YOU." In John 15:12-13, we have the Lord repeating with emphasis this thought: "This is my commandment, That ye love one another, as I have loved you. Greater love hath no man than this, that a man lay down his life for his friends." We must understand how great Christ's love really was at that time and is today. If I am to love others as Christ has loved ME, then I must know how great His love is.

The Bible teaches that because of love He died for us. In Romans 5:8, "But God commendeth his love toward us, in that, while we were yet sinners, Christ died for us." Notice the contrast with man's love. In Romans 5:7, man's love is expressed in these words, "For scarcely for a righteous man will one die: yet peradventure for a good man some would even dare to die." You know, we may admire the strict honesty of the righteous man who is just in his dealings with others, but we do not feel moved to die for him. And the good man who is more than just, he is so good in the sense that he is kind and amiable and generous. As Brother R. L. Whiteside points out, such a man may stir our emotions and get hold of the affections of our hearts. For such a man, some might dare to die but even that would be unusual. But our Lord died for sinners. He died even for His enemies. He died for those who hated and abused Him. He died for those who mocked Him and scourged Him and crucified Him. He died for those who rejected Him, who refused His teachings. He died for those who were opposed to His Father, and who had sinned against Him. He shed His blood that they might live. Never ... never has such love been known. And here is the measure of the Lord's new commandment, "As I have loved YOU, that ye also love one another."

Christ died for our sins. Paul says, "While we were yet SINNERS, Christ died for us" (Romans 5:8). He died in our stead. He died to save us from eternal death. He took our place on the cross. As Peter says, "Who his own self bare our sins in his own body on the tree, that we, being dead to sins, should live unto righteousness" (1 Peter 2:24). And by His love in dying in our place, Christ provided the way for our salvation from the eternal suffering of hell. Such love should kindle a love within us. John thinking of God's love says, "We love him, because he first loved us" (1 John 4:19). And when we consider the great love of our Lord and Saviour, it should create within us a desire to return the same love in our lives. Christ is our example in all things, but especially we see here the greatness of His example of love. And our constant desire and prayer should be to obey the Lord's command to "love one another" even—listen—even "as I have loved you." So love should kindle love within us.

Love should cause us to obey Him. Jesus says, "If ye love me, keep my commandments" (John 14:15). Again, "If a man love me, he will keep my words" (John 14:23). And "He that hath my commandments, and keepeth them, he it is that loveth me" (verse 21). Again, "Ye are my friends, if ye do whatsoever I command you" (John 15:14). 1 John 5:3 teaches, "For this is the love of God, that we keep his commandments: and his commandments are not grevious." Here is the test of our love for God and the promise is, "If ye keep my commandments, ye shall abide in my love; even as I kept my Father's commandments, and abide in his love" (John 15:10). Our love should stand the test so that we can receive the promise. The question is "Have you loved Christ enough to obey Him?" The question is not just "Have you loved Christ?" But have you loved Him enough to obey Him?

The Lord teaches men to believe in Him as the Son of God (John 8:24). Have you believed? He teaches men to repent of their sins (Luke 13:3). Have you repented? Jesus teaches men to be baptized in order to be saved (Mark 16:16). Have you been baptized for the remission of your sins (Acts 2:38)? The Lord's kind of baptism is a burial in water (Romans 6:4). And when He was baptized in Jordan, He "went up straightway out of the water" (Matthew 3:16). This is the Lord's plan. It is ours to obey and not to substitute. We are not to substitute sprinkling or pouring for the Lord's kind of baptism. It is for us to obey. And in so doing, we can be "the children of God by faith in Christ Jesus. For as many of you as have been baptized into Christ have put on Christ" (Galatians 3:26-27).

There should be no doubt in your mind as to whether you are a child of God. Your love for Christ should be great enough and strong enough to move you to obey the Lord as you have faith in Him. And in penitence you should be willing to do as Ananias told Saul, "And now why tarriest thou? arise, and be baptized, and wash away thy sins, calling on the name of the Lord" (Acts 22:16). In obeying these, because of your love for the Saviour who died for your sins, you can be without any doubt a child of God, born into God's family, the church of our Lord. As a Christian you can wear the name of Christ (1 Peter 4:16). And in obeying all of these things, you can become without a doubt a child of God, and you can give your life as a living sacrifice in His service (Romans 12:1-2).

Your faithfulness in worship and in service will depend on your love for Christ. Let His words be impressed upon your heart. "If a man love me, he WILL keep my words" (John 14:23) and "if you love me, keep my commandments" (John 14:15). Not one—listen—not one single duty will fall upon you in living the Christian life that you cannot willingly and cheerfully accomplish when you have the proper love for Christ. Love will make sacrifice a joy in service to the Lord. If hardships and sufferings must be endured, think about what the Lord suffered for us. Remember how He died for us. And then let us love one another. The Bible states, "Love thy neighbour as thyself" (Matthew 19:19). And more, as Jesus says, "Love one another; AS I have loved you" (John 13:34). Seek the good of others even as you would seek your own good. Treat others as you want to be treated (Matthew 7:12). Love them as you love yourself ... but don't stop with your friends. Jesus says:

> Love your enemies, bless them that curse you, do good to them that hate you, and pray for them which despitefully use you, and persecute you; that ye may be the children of your Father which is in heaven (Matthew 5:44-45).

Let your righteousness exceed that of the scribes and Pharisees (Matthew 5:20). And rise to the standard of our Lord's example. What is the standard? "Love one another; AS I have loved you."

There is one thing that should be apparent to us as we go down the road of life ... that people need love. The world is filled with hate; there are troubles and sin and war and crime and bloodshed all around us. So many people have so little regard for others about them. The rights and welfare and even the lives of others are so lightly considered. Men are hungering and thirsting for love, not hate. It is love that can comfort the troubled heart and can remember the neglected. It is love that can care for the needy and love can see that the widows and orphans are not forgotten. Love can lift up the fallen and minister to the sick and sustain the aged and the infirm. It is love that can find a way when those prompted by lesser motives of mere duty or some remuneration or a personal consideration have all failed. Love can make this world into a paradise of God, and how much better a place this would be if men could learn the lesson of love, and by love serve one another as we are taught in Galatians 5:13 and in Romans 13:8—"Owe no man anything, BUT to love one another."

Love should abound in our homes. Love is absolutely essential to the happiness of a family. The Bible teaches the husband to love his wife and the wife to love her husband (Ephesians 5:28-29; Titus 2:4). Children are to love their parents and to remember the command, "Obey your parents in the Lord for this is right" (Ephesians 6:1-2). Parents are to love and provide for their children and "bring them up in the nurture and admonition of the Lord" (Ephesians 6:4). Love can help solve the problems of marriage. It will bring patience and tenderness and forgiveness and thoughtfulness. When love is absent, the bonds of marriage are neglected, and the children are robbed of the affection and devotion they need to fashion their lives for God and for eternity. God wants Christian homes where love reigns and where children are reared to know the blessings and the meaning of true Christian love.

Christians are to love each other. Jesus says, "By this shall all men know that ye are my disciples"—I want you to think about this statement; one of the great statements of the Bible and seemingly so neglected—"By this shall all men know that ye are my disciples, IF ye have love one to another" (John 13:34-35). In 1 John 4:21, He says, "He who loveth God love his brother also," AND "If any man say, I love God, and hateth his brother, he is a liar: for he that loveth not his brother whom he hath seen, how can he love God whom he hath not seen?" (1 John 4:20). Love should move us to "bear one another's burdens and so fulfill the law of Christ" (Galatians 6:2).

Peter says, "Love one another with a pure heart fervently" (1 Peter 1:22). Love would make us "kind ... tender hearted, forgiving" (Ephesians 4:32). But where love is not found, there is trouble and discord and strife and division, even among the disciples of the Lord. Many professed Christians have never learned the meaning of 1 John 3:14, "He that loveth not his brother abideth in death." The most powerful uniting force on earth is love. It is the blessed tie that "binds our hearts in Christian love" to God and to each other. Love makes happy Christians. It rejoices in the opportunity to work together, to worship together, to pray together, and in all things to serve God together. Through love we can keep the "unity of the spirit in the bond of peace" (Ephesians 4:3).

Sectarianism and denominational barriers would be destroyed if Christian love were cultivated and practiced as our Lord has taught. Religious division is sinful, and it opposes the Lord's teaching on love. It is not a question of your accepting MY doctrine and MY church. It is simply the matter of loving the Lord and obeying HIS teaching of love. Then love will bind us to the Lord; and one thing is sure, if we are bound to the Lord, then we will be bound to each other.

The problem, then, must lie with us. The problem is not in saying that we love God or in professing to love one another—most men can do that. The real crux of the whole matter is, Have we learned the Lord's teaching of love? Are we able to go beyond the law and make love the controlling and directing principle of our thinking and of our actions?

Let each one of us examine his own heart. Let us as individuals in the privacy of our meditation and self evaluation determine our own personal condition. May we pray the Lord's wisdom and His blessings of strength and health to the end that we may be able always to be aware of this great need. Certainly we ought to close today with the fervent and humble prayer that God may help us, each one of us, to love God and to love one another even as Christ has loved us.

Pentecost – Creation Day

Ladies and gentlemen, we invite your attention today to the subject, "Pentecost, the Church Creation Day." About one year before His death, Jesus says, "Upon this rock I will build my church; and the gates of hell shall not prevail against it" (Matthew 16:18). When our Lord made the statement: "upon this rock I will build my church," it is evident that He promised to build only one church, and that was His!

The questions often arise: "What church was that?" and "what is the church? And we answer these questions: the church is His body (Colossians 1:18-24; Ephesians 1:22-23)! Then, the church of Jesus Christ and the body of Jesus Christ are the same thing because the church is the body of Christ. And, as Paul has said, Jesus is the head of that body; and every baptized believer is a member of His body, the church (Ephesians 5:30; 1 Corinthians 12:12-20). It is the very church He said He would build on the "rock," which refers to the confession of faith in Him as the Son of God that the Apostle Peter had just made.

Often times, this question is raised: "When was this church built?" It was sometime between the declaration He would build it and the subsequent statement: "the Lord added to the church." In the former declaration, the building of the church was yet in the future; in the latter statement, it had been accomplished: the church was built. Now, between the two statements, there was a period of just one year, one month, and about eleven days. To give another point of reference, there was a length of time between the Savior's discourse at Caesarea Philippi (Matthew 16:18) and the actual adding to that church on the day of Pentecost (Acts 2). Jesus said that He would build it. In AD 33, members were added to it. So, it must have been actually built in the spring of AD 33.

But the question is: When did this event occur? To ascertain when and where Christ built His church, we need but to learn when Christ was made head of the church; for the head of the body must of necessity be created at the same time. Paul told us exactly when Christ was made head:

> According to the working of his mighty power, which he wrought in Christ, when he raised him from the dead, and set him at his own right hand in the heavenly places, far above all principality, and power, and might, and dominion, and every name that is named, not only in this world, but also in that which is to come: And hath put all things under his feet, and gave him to be the head over all things to the church, which is his body, the fulness of him that filleth all in all (Ephesians 1:19-23).

Paul reiterates this idea to the Colossians: "And he is before all things, and by him all things consist. And he is the head of the body, the church: who is the beginning, the firstborn from the dead; that in all things he might have the preeminence" (Colossians 1:17-18).

These passages show; (1) that Christ, to be head of the church, had to have preeminence over all things both in heaven and on earth; (2) that this preeminence had to be made, or accorded Him on account of His triumph over death; (3) that such a place of honor could be bestowed only upon a throne at God's right hand in heaven—not on earth—and it could not have been done until God raised Him from the dead because it was from the dead that God raised Him to sit at His right hand as exalted ruler over all things. Christ, therefore, never became head of the church until he ascended to heaven and was crowned as King of Kings at God's right hand. Consequently, the church, the body of Christ, was not built until Christ was crowned King of Kings at God's right hand in the heavens **after** His ascension.

Let us consider the coronation: The crowning of the King of Kings occurred, according to Acts 2, on the day of Pentecost, AD 33. The life principle—the Holy Spirit Who united the head in heaven with the body on earth—came from God into the body on that day (Acts 2:1-5). Here, then, was the day the Church of Christ was built. As there could have been no head without the body and no body without the head, so there could have been neither head nor body without the vitalizing Spirit Who descended from God into the body on the day of Pentecost, AD 33. Here is the completed building to which Christ referred when he said, "I will build my church." The church existed from the moment the Holy Spirit filled the apostles on that day.

The apostles were living charter members of Christ's church on the day of Pentecost; hence, there were added to them that day about three thousand souls (Acts 2:41). The expression "there was added unto them," refers to the apostles alone. This exclusive reference to the apostles begins in Acts 1:17, where the ministry of Judas Iscariot is named. He was an apostle (Matthew 10:2-5), and his ministry was the same as the other apostles. But Judas fell away from all rights of that ministry, and another had to take his place as the twelfth apostle. Matthias was selected by God to fill Judas' place (Acts 1:26). Because Christ would build His church with precisely twelve human beings, or earthen vessels (2 Corinthians 4:7), to form the body, there had to be twelve intact when the time came. Following the pronoun, we connect the last verse of Acts 1, with the first verse of Acts 2:

> And they gave forth their lots; and the lot fell upon Matthias; and he was numbered with the eleven apostles. And when the day of Pentecost was fully come, they (the eleven plus Matthias) were all with one accord in one place.

The same twelve were next baptized in the Holy Spirit and spoke with other tongues—still just the twelve (verse 4). All who spoke were Galilaeans (verse 7), the home of all the apostles. In verse 14, we read, "But Peter, standing up with the eleven, lifted up his voice, and said unto them ... ." Unto them, the chosen twelve, the three thousand were added. Paul tells us we are of the household, (church) of God, being built on the foundation of the apostles and prophets, Christ Jesus himself being the chief corner stone (Ephesians 2:20).

Peter's discourse on the day of Pentecost emphatically explained the death, burial, resurrection, and coronation of Jesus. He pointed to the prophets' declaration that these things would so occur, quoting both Joel and David in confirmation of those truths. But the men, Joel and David, were long since dead, so they could not themselves be the foundation of the church; it was only that they predicted the founding. Peter explained that these prophets had predicted these events; that is, all of the events surrounding the promised Messiah as well as the outpouring of the Holy Spirit on this day. So, Pentecost is, of necessity, the birthday of the church.

You recall in an apocalyptic vision, John saw the future holy city, and the wall of the city had twelve foundations, and on them the names of the twelve apostles of the Lamb (Revelation 21:14). This corresponds with the selection of twelve apostles with whom to inaugurate the church. The twelve were the living foundation … that is the human part of Christ's church. They were its sole charter members. They then automatically became the first members when Christ became the head on the day of Pentecost. Christ in heaven, the apostles on earth, were builded into a form, the church of Our Lord on that day; and unto **them** were added on that day about three thousand souls. The church was created on that day and immediately became a living soul! This explains what Christ meant when He says to His apostles, "In the regeneration when the Son of man shall sit in the throne of his glory, ye also shall sit upon twelve thrones, judging the twelve tribes of Israel" (Matthew 19:28). The regeneration is the time when men are being regenerated through the gospel: the age of Christianity. This regeneration began on the day of Pentecost, and it will continue until Jesus comes again.

I propose to you today, that Jesus Christ is now (not future) seated upon the throne of His glory. He sat down on it on the day of Pentecost, and on that day the twelve began to judge men by laying before them the terms for the remission of sins dictated by the Holy Spirit. The twelve thrones clearly refer to the position in which the apostles were set (1 Corinthians 12:28). They were charter members, first to instruct by unfolding the plan of salvation. Christ, as head, dictated the plan. They, as members, executed that plan. I think that is important! To them, every soul that is saved will be added (Acts 2:47). All are added to the apostles or added to Christ. There is no other church of God open to men save the one that originated on that day of Pentecost.

The question of Paul's apostleship is not really of concern here. He was a special apostle! He was commissioned to the Gentile world (Acts 25; Galatians 2). And he preached to the Gentiles precisely what the twelve preached to the Jews; there is but one gospel for both Jew and Gentile. Paul was not one of the twelve; hence, he was not in the original foundation, as such. He says he was a child born out of due season; or as one translation puts it: "a child untimely born," born as an apostle several years too late to be in the original foundation. Hence, he speaks of certain ones having been in Christ "before me" (Romans 16:7). This statement shows that the body of the church was fully formed—completed, (foundation and all) even before Paul became an apostle. Otherwise, the building of the church would have rested upon an incomplete foundation; hence, an unfounded building until the day of Paul! But the church **was** complete on the day of Pentecost, with the twelve forming its complete foundation, and their names were transferred to the twelve foundations of the New Jerusalem (Revelation 21:12).

I think we must realize then that what we are looking at is the divine church. The church built, or created, on the day of Pentecost is the one and only church of God or Christ upon the earth. To enter that church is to build upon the divine foundation and have communion with Jesus Christ as head.

Any church founded this side of Pentecost is purely a human sect! Having in its foundation neither Christ, the apostles, nor the inspired prophecies of the Old Testament period, it possesses nothing of worth to human souls: it becomes a vain religion (Matthew 15:9).

As when God made Adam a perfect man on the day He created him, so Jesus made a perfect church on the day of Pentecost. It lacked nothing! Its head was perfect; its members were perfectly set in it; its law was perfect—a perfect gospel. God's power to save men (Romans 1:16) was first preached on that day. The terms for remission of sins were perfectly presented on that day (Acts 2:36-41). The result was about three thousand perfect additions to that church. Here, then, is the perfect church—the **only** Church of Christ! As such, it is the model church—a church whose every characteristic must exist in all subsequent congregations of Christ's church.

All churches of Christ, therefore, must possess Christ alone as builder and head and must contain the original twelve apostles as its charter members. Any church to which the apostles did not belong is not God's! To be in fellowship with Christ and God, we must be in fellowship with the original apostles, not some modern apostles or modern successors of apostles. I assure you that Christ's apostles have had no successors! Also, any Church of Christ today must preach the gospel alone as the only means of reaching, adding, or enlisting men.

The church must command all men who would enter it to believe on Christ, to repent of their sins, and to be baptized in Christ's name for the remission of their sins (Acts 2:38). Not only this, but that church must teach all who truly do these things, to know that the Lord has added them to the **only** church He has, which includes and consists of all Christians, from the apostles until now; and that, therefore, it is their duty to love and fellowship those who have obeyed the same divine instructions with them.

People today who do precisely and only what the people did on the day of Pentecost become members of that same church. They are united to Christ and to His apostles in the church that Christ built.

I think it is such a wicked calamity to charge that such people belong to some "new church" that was established by Alexander Campbell or some other man. They belong to nothing except the church built by Christ on the day of Pentecost. It is those who will not do what the apostles commanded, who belong to the new ones. On that day, in obedience to Peter's command of Acts 2:38, they that gladly received his word were baptized; and it is so today! Those who receive God's word are baptized. All who are unbaptized have (in every essential element) rejected God's council and words and really, His salvation.

As we have seen, the church founded at that time is the only church of Jesus Christ upon the earth! Any church that claims to have been established either before or after the day of Pentecost is of human origin, however good it may be, however benevolent its claims! The church **must** rest upon Christ crucified and, hence, could not have been established before His death. And, of course, any church that claims to have been established after the day of Pentecost is essentially post-apostolic and, therefore, without the Holy Spirit Who was fully dispatched on the day of Pentecost to abide with Christians forever.

Certainly, these are grand and glorious truths, and those who do today what Peter there commanded and what the people did on the day of Pentecost, will be, by the same Lord, added to the same church, the only one that Christ ever established and the only one He now claims as His own. As soon as one is baptized, he is added to the church, leaving no saved man out of the church; for the Lord adds to them, day by day, those who are saved. There are no saved people outside of the church. God has no children outside His family.

God Is, Sermon #1

This morning I have chosen to speak to you on the existence of God and the origin of life. It is no little matter to approach this subject; and I suppose if one ever feels insignificant, it would be when we attempt to comprehend something so vast and so great as the eternal God. The Bible states in Hebrews 11:6, "But without faith it is impossible to please him: for he that cometh to God must believe that he is, and that he is a rewarder of them that diligently seek him."

We **must** come to the Lord or draw near to Him, but it is impossible to draw near to one that we know nothing about or that we do not believe in. I begin our lesson upon the premise that God either is or He isn't. And as simple as that may sound, I think it is important. He either is or He isn't; He either was or He wasn't; He either lives or He doesn't. And if God lives, then all matters. There is no middle ground. To remain neutral, or attempt to remain neutral, is worse than bad when you really think about what the scriptures have to say. If He exists, **all** matters; if He does not exist, **nothing** matters.

Atheists and agnostics of all time have said their main argument is that the presence of evil in the world argues the fact that there is no God. If, they say, God exists, then why do we have evil, injustice, and inequity in the world? I propose to you that that is not a valid argument. If God does not exist, there is no evil. There are no inequities. There is no injustice. God is the **source** of right; and if He does not exist, I submit to you that you cannot tell me that this is right and that is wrong; without Him there is no standard of right and wrong.

In our day, it is not enough to just say, "Well, I think God lives," or "I don't think He lives," or "I don't see how He could live." We must "Be ready always to give an answer to every man that asketh (us) a reason of the hope that is in (us) with meekness and fear" (1 Peter 3:15). In these days, carrying the gospel into the world is first to sustain the fact that He lives. There was a time in this country during which one could go into any given community to preach the gospel of Christ and assume that at least 95 percent of the people believed in the

Bible and believed in God. About all you had to do was show the difference between what the Bible says and what they were practicing. But now, as we take the gospel into the various parts of the world, that isn't the case at all. You don't have to travel far from here to find that many don't believe God exists.

I believe God is knowable. The Bible teaches we can know He exists. When Mr. Flew came to this country recently from England and debated Thomas Warren, the proposition was clearly stated. The proposition was, "I know that God exists." Mr. Flew defended the proposition, "I know that God does not exist." I like that because it is getting it down to where it really is. I do believe God is **knowable.** The atheist says He doesn't exist. An agnostic says He exists, but you can't prove it. The Christian says God lives, and you can know Him and He is provable. In Psalm 46:10, the Lord says, "Be still and know that I am God." I submit that God is **knowable**; and if God is knowable, then God is **provable.** When we start talking about the existence of God, we are discussing thorny and controversial matters; but that shouldn't bother us. It should cause us to study a little more and try to determine carefully what this Book has to say. When we start discussing Christian evidences, we are discussing the existence of God, the deity of Christ, and the inspiration of the word of God.

There are three basic positions in regard to why life exists on earth today. There isn't any doubt that life is here. **You** are living today; you **exist.** Let me say to you in the beginning that our young people need to know these positions because they deal with them in school. For that reason, some of us who are older need to be setting forth what the Bible has to say.

> First of all, there is the position of the atheist, who believes in biological organic evolution of the species, who says that man and the world that exist today are the result of purely naturalistic, mechanistic, uniformitarian forces that operate externally in nature.
>
> Another position is special creation—that is, "In the beginning God created the heaven and the earth ... and all things therein." By the way, that is precisely what I believe; and it fits all the facts of science that I have ever learned or have ever read about. It fits the basic law of causality; it fits the basic laws of biogenesis and thermodynamics.

> The third position, and it is growing every day, is theistic evolution. I worked two years with a professor who believed this. She was a theistic evolutionist. As the years passed, I came to understand the theory quite well. She believed in God. She went to church. She considered herself a fine member of her church but believed in religious evolution, mitigated evolution, and progressive evolution or sometimes referred to as threshold evolution. It afforded her an opportunity to hang onto religion and yet rub shoulders with the rank and file of biological evolutionists in her field. Her basic belief was—God created and developed the universe we are in, but He did it through evolutionary process. He supervised it all. God wanted it to happen this way—spontaneous formation of life from chemicals, from amoeba to man. It is a popular way. I suspect that it is a way out. You don't have to make a decision. You believe in God, and you believe in theistic evolution.

The greatest problem with theistic evolution is that it is wrong … It is flat wrong!! The Bible does not teach any such thing. I would like to point out just two or three things about this theory before we go on to the rest of the lesson. First of all, Genesis 1:1 says, "In the **beginning** God **CREATED** ... ." In the beginning, God did not **begin** to create. "In the beginning God **CREATED** the heaven and the earth." In Exodus 20:11, the Bible states that in **one week** the Lord created all that He created, and it was done.

One of the problems that theistic evolutionists have is how to explain the spirit of man. They explain that man evolved from a lower form of life through spontaneous generation—God supervising it, of course—and that man evolved from the lower to the higher. But the theistic evolutionist believes in the spirit of man, too. And I have a real problem with their idea of evolving the spirit of man until man is finally made in God's own image when, in fact, the Bible states that when God created man, he "breathed into his nostrils the breath of life; and man became a living soul" (Genesis 2:7). God gave him His image in the beginning, not through a long, long process. They also teach that it takes a miracle to get the image of God into man (conversion) yet do not believe in the miracle of creation!

Another problem the theistic evolutionist has is the very difficult time of explaining Eve. This theory cannot explain how two different sexes evolved in the same geographical region at approximately the same time. It is difficult to explain how Adam, if indeed he was the product of blind chance or at least if he began at the lowest level, having looked at all the animals that God had made did not find among them—if indeed he was an animal, too—one who was suitable for him and how it took a special act of creation—not evolution—to create a being who could stand by his side as his counterpart. The Bible teaches that Adam was the first **man**—not homo erectus—**Adam** was the first **man** according to 1 Corinthians 15:45. Theistic evolution cannot explain creation in one week because it must take thousands and millions of years to bring these things to pass while Exodus 20:11, Nehemiah 9:6, and Genesis 1, all teach that in **one week** God created all the heavens and the earth and everything that therein is.

Theistic evolution cannot explain a full grown man, a full grown woman, and a full grown universe. You see, when God created, He created with the appearance of age. Someone has asked, "If you were to cut down a tree in the Garden of Eden, how many rings would you find?" I don't know because it just fell from the hand of God. But I do know that that tree was grown and could bear fruit and bear seed, and reproduce after its kind. Adam and Eve were also created full grown, perfectly capable of reproduction and carrying on the plan of God. The Bible is either right or it's wrong. The Bible says that God just made them that way. He created with the appearance of age.

The Bible teaches the doctrine of catastrophism. It teaches that certain catastrophes have occurred, while evolution—both biological and theistic—teach that these things gradually evolved and that nothing drastic has intervened. It reminds me of the Apostle Peter when he says:

> ...for since the fathers fell asleep, all things continue as they were from the beginning of creation. For this they willingly are ignorant of, that by the word of God the heavens were of old, and the earth standing out of the water and in the water: Whereby the world that then was, being overflowed with water, perished (2 Peter 3:4-6).

The Bible teaches catastrophe. Theistic evolution teaches uniformitarianism—that everything has been gradually and uniformly evolving to bring us to where we are.

Theistic evolution makes a liar of Jesus Christ. I am being very blunt, but that is precisely what it does. It makes a liar of Jesus Christ because in Matthew 19—having been approached by the Pharisees who says, "Is it lawful for a man to put away his wife for every cause?"—He says, "Have ye not read ... ?" Notice this little bit of biting irony. Jesus says, "Haven't you read ... ?" By the way, when He does that, He places His stamp of approval upon the book of Genesis. He not only places a stamp of approval on the book of Genesis, He places it as far back as Genesis 2, when He says, "Have ye not read, that he which **made them AT THE BEGINNING** ... "—not began to make, but He "made them at the beginning ... And said, for this cause shall a man leave father and mother, and shall cleave to his wife: and they two shall be one flesh?" He says that was the beginning. God made it that way. This is what Jesus thought about the matter. And Genesis 2:2 says that "God ended his work." The heaven and the earth were **finished—IN THE BEGINNING.**

Some of the foregoing may seem tedious to some, but I think these are important things to know when we talk about the existence of God. I believe He is knowable, and I do not believe that a Christian's faith is a blind emotional subjective "leap in the dark." I believe that God can be proved.

A Christian's faith may be expressed in a few words—**something IS**, therefore **Someone eternally WAS**. There isn't any doubt today that something is. We are here. The world is here. We are sailing through unlimited space at a tremendous rate of speed. Everything moves with precision; everything is beautifully and wonderfully made. God runs a beautiful and orderly universe. Something IS, therefore Someone always WAS. These things did not just happen to be. AH! but one says, "Where is the emperical evidence of God?" Let me remind you that there are some things that are not based purely on empirical evidence or on observation and experimentation. That is not the only way to learn.

I was reading just recently about a court case in which the accepted evidence that turned the tide was based on the doctrine of evidence that they call prima facie, and by that they mean adequate evidence that is given that cannot be successfully refuted. A culmination of lines of thought and evidence that can run into only one possible conclusion. I propose to you that this is what you see when you read the Bible because the Bible is not a science book, although it never contradicts true science. The Bible is not written as a science book, but there is a culmination of lines and evidences that move into one conclusion—that **something IS** therefore **Someone eternally WAS.** From that, we find no escape.

From whence came our idea of God? Do we worship God because our fathers and our grandfathers and the ones before just dreamed all this up? Are we singing songs to Somebody and we really don't know whether He is there or not? From whence came the idea of God? If you haven't had to deal with that, you **will.** If you are a young person, especially, you are going to deal with that somewhere. Where did God come from?

I believe the Bible teaches that the idea of God is innate, that it is inherent in man. One of the things that separates us from the animal kingdom is that we have the inclination, if I may call it so, to be religious. We sometimes really work at being everything else, but there is in mankind an inclination to be religious. Question: Why? From whence came the idea of our God? I propose to you it is a human trait.

On April 13 through 23, 1829, in Cincinnati, Ohio, Alexander Campbell met Robert Owen, an atheist. Robert Owen came from Scotland, advertised in the United States as the Goliath of atheism, and that he was! He went about the country challenging the religious leaders of the time, and **nobody** was willing to deal with this man because he was quite good at what he was doing. But on April 13 through April 23, Mr. Campbell and Mr. Owen squared off to discuss the existence of God. And if you haven't read the account, you should. During the course of the discussion, Mr. Campbell asked Mr. Owen, "Where did the idea of God originate?" It took a long time to get an answer out of Mr. Owen, but finally he answered with the word, **"Imagination."** The idea that exists in peoples' minds about God is strictly the product of man's imagination. Mr. Campbell then quoted two respected philosophers and psychologists, John Locke and David Hume. The quotations were to the effect that the creative power of the mind amounts to nothing more than the faculty of combining, transposing, augmenting, and diminishing the materials afforded to us by sense and experience. Now think about what he is saying. He is saying that imagination has no creative power. With all the imagination you can get together, you can't create anything. Reason and imagination do not create.

Sigmund Freud, the German psychoanalyst, said the only reason a person calls upon his Heavenly Father is that he has formed that concept from the fact that he has an earthly father. However, I cannot believe, in reading this Book, that the God of the Bible is a God we would create. I want to tell you, I would not create ... I don't know how I could create a God like this. I think I might come up with a god in my mind, but I don't think I would come up with one like our God. I want to read from Habakkuk:

> What profiteth the graven image that the maker thereof hath graven it; the molten image, and a teacher of lies, that the maker of his work trusteth therein, to make dumb idols? Woe unto him that saith unto the wood, Awake; to the dumb stone, Arise, it shall teach! Behold, it is laid over with gold and silver, and there is no breath at all in the midst of it. But the Lord is in his holy temple: let all the earth keep silence before him (Habakkuk 2:18-20).

The Apostle Paul says it so beautifully in Acts. I think it is one of the greatest sermons of all time! He stood in the Areopagus in Athens, Greece, and spoke to the most informed men of his day, preaching to them about the unknown God.

> Whom therefore ye ignorantly worship, **HIM** declare I unto you. God that made the world and all things therein, seeing that he is Lord of heaven and earth, dwelleth not in temples made with hands; Neither is worshipped with men's hands, as though he needed any thing, seeing he giveth to all life, and breath and all things; And hath made of one blood all nations of men for to dwell on all the face of the earth, and hath determined the times before appointed, and the bounds of their habitation; That they should seek the Lord, if haply they might feel after him and find him, though he be not far from every one of us: For in **HIM** we live, and move, and have our being; as certain also of your own poets have said, For we are also his offspring (Acts 17:23-29).

He says since "we are the offspring of God, we ought not to think that the Godhead is like unto gold, or silver or stone, graven by art and man's device." Then he says, "The times of this ignorance God winked at; but now commandeth all men everywhere to repent." Why? "Because he hath appointed a day, in the which he will judge the world in righteousness by that man whom he hath ordained." I propose to you that the human mind is not capable of coming up with a God like that! If you want to see what kind of gods the human mind concocts, turn to the book of Habakkuk. He said it is insensible stone, it is a dumb idol, it neither sees nor hears nor speaks—there is no life therein. Indeed, the God of the Bible is not one we would ever create!

Thank you for listening. We will conclude this Sermon next Lord's Day as we present more evidence that "God Is."

God Is, Sermon #2

Good morning, everyone. Today we will continue the subject, "God Is," which we began last Lord's Day. If you missed the program last week, we invite you to write for a free printed copy or free cassette tape.

The inclination to be religious is innate. An objection raised to this truth is often stated as follows: If the idea of God is innate, if it is inherent within us, then there could be no unbelievers. There would be no agnostics because if it's basic and it's innate, then no one could deny it. Let me answer by saying this, man **can deny anything!** Some have even denied the flood of Noah's day. I mean a universal flood—and yet Peter says there were those who denied that it ever occurred.

I was in Kansas City some time ago in a meeting; and while waiting downtown one day, I had a little extra time; so I wandered into a Christian Science Reading Room—and that is a misnomer, it is neither Christian nor Science. One of the basic doctrines of Christian Science is that many things are illusions. They deny matter, and they deny death. You don't really die: you think you do! You don't really exist. I want to tell you that is quite an amazing thing for somebody as big as I am to be denied existence! **I exist!** You exist! We're not illusions. What I am saying is that if you can look at an individual and deny he is even there or if you can look at death—which is universal and will be until our Lord comes again—and say it doesn't exist, you are capable of denying anything under the sun! However, a denial of fact does not negate the fact. A denial of truth, or having a poor attitude toward truth, does not negate truth. The Bible sets forth mind and matter: mind the cause—matter the result.

The Creator always transcends creation, and that makes sense doesn't it? **Something IS** therefore **Someone eternally WAS.** There are resident forces in our world; there isn't any doubt about that. Plants reproduce by means of seed, and that goes on every day whether we have anything to do with it or not ... it just goes on all the time. I often think of this. Every blade of grass, every blade of grass in every field all over the world is carrying on its complicated process of photosynthesis. It is going on all the time. Animals have the power to reproduce, and that goes on all the time. The movements and the processes of this universe are constant and dependable; and the process goes on day by day and night by night whether we do one thing about it or even think about it—it goes on. However, that does not argue that He is not there and that nature is an independent entity.

Let me give you same passages that speak of this matter. In Matthew 6:30, Jesus tells us He clothes "the grass of the field" and that "Solomon in all his glory was not arrayed like one of these" (Matthew 6:29). Matthew 6:26 says He feeds "the fowls of the air." In Matthew 10:29, He says not one sparrow falls without His taking note of that matter. Job 37:10 says, "By the breath of God frost is given." What is he saying? God is still connected. God didn't just create and back out of this world. He is not separate from the world that He has made. Nature is not an independent entity: God is still there. **Something IS**, therefore **Someone eternally WAS.**

Stimulus—response. I don't have any problem with that. I don't have any problem with cause—effect because the Bible teaches it. In Hebrews 3:4, the writer says, "Every house is builded by some man." Cause—effect. There is no house that just happened to be. In Romans 5:12, for example, he says, "Wherefore, as by one man sin entered into the world, and death by sin; and so death passed upon all men." There are many effects that come out of that fact. Listen to Him! He is saying that death is universal. What causes death? He says it comes because of sin. So anytime a person dies, it argues the fact of sin. But when you think about sin, it argues the fact of transgression because that is what sin is. And when you think about transgression, it argues the fact of law because sin is a transgression of law. And when you talk about law, it argues the fact of a law giver because there is no such thing as law without a law giver. And when you talk about a law giver, you are talking about the eternal God. "Cause—effect" is very much with us; it is very basic, very fundamental. Every effect must have an adequate cause, but no effect can be quantitatively or qualitatively greater than the cause; and the cause, of course, is eternal God.

The universe is here. It is not an illusion. There are four basic explanations for the universe.

(1) It was spontaneously generated; just out of nothing, it created itself. Now I am not prepared for that, and I haven't met many people who are.

(2) It is an illusion; it doesn't exist. Not many people are ready for that.

(3) One of the easy ways out—it has just always existed. I think we tend to fall into that sometimes. I want to tell you that is scientifically untenable. I want to know why has it always existed? What do we mean when we talk about **always?**

The second law of thermodynamics says the stars are gradually burning up, the sun is cooling off, the earth is wearing out. Well, maybe so. But I want to tell you, if the clock is running down, there was a time when the clock was wound! And if the clock was one time wound, somebody wound it! I think **that** is what is important for us to remember. You can't get away from the fact that God lives—that God exists.

(4) And, of course, the fourth is that it was created. That is what I believe—that our finite, dependent, even contingent earth argues an infinite, independent, eternal mind, and that's **God.** And I don't think there is any other way out for any thinking person except to believe in Him. The poem argues the poet. The law argues the law giver. The mathematical theorem argues the mathematician. Order, arrangement and design argue intelligence, purpose, and production. From a tiny world of atoms to the vastness of multiplied solar systems, there is beautiful and perfect order. You don't have to know a great deal to find that out.

In Psalm 19:1, David says, "The heavens declare the glory of God; and the firmament showeth his handiwork. Day unto day uttereth speech, night unto night showeth knowledge." In Acts 14:17, the Apostle Paul says the Lord sends the rain and fruitful seasons. In Romans 1:19, he says, "Because that which may be known of God is manifest in them; for God hath shown it unto them." He says they are without excuse.

We repeatedly experience a change of seasons. When we get up in the morning, we smell it in the air—we "feel it in the air" as we sometimes say. There is a definite change that occurs in this old world of ours and that is because this earth is tilted a little bit. In fact, they tell us it is tilted precisely 23.5 degrees on its axis. That is why the poles are in a twilight zone and why they have an accumulation of ice. If you were to change that five tenths of a degree, it would cause some unbelievable problems in this world of ours. The rotation of the earth is so very accurate. In fact, it is so accurate that a one second variation would cause some unbelievable problems.

Isn't it amazing that our atmospheric pressure in this world is a precise 14.7 pounds per square inch at sea level? The atmosphere just happens to be the proper density to keep meteors from bombing this world, and it allows only certain amounts of rays to get through to us down here. How amazing that it just happens to be 78 percent nitrogen and 21 percent oxygen. Everything is set for the habitation of man. I find it amazing to think about "what the Lord hath made"! A piano can strike out 88 tones; the human ear is capable of picking up 1,500 tones. The human eye has 300,000 nerve line connections between the brain and the eye—that fact can boggle the world's best computers. I find, as David says that we are fearfully and wonderfully made (Psalm 139:14).

It is amazing how long it takes for **fact** to catch up with **faith**. Faith speaks in Proverbs 8:27 (ASV) of "the circle upon the face of the deep." Isaiah 40:22 says, "It is he that sitteth upon the circle of the earth." That was 1,000 years before Christ. How did Isaiah know that the earth was a sphere? Just faith in God! **Fact** finally caught up with **faith** when Mr. Newton became aware of the law of gravitation and figured out a few things. Faith says the earth hangs in space. Have you ever seen some of the drawings that have been made to show how this earth is suspended? The earth is shown on the back of elephants who are setting on turtles who are setting on snakes and so on it goes. We must set this earth on something! Of course, we always have the problem with that last thing it is setting on. The Bible has been saying all along in Job 26:7 that He "hangeth the earth upon nothing." In 1475, Mr. Copernicus said that's a fact—that's the way it is.

Faith says the moon is a smaller non-light-generating body. Genesis 1:16 says He made a "greater light to rule the day, and a lesser light to rule the night." Job 25:5 says, "The moon, it shineth not"—a non-light-generating body ... a reflective body. It was not until the late eighteenth century that fact finally caught up with that and said that is the way it actually is. Faith has been saying to people as long as they could read this Book that there is a great empty space in the north. Job says, "He stretcheth out the north over the empty place, and hangeth the earth upon nothing" (Job 26:7). I read with interest some time ago in Scientific American about the great black holes in space. We build bigger scopes and look out through space and there is, indeed, a place in the northern skies where there is nothing. **Nothing!** Reaching out beyond all that man can possibly see with the most powerful telescopes he can build, there is still nothing out there!

Another thing I found of interest in this study is that scientists tell us light beams emit musical sounds. Psalm 19:1 says, "The heavens declare the glory of God; and the firmament showeth his handiwork." Artificial light emits a static sound, while stellar light, coming from the stars, gives off a sound like a musical top. Job 38:7 says, "The morning stars sang together;" and Isaiah 24:16 says, "From the uttermost part of the earth have we heard songs."

Faith has been saying for a long time that the stars are innumerable (Genesis 15:5; Jeremiah 33:22). You remember he says the descendants of Abraham would be like the stars of heaven and the sands of the sea. I thought it interesting that in the year 150 BC, a man counted the stars and said there are precisely 1,026 stars. Ptolemy, in 150 AD, counted them and said there are 1,056 stars. Mr. Brack, in 1575, said he counted them and found 777 stars. Dr. Carl Sagan said recently, with the aid of one of the biggest scopes we have, there are now 25 sextillion—that is (twenty-five) 25 with twenty-one zeroes behind it. He also said when we build a bigger scope, we will see more. They are as the scripture said all along—**innumerable**.

One of the things that is most amazing about it all is that all this was done for man. I would like to close with that thought. Every bit of this spectacular universe He has done for us! Why? Because we are those made in His own image (Genesis 1:26). I have an old book Ashley S. Johnson wrote many, many years ago called "The Life of Trust." He wrote a piece that I think is very well done. I want to read it to you:

> For man, the sun rules the day and the moon rules the night; and for his happiness, the countless and unnamed worlds exist in fathomless space. For him, the seasons, winter with her ice

and snow, spring with her swelling buds and enchanting prophecies, summer with her harvest and fragrance, and autumn with her bursting garners crimson and gold, roll on in endless progression. For him, nature attunes her voice, and for him, changing and yet changeless beauty lives in perennial youth. For him, the oceans wash their shores, the rivers murmur anthems of peace, mountains lift up their snow-crowned peaks into the blue vaults above, and grass carpets the valleys on which he walks. Nature's God has written in every language and dialect, in words too plain to be misunderstood, that all these things are for the happiness of man. Imagine, if you can, the instantaneous depopulation of the earth. The stupendous and incomparable realm of creation would appear worse than folly's wildest dream. Without man's eye, the heavens would be but desolate waste, and without his ever multiplying and ever increasing wants, the fertile fields might as well be a sandy and boundless desert.

I think that is so well said. It is for man that all this was done; and yet it is to our everlasting shame that man is the only creature that ever fell from the hand of God that has said, "There is no God."

"All thy works shall praise thee, O Lord" (Psalm 145:10). "Praise ye him, sun and moon: praise him, all ye stars of light. Praise him, ye heavens of heavens, and ye waters that be above the heavens. Let them praise the name of the Lord: for he commanded, and they were created" (Psalm 148:3-5). He spoke and they were. He commanded and they stood fast.

In the presence of God today, remember that "without faith it is impossible to please him" (Hebrews 11:6). You must believe that He is. I believe that He is knowable. I believe that He is provable, that all these lines converge into one inescapable conclusion—**HE LIVES!** There is Somebody bigger than you and I; and He has revealed His will to us. His will for you is that you become a Christian through faith in Him, repentance of your sins, confession of His Son, and through baptism in His precious name for the remission of your sins. God lives, and we don't live for Him?? God lives, and we are depressed and we want to give it up and quit?? Think about it!! If God is, EVERYTHING MATTERS!

Not My Will

Good morning, everyone. We are very grateful that you are with us this morning. We would like to express to you the gratitude in our hearts for your continued interest in this broadcast. Certainly any letter or any word from you is encouraging to those of us who are sustaining and delivering this broadcast. So may I encourage you to write us a card or letter? We hope you will continue to listen each Lord's Day as we search the scripture, as the Bible states, to see whether these things are so.

For our lesson this morning, we invite you to turn to Luke 22:42 and read with us, "Father, if thou be willing, remove this cup from me: nevertheless not my will, but thine, be done." Our theme for today comes from this verse—"Not my will, but thy will be done." These words are from the prayer of Christ when He prayed to our Father in Gethsemane. The time was at hand for Him to be delivered into the hands of the enemy to be crucified. You will remember that Jesus took with Him Peter, James and John and departed into the garden to pray. He withdrew Himself from them about a stones throw and prayed the words that we read. He then went back and found His disciples sleeping. To them He says, "Watch and pray, that ye enter not into temptation: the spirit indeed is willing, but the flesh is weak" (Matthew 26:41).

Matthew says that, "He went away again the second time, and prayed saying, O my Father, if this cup may not pass away from me, except I drink it, thy will be done. And he came and found them asleep again: for their eyes were heavy. And he left them, and went away again, and prayed the third time, saying the same words. Then cometh he to his disciples, and saith unto them, Sleep on now, and take your rest: behold, the hour is at hand, and the Son of man is betrayed into the hands of sinners" (Matthew 26:42-45).

Thus, our Lord was willing to humbly submit to the Father's will, even to the point of dying on the cross—"even the death of the cross" as Paul says in Philippians 2:8. It was easy for our Lord to say, "For I came down from heaven, not to do mine own will, but the will of him that sent me" (John 6:38). Our Lord always lived in this spirit, and this is the frame of mind we should always have—that is, "Not our will Father, but thine be done." The child of God, like the Lord Jesus, will desire to do the Father's will and to accomplish His purpose on earth because it will be the most satisfying thing we can do.

Let us observe, with Christ as our example, how the Father's will must be done. First, God's will should always be done in the church. Paul says, "Unto him be glory in the church by Christ Jesus throughout all ages, world without end" (Ephesians 3:21). Could there ever be any misunderstanding between brethren that would result in church fusses and factions if every member prayed, "Father, not my will but thine be done," and then lived in that particular spirit? Is it not God's will "that there be no divisions among you; but that ye be perfectly joined together in the same mind and in the same judgment"? (1 Corinthians 1:10). Jesus says to His disciples, "It is impossible but that offenses will come: but woe unto him, through whom they come!" (Luke 17:1). So it is that differences sometimes arise between us but if we are willing to let God's will be done instead of our own, then all matters could be settled for the good of all and the glory of God. The main difficulty in settling such disturbances is that so many say, "I will have my own will and my own way instead of the Father's will." If all would sincerely pray, "Father, not my will but thine be done," there would never be any unfaithful members of the Lord's church, for God wills that we be faithful "unto death" (Revelation 2:10; Matthew 10:22).

It is the Father's will that Christians assemble for worship and observe the Lord's Supper upon the first day of the week as the first Christians did (Acts 20:7). The Hebrew writer says, "Not forsaking the assembling of ourselves together, as the manner of some is; but exhorting one another: and so much the more, as ye see the day approaching" (Hebrews 10:25). Therefore, when a member of the church sleeps too late to come to worship on the Lord's Day or he spends the day in pleasure, he does not have the desire of the Father in mind. It is the will of the Father that we "go ye into all the world, and preach the gospel to every creature" (Mark 16:15). Luke says of the Jerusalem church, "And daily in the temple, and in every house, they ceased not to teach and preach Jesus Christ" (Acts 5:42). Hence, a church that has no program of evangelism has no disposition that the Father's will be done through its members. If we would sincerely pray, "Father, not my will but thine be done," there would never be introduced into the doctrine of Jesus Christ the doctrines and commandments of men. Neither would there be imposed upon the church any practice that is unlike the practice of the New Testament church. In 2 John 9, we read, "Whosoever transgresseth, and abideth not in the doctrine of Christ, hath not God. He that abideth in the doctrine of Christ, he hath both the Father and the Son." Why will men teach the doctrine of justification by faith only when the New Testament says, "Ye see then how that by works a man is justified, and not by faith only" (James 2:24). Why will men teach that it is impossible for a child of God to apostatize, or to fall from grace, when we read in the New Testament such divine declarations as this, "Wherefore let him that thinketh he standeth take heed lest he fall" (1 Corinthians 10:12).

Here is another question. Why will men practice sprinkling for baptism when the Bible authorizes immersion? In recording the baptism of the Ethiopian eunuch, Luke says:

> And he commanded the chariot to stand still: and they went down both into the water, both Philip and the eunuch; and he baptized him. And when they were come up out of the water, the Spirit of the Lord caught away Philip, that the eunuch saw him no more: and he went on his way rejoicing (Acts 8:38-39).

Paul says, "Buried with him in baptism, wherein also ye are risen with him through the faith of the operation of God, who hath raised him from the dead" (Colossians 2:12). The New Testament teaches beyond a doubt that baptism of the first century was by immersion. Baptism has not come from men, and it is impossible to prove the New Testament teaches sprinkling and pouring as well as immersion. The New Testament contains the will of the Father. The point is that many now will admit the Bible teaches immersion and when asked, "Why do you practice this?" will reply, "What difference does it make? Who still believes the Bible contains the will of God?" Many honest souls have been sprinkled or had water poured upon them, thinking that this is what the New Testament teaches and believing that their minister would define this as New Testament teaching when he would not. Why is it hard for many to accept what the Lord Jesus and His disciples taught on this subject? Is not the answer simply, "My will be done and not yours, Lord"?

If all would pray devotedly, "Father, not my will but thine be done," there would not be given to the professed followers of Christ any name but the divine name of Christian (Acts 11:26). For in this name we glorify God. Peter says, "Yet if any man suffer as a Christian, let him not be ashamed; but let him glorify God on this behalf" (1 Peter 4:16). We have noticed briefly that God's will is to be done in the church. Let's observe another place where God's will is to be done.

God's will is to be done in the home. If the Father's will were accomplished in every home in our land, there would never be another divorce case brought into the courts. God's will in this relationship is well expressed in Matthew 19:8-9. No, I don't think we are left any doubt about what the Father's will is in the home. He has spoken to every member of the family declaring just how they should feel and act toward each other. To the husband, He says, "Husbands, love your wives, even as Christ also loved the church, and gave himself for it" (Ephesians 5:25). In Colossians 3:19, the same writer says, "Husbands, love your wives, and be not bitter against them." To the wife, He says, "Wives, submit yourselves unto your own husbands, as it is fit in the Lord ... . Therefore as the church is subject unto Christ, so let the wives be to their own husbands in every thing" (Ephesians 5:22-24). To the parents, He says, "Train up a child in the way he should go: and when he is old, he will not depart from it" (Proverbs 22:6). "And, ye fathers, provoke not your children to wrath: but bring them up in the nurture and admonition of the Lord" (Ephesians 6:4). "Fathers, provoke not your children to anger, lest they be discouraged" (Colossians 3:21). To the children, He says, "My son, hear the instruction of thy father, and forsake not the law of thy mother" (Proverbs 1:8). "Children, obey your parents in the Lord: for this is right. Honour thy father and mother; (which is the first commandment with promise;)" (Ephesians 6:1-2). "Children, obey your parents in all things: for this is well pleasing unto the Lord" (Colossians 3:20). What a wonderful home your home and mine would be if every father, mother, husband, wife, and youth would truly say, "Father, not my will but thine be done in our home." Think what a change would occur in this world and in our lives if all of us would say, "Father, simply let me become a doer of your will."

I would like, in the remaining time, to cite an example I have learned in the Old Testament about this matter of doing and not doing the will of the Father. It has to do with a study about the rebellion of Jeroboam. You recall the efforts Jeroboam made to establish his own religion for the people. He fled into Egypt for plotting against Solomon, when a young man, after Solomon had given him an office of honor according to 1 Kings 11. You recall that on the death of Solomon and upon the request of his friends, Jeroboam returned from Egypt. Ahijah had prophesied that ten of the twelve tribes would be given into his hands, and he made haste to fulfill this prophecy. So Jeroboam and all the congregation of Israel came to Rehoboam, the son of Solomon, and he said:

> Thy father made our yoke grievous: now therefore make thou the grievous service of thy father, and his heavy yoke which he put upon us, lighter, and we will serve thee. And he said unto them, Depart yet for three days, then come again to me. And the people departed. And king Rehoboam consulted with the old men, that stood before Solomon his father while he yet lived, and said, How do ye advise that I may answer this people? (1 Kings 12:4-6).

And I want you to notice the answer the older, wiser men gave to him. "If thou wilt be a servant unto this people this day, and wilt serve them, and answer them, and speak good words to them, then they will be thy servants for ever" (1 Kings 12:7). You recall that Rehoboam forsook the advice of the older men and consulted the young men who grew up with him and who stood before him. They answered him by saying:

> Thus shalt thou speak unto this people that spake unto thee, saying, Thy father made our yoke heavy, but make thou it lighter unto us; thus shalt thou say unto them, My little finger shall be thicker than my father's loins. And now whereas my father did lade you with a heavy yoke, I will add to your yoke: my father hath chastised you with whips, but I will chastise you with scorpions (1 Kings 12:10-11).

When Jeroboam and the people heard this, they cried, "What portion have we in David? neither have we inheritance in the son of Jesse: to your tents, O Israel: now see to thine own house, David. So Israel departed unto their tents" (1 Kings 12:16). Thus, the once united kingdom of Israel is now divided, but the matter didn't stop here, you remember, because Jeroboam built Shechem in mount Ephraim and dwelt there:

> And Jeroboam said in his heart, Now shall the kingdom return to the house of David: If this people go up to do sacrifice in the house of the Lord at Jerusalem, then shall the heart of this people turn again unto their lord, even unto Rehoboam king of Judah, and they shall kill me, and go again to Rehoboam king of Judah. Whereupon the king took counsel, and made two calves of gold, and said unto them, It is too much for you to go up to Jerusalem: behold thy gods, O Israel, which brought thee up out of the land of Egypt. And he set the one in Bethel, and the other put he in Dan. And this thing became a sin: for the people went to worship before the one, even unto Dan. And he made an house of high places, and made priests of the lowest of the people, which were not of the sons of Levi (1 Kings 12:26-31).

In the thirteenth chapter of 1 Kings, God sent a young prophet to cry out against the altar worship at Bethel. My point in reading this account is this—there is a lesson for us today. First, we notice that this matter was the product of Jeroboam's imagination. He conceived this thing in his heart (1 Kings 12:26). He had no concept whatsoever of saying, "Father, not my will but thine be done." It is evident that he was concerned only with his will and his desires. It seems that his chief concern was not abiding by the will of God—a willingness to do right and have God's will thus come about—he simply wanted what he wanted and what he thought. God declared that His thoughts are not man's thoughts, you remember? And it is always true that religious effort that follows man's opinion, in preference to the plain and explicit word of God, is the product of man's imagination. Jesus says, "In vain do they worship me, teaching for doctrines the commandments of men" (Mark 7:7). In the religious world today, men make the same tragic mistake. How many times have you heard people contend that one does not have to be baptized to be saved? Or they say I surely don't believe baptism has anything to do with one's salvation. But who do we think we are to follow our own judgment, people? Our own judgment—in rebellion to the will of the Almighty God!! We can never, by any wild stretch of the imagination, think that we are saying, "Not our will. Father, but thine be done."

Second, we notice again that Jeroboam's effort had a selfish view in mind. You remember he set up golden calves in Bethel and Dan. He did so lest the people continue to go to Jerusalem and worship and the hearts of the people be turned from himself back to Rehoboam. So it is today that many religious efforts crowd God entirely out and they become efforts that exist with the sole purpose of honor and aggrandizement of some individual. The Papal system with all its pomp and ceremony bestows undue honor upon a mere man. God only is to be the object of our devotion—not man. His will is to be our aim—not the satisfaction of our own selfish whims. The validity of religious things can largely be measured by a consideration of the respect shown to God. I would like to re-emphasize that. The validity of religious things can largely be measured by a consideration of the respect shown to God. Jesus says, "My meat is to do the will of him that sent me." Acceptable service is not concerned with the desires and the aims of man, but those of God. The pride of life, man's desire to selfishly do his will rather than God's, is the basis of all sorts of schemes that are palmed off on men in the name of religion today.

Third, I would like for you to notice this thing that Jeroboam did fostered convenience rather than conviction. God had decreed that Jerusalem was the place for men to worship, but Jeroboam said it was too much for the people to go to Jerusalem. He was catering to the people: he was a man pleaser. He was not the last one, however, to make this mistake. Many a man is willing to sell out today—I mean, all the way—they are willing to sell out to soothe the feelings of the people. The religion of the Lord demands that we serve through conviction rather than through convenience. It is concerned with obedience—not ease. It may lead us into some rough and difficult places. It may well demand that we make costly sacrifices, but God requires obedience. Jeroboam pleased men but displeased God, and that was a sin.

Last, we notice that Jeroboam did not respect the law of God because he built altars in Bethel and altars in Dan rather than allowing the people to go to Jerusalem to worship. Jerusalem was the place where God had decreed for men to worship Him. It is tragic but true that men still follow their own desires rather than the plain declaration of the scripture.

Let us learn these valuable lessons from this tragic story of one who rebelled against God. May we be inspired to follow, without question, our Father's will? We should remember that Jesus has said, "Not everyone that saith unto me, Lord, Lord, shall enter into the kingdom of heaven; but he that doeth the will of my Father which is in heaven" (Matthew 7:21). Our entrance into the celestial city is dependent upon our doing the Father's will. The question today: What are you doing to accomplish the Father's will in the church and in your life and in your home? It does no good to pray, "Father, not my will but thine be done," unless we endeavor to live in harmony with this, the Father's will.

Thank you for listening.

www.ingramcontent.com/pod-product-compliance
Lightning Source LLC
LaVergne TN
LVHW091029080826
845145LV00002B/418

9780997258943